AUSTRALIA
IMAGE OF A NATION 1850~1950

2

AUSTRALIA
IMAGE OF A NATION 1850~1950
David Moore · Rodney Hall

Front endpaper
'On the Yarra'. *N. J. Caire, n.d.*

Back endpaper
King Street, Sydney, taken from Pitt Street looking towards George Street.
NSWGP, 1907

Half-title page
Dressed with style to do her duty for the suffragist publication *Votes for Women*,
Miss Vida Goldstein of Melbourne. *T. Humphrey and Co., 1912*

Title page
An ambrotype of Miss Elanor Elizabeth Stephen. *Unknown, c. 1854*

Caption Credits

The names of some institutions had to be shortened to initials only. They are as
follows:-
CIO: Commonwealth Immigration Office
MIO: Ministry of Information, London
NSWGP: New South Wales Government Printer
WAGP: Western Australian Government Printer
WAN: Western Australian Newspapers

This edition published in 1989 by PR Books,
5 Skyline Place, Frenchs Forest, NSW, Australia, 2086
Telephone: (02) 975 1700, facsimile (02) 975 1711
© This collection of photographs David Moore 1983, 1989
© Text and captions Rodney Hall 1983, 1989
First published in 1983 by William Collins Pty Ltd, Sydney
Designed by Patrick Coyle
Typeset by Savage & Co. Brisbane
Printed in Hong Kong by South China Printing Co. (1988) Ltd

National Library of Australia Cataloguing-in-Publication data

Moore, David, 1927– .
    Australia, image of a nation 1850–1950.

    Bibliography
    ISBN 1 875113 20 7.

    1. Australia—History—Pictorial works.
    I. Hall, Rodney, 1935– . II. Title.

994

Acknowledgements

Publication of any book requires the generous assistance and professional expertise of many people working in separate, yet allied, fields. Production of this volume has been an exceptional team effort requiring knowledge, skill and devotion. Wherever help was required it was forthcoming with enthusiasm. Further, there existed an understanding that a pursuit of excellence was mandatory if the book was to achieve its aim.

To merely list those whose assistance has been so invaluable seems to do them an injustice for they deserve much greater acknowledgement than this. However, space limitations decree that my thanks be brief.

All the researchers of photography who have so readily contributed their time and accepted my endless requests deserve special mention. To a very real extent this is *their* book for it is they who have unearthed the riches.

Both senior and junior staff members of many institutional archives have been most helpful and encouraging. Important collections of pictures throughout Australia and in London have been made freely available for research over a period of many months. Belief in the need for this book by archivists everywhere has enabled much previously unpublished material to be located. I hope that the final selection of pictures will in some way express my thanks to those who love photographs and are responsible for their preservation. Additionally, where private collectors of old photographs have been approached they have all responded with willingness and grace.

In order that the highest possible quality of reproduction could be obtained from archive prints (where no original negatives existed) photographers were commissioned to make standard formula, large-format copy negatives. This work has been handled with superior professionalism and grateful thanks are due to all these craftsmen who have so expertly contributed their skill.

Perhaps inevitably there will be accidental omissions of some who deserve to be recognized for the help they have given. To those my sincere apologies and to all those listed my unreserved gratitude.

John Cross, Dawn Troy and Leone Dawson of the Archives Office of New South Wales; Gael Newton, David Millar and Kerry Dundas of the Art Gallery of New South Wales; Sigrid McCausland and Elizabeth Nathan of the Australian Archives; Christine Godden of The Australian Centre for Photography; Graham Goodman of Australian Consolidated Press; Francesca Baas Becking and Luke Taylor of the Australian Institute of Aboriginal Studies; John Field of The Australian Museum; Ian North of the Australian National Gallery; Jan Mulqueen and Peter West of the Australian War Memorial; Graham Parks of Cinesound Productions; Sue Motherwell of The Herald and Weekly Times; Alan Blandford of John Fairfax and Sons; Peter Hunter and Don Pitkethly of Kodak; Margaret Medcalf and Robin South of The Library Board of Western Australia; Peter Stanbury and Alan Davies of the Macleay Museum at the University of Sydney; Margaret Calder, Julie Wood, Christine Pryke and Cheryl Evans of the Mitchell Library; Barbara Perry and Sylvia Carr of the National Library of Australia; Alan Leishman and Alan Clifford of the Government Printing Office of New South Wales; John Forsyth of the State Rail Authority of New South Wales; Warren Clark, John Squire and Janice Ball of Qantas; Rhonda Hamilton of the Queen Victoria Museum and Art Gallery; J. H. Love and Carolyn Spooner of the State Library Division of South Australia; Ian Pearce of the State Library of Tasmania; Shar Jones of the State Library of Victoria; Barbara Pretyman of the Tasmanian Museum and Art Gallery; Chris Gillard of West Australian Newspapers; also Gordon Andrews, Ted Bezzant, Jean Blundell, Elizabeth Bradhurst, Anthony Browell, John Cato, Herbert Chargois, John Delacour, Max Dupain, Graham Garrett, Stuart Gore, Geoff Harrisson, Cyril Hume, David McCarthy, Toni McDowell, Ian McKenzie, Jean McKinley, Dame Mary Durack Miller, Peter J. Phillips, Mrs Gordon Pullar, Mr and Mrs Quentin Macarthur-Stanham, Richard Stringer, Peter Whyte, Richard Woldendorp and Heather Wippell, my uncomplaining, tireless and meticulous assistant without whose help this collection would not have been assembled.
D. M.

Photographic Researchers

Queensland   Robert Longhurst
New South Wales and the ACT   David Moore
Victoria   Jenny Carew
Tasmania   Carol Smithies
South Australia   Susan Woodburn
Western Australia   Anne Pheloung
London   Mary Andrews and Richard Doust

Copy Photographers

Queensland   David McCarthy
New South Wales   John Delacour
Victoria   Ian McKenzie
Tasmania   Geoff Harrisson
South Australia   Staff of the State Library of South Australia
Western Australia   Peter Whyte
London   John Summerhays

Contents

Preface 9

Introduction 13
Home Away from Home 19
Men in Conflict 43
The Land of Sacred Water 61
Life in the Backblocks 83
God made them High or Lowly 113
Getting Through—and Answering Back 147
By the Sweat of Their Brows 177
In Pursuit of Happiness 211
Luxuries and Slums 237
Independent, More or Less 267
You Win Some, You Win Some More 295

Archive Credits 328
Bibliography 331
Index 332

Preface
by David Moore

The documentary photographer has long shouldered the responsibility of saying to the world 'it is like this'. We look back thirty, fifty, a hundred years or more and marvel at the apparent exactness of photographic information. The time-machine of the camera can instantly transport us through the past, place us in the very spot where the tripod once left its marks in the dust and permit us the privilege of being witness to a time which cannot be repeated.

The still, silent scene is confronted with wonder, almost as if we expect to hear a dog bark in the distance or see leaves moved by the breeze. Yet all will be forever frozen in the grip of the emulsion. People, animals, trains and ships will remain trapped by the release of the camera shutter. The photographer—master craftsman of image—has embalmed a corner of the world for our future study.

Since the 1830s, the continuous flow of photographs has created an ever rising flood. Each day the volume increases and each day more pictures of interest become buried. John Szarkowski, director of the department of photography at the Museum of Modern Art in New York, once said that there are more photographs in the world than bricks. Research for this book shows evidence that his statement is probably true.

One of the starting points for the project was a belief that major institutional archives in Australia and London contained many rich and absorbing photographs that previously had not been seen by the public. There was indeed much to discover, however we have not attempted an encyclopaedic coverage of all that occurred in one hundred years of the nation's history. Instead we have tried to give a feeling of the changing times which cast the mould for what Australia has become in the 1980s.

Photography of value has required an attitude of care and attention since the beginnings of the science. Today we tend to overlook this fact in the age of automation. In the mid-nineteenth century, relatively insensitive emulsions coupled with lenses that seriously restricted the amount of light which could pass to the plate made the recording of images a meticulous task. Also, because of the need to produce huge negatives (before the technique of enlargement had been developed), equipment was often of gargantuan proportions. Glass plates up to a size of 15 × 12 inches were common and the camera itself was consequently enormous in order to accept these precious vehicles for the light-sensitive emulsion. Transport—over rough tracks, across deserts and through forests—was a difficult and delicate exercise demanding great stamina from the pioneer photographers.

There was the even greater challenge faced by photographers before the introduction of the dry plate around 1880. Although it was a technical revolution when it became available in 1851, the wet collodion process was something of a headache for photographers. The light-sensitive emulsion needed to be applied to the glass plate, the

Gold prospecting was hard and lonely work, often in very primitive conditions. A group of miners takes time off to pose for their photograph near Warburton, Vic. *N. J. Caire, c. 1878*

exposure made and the negative developed before the emulsion had dried: a matter of a few short minutes.

Should the photograph be one made in a studio, with all darkroom facilities readily at hand, the process—although exacting—was not particularly arduous. However, in order to make pictures in the field, photographers were forced to include a portable darkroom and chemicals, along with all other necessary equipment when they set off from their base. The photographer's horse-drawn caravan became a familiar sight as it trundled into outback towns and camps across the nation for a period of three decades until the blessed, pre-packaged dry plate was marketed.

If the sheer size and bulk of equipment was a hindrance to some early masters of the camera, we can but applaud the efforts of the enterprising Bernard Otto Holtermann, as an example of Victorian ingenuity.

Wishing to produce a series of panoramic photographs of Sydney Harbour in 1874, Holtermann first built a masonry tower in North Sydney some seventy-three feet high. With his twenty-four year old associate Charles Bayliss in charge of technical requirements Holtermann then proceeded to construct the world's largest camera.

Into the wall of the top room in the tower was fitted a specially imported 100 inch focal length lens which faced the harbour. Opposite, on the northern wall, a construction for holding an enormous sheet of glass was fixed.

When conditions were judged to be right for photography, Bayliss set to work under the red glow of illumination to which the plates would not be sensitive. Carefully, he coated a plate of glass with emulsion then transferred it to the plate-holder construction. Next he uncapped the inside of the huge lens for the desired exposure time, recapped it and removed the now-exposed plate carrying its latent image. The negative was immediately processed and fixed in previously prepared baths of chemicals. The precious glass plate was then manhandled down several flights of narrow stairs to be dried by the heat of an open fire.

Returning to the camera room, Bayliss altered the direction of the lens and repeated the laborious process twice more until he finished with three distinct images of the harbour. Whether it was intended that these three pictures would be sequentially panoramic, so the total view could be mounted as one enormous sweep, is not clear for two of the negatives cover a similar area of the landscape whilst the third leaves an unexplained gap covering part of McMahon's Point. Perhaps there was a fourth negative which showed the missing area or could it have been that an error of lens alignment omitted part of the view?

Unfortunately, it is likely that this intriguing puzzle will remain unsolved for today only three negatives of this size exist. Nevertheless, despite apparent inaccuracies, the achievement of Bayliss and Holtermann was an astounding technical feat for they were not working with plates of 12″ × 10″ or even 15″ × 12″, rather they were making history with what were then the world's largest sensitized sheets of glass. Two measured 4′6″ × 3′2″ and the other 5′0″ × 3′2″. These unique documents of photography are now safely housed in the Mitchell Library of New South Wales.

Holtermann was delighted with the results and in 1876 he exhibited prints from these remarkable negatives in San Francisco and Philadelphia. Then in 1878, he took them to Paris to be displayed at the *Exposition Universelle Internationale* where he was honoured by the award of a silver medal.

The diligence of early photographers and the obvious pride they took in their work fills us with respect. It is apparent in much surviving material that there was a pursuit of excellence to the very highest standards current in the field.

Part of B. O. Holtermann's panorama of Sydney Harbour looking from North Sydney across Lavender Bay. *Charles Bayliss for B. O. Holtermann, 1874*

MITCHELL LIBRARY

From the precious, mirror-backed daguerreotypes, dating from 1839 (from which it was not possible to make duplicate images) through to the later development of prints on sensitized paper where multiple printing from the original negative became commonplace, we can see that photographers throughout the world respected the medium as a vehicle for communication where fidelity of rendition was of paramount importance. Visual information was recorded for all time as it had never been recorded before. The documentary artist with his pen or brush finally had to admit that the line the camera could draw was more faithful to reality than that which flowed from his hand.

For this reason alone, if for no other, archives housing historic photographs bear an awesome custodial responsibility. Destruction of just one glass plate or original print means an extinguished light leaving a black hole in the rich fabric of our past.

Sadly, we cannot remain totally convinced that the same high standards exhibited by many nineteenth century photographers applied in the first half of the century which followed.

It seems reasonable to assume that the simplification of the process and the invention of the roll film camera played some part in the decline. After all, if pictures are being made with 15 × 12 inch glass plates, the shutter release is not tripped until the total picture has been most carefully considered and all technical variables determined.

The concern for structure and tonal balance became less evident in much twentieth century photography. In some cases, technique became downright sloppy and often the sharpness of detail was poor compared to photography which had been produced fifty to seventy-five years earlier.

The 'pictorial movement' of 'Art' photography did little for factual documentation of our land or society. After being presented with the glorious gift of clear vision by dedicated optical engineers, many photographers turned their backs on technical precision and wasted a great deal of time—and film—trying to make their images resemble inept and meaningless paintings. It was only the really sincere and capable photographers, such as Harold Cazneaux, who managed to hold the medium in relative control. This was achieved by a genuine understanding of light and form as well as structure and balance within the frame.

The first photographs ever made in Australia date from some time in the early 1840s. Probably the very first was taken by a visiting Frenchman who seems to have returned to Europe with his image This effectively deprived Australia of a unique artefact as numerous searches in the archives of France have so far failed to trace this important picture of Bridge Street, Sydney.

The collection of photographs in this book spans a period of slightly more than a century. At the outset it was intended that the limits of enquiry would be established by the dates 1850–1950. However, research identified two images which pre-date the middle of the last century so it seemed reasonable to include them not only because of their historical significance but also as examples of fine photographic vision.

The period immediately following the end of the Second World War witnessed the beginnings of much social change across the nation. By 1950 Australia, together with most of the western world, looked forward to a future vastly different from the familiar patterns and attitudes which were so traumatically terminated in 1939 by world conflict. The mid point of the century became a dividing line and this was where we decided to leave our examination of the country and its peoples.

This volume seeks to acknowledge and celebrate the finest photography of the past. Additionally it may provide a framework of understanding for the identity of Australia's future generations.

MITCHELL LIBRARY

A photographic freak, caused perhaps by overheating of the emulsion: the Goldfields Express, Kalgoorlie, WA. *J. J. Dwyer, c. 1890*

THE RED BLUFF

Introduction

In 1837 Louis Daguerre pointed his camera at a subject and uncovered the lens. During the next half-hour he could only guess at what might be happening in the dark of that closed box, the sensitive plate receiving an upside-down picture. Gradually and miraculously details were imprinted by their own volition, to be discovered later, washed in salt water, displayed in a case and glimpsed by angling the image to catch a partial light.

Three hundred years earlier, the image of Terra Australis del Espiritu Santo haunted the European imagination. Tantalized by the unknown, by hints of an inverted hemisphere, they set out in ships from the safety of the old mediaeval horizons for the risky world of speculation.

Two Portuguese ships sailed south from Java in 1528 into a void of sea and sky, right in the middle of the cyclone season where calm blue days suddenly swirl into furious tempests, the tiny vessels wallowing, their square-rigged sails useful only for running before the wind, unable to turn back even if their masters wished to give up and head home. They had no notion of what lay before them. The edge of the world and a drop into hell was still a living possibility, so was the fabled kingdom of Prester John the most pious and, hopefully, the wealthiest of all Christian monarchs.

And then out of the flat sea, a flat horizon of land appearing, all hands staring at it with relief and apprehension. Advancing closer, the land being seen to stretch its immense featureless length far into the distance, perhaps as huge as the ocean they had crossed to get there. Yet when they sailed in to explore the coast they were met by a baffling wilderness of warm mud; an unapproachable silence and stillness. The day mysteriously darkened, night briefly flooding the sky: it was an eclipse of the sun.

On this day of portents people were most certainly watching them. And during their slow progress down the west coast messages were already passing by immemorial means across the island continent. Very likely the Aborigines of the territory later to become Sydney knew of the intruders before the Portuguese sovereign received his reports.

No people on earth could be less like Europeans than these naked nomads.

The Portuguese respected wealth and display, coming from a Renaissance court where nobles dressed in elaborately stitched doublets, their ladies' colossal farthingales so thickly embroidered with beads and gems they might stand up by themselves even without the framework of whalebone stays worn under them. These same nobles could tolerate inflicting squalor and cruelty on others for the sake of a place at court, to breathe the palace air filled with elegant music and stinking of excrement. And their cathedrals, too, were palaces to God and His bishops, repositories of treasure. The Portuguese ships were a microcosm of their society: commanded by noblemen-soldiers,

The Red Bluff. The roadway has opened a great wound across the hillside to provide settlers with welcome contact from the town. As an unseen presence the photographer, photographing a painter painting a couple of houses in the bush, makes his statement about the function of the camera. And, perhaps, about art. *Unknown, n.d.*

guided by the new technicians, and accountable to their own priest, the crew living in filth between-decks where there was no room to stand up and having to crawl to their quarters after exhausting days and nights slaving in the interests of their merchant owners.

These were the Europeans who sought contact with Aboriginal tribes governed by a free association of elders, whose sole possessions were weapons for hunting, baskets for roots and berries, wooden artefacts bearing the mythology that gave meaning to life, and whose greatest works of art were washed off their bodies the following morning. These were people whose territory, though exactly and spiritually known to them, was unfenced, and whose shelters were temporary. The land under their feet lay rich in gold and jewels but they showed no interest in either; their treasures were their monumental languages of sacred words and ceremonial dances.

Small wonder the Portuguese, and the Dutch who followed them later in the sixteenth century, sailed away without any apparent desire to invade or take possession of what they found there. Compared with the sumptuous spoils witnessed in Cathay by Marco Polo, in India by Vasco da Gama and the Indies by Christopher Columbus, not to mention their own observations in the Spice Islands, this vast country was barren of interest.

They were not to know—and perhaps wouldn't have cared if they had—that here lay the largest of all islands, rich with unique animals and plants, a complex ecology more self-contained than anywhere else in the world, that the tops of mountains in the innermost desert still bore marks of the sea and its fossils, that the gnarled flatness of the land was evidence of extreme age, worn smooth millions of years before the upstart Himalayas cracked open and broke skywards with the heaving of earth's crust; a country where gentle regions and harsh were all on a gigantic scale, a stony desert as big as Portugal itself, the fertile coastal plain stretching as far as from Oslo to Athens, snow-covered mountains and steamy rainforest. The Great Barrier Reef,

which might at first look featureless, a trail of scrubby rocks just above waterlevel, on closer inspection reveals miraculous colour and life; Australia as a whole was rather like that too. This would eventually be realized and interpreted by men and women very different from those hard-driven sailors; the naturalists, the artists, the settlers who grew to be intrigued by the land.

In Aboriginal time, the several hundred years from this first European arrival up till 1770 might have represented no more than a passing phase. But two centuries after the Portuguese visit, Europeans had changed. Captain James Cook sailed from an England profoundly altered since the Renaissance court of Henry VIII. The Industrial Revolution had begun, the working class had come into being, and as further proof of change, here was a working-class boy risen to be master of his own vessel, one of the great navigators, scouting for ports to secure England's mercantile supremacy in the east under the guise of speculative science. The transit of Venus having been observed, the real business of the voyage began.

The treasure Cook had been sent to find was a harbour, and he obliged with a magnificent specimen. His contact with the Aborigines proved irrelevant except for observing their simple weaponry and lack of martial organization: the British were not expecting them to have anything worth robbing. And when the penal colony was established they were left alone in what was taken to be childlike innocence to pursue Arcadian simplicities of hunting, food gathering and dancing.

So the convicts landed, transported as unpaid labour to build the port of Sydney. (That Sydney was never intended just as a dumping place for convicts is evident in the report that 'a large town has already been planned and several houses built' in April 1789, just one year after the landing of the First Fleet.)

Before long, farming became necessary for survival. This and the habit of acquisitiveness led to a hinterland being occupied to support the garrison. The invasion began in earnest.

'Kang-oo-roo' and 'Woman of New South Wales' from John (later Governor) Hunter's Sketchbook, 1790.

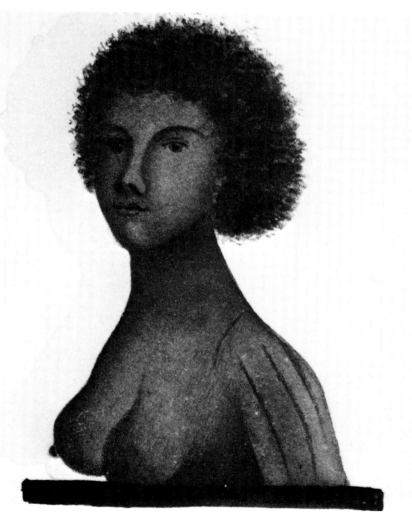

Not surprisingly, the owners of the land fought back; there were no great battles, but countless local skirmishes, a guerrilla warfare that didn't stop till the 1930s and has some sporadic continuance even today. To the pioneer farmer the attacks often seemed arbitrary, especially if he was not one of those to actually chase native people away from land that was to be his. Ignorant that a tribe might take many months to complete the food-gathering circuit of its territory, he and his family occupied a vacant district, built a hut and settled in. They laboured to clear the scrub, prepare the soil for planting and fence their livestock. It was hard work with virgin ground which they soon regarded as wholly theirs to live off and defend. And defend it they did when the tribe came round again. Murders took place on both sides and some of the most unsolvable repetitions of violence were pay-back killings, revenge taken, often years later.

Through all this it seemed never to have occurred to the champions of Western civilization that they were the foreigners. Just how foreign, their art and their diaries show.
(See illustrations on opposite page.)

Before we laugh at these idealized people and caricatured animals, we should pause to consider the silent partner in every work of art, the audience, whose interest and imagination is to be sparked by the picture for it to work. Were these inaccuracies really as inaccurate as they seem? Or were they rather more astutely pitched to win serious attention in their day than we give them credit for? Even Captain Cook's journal and Joseph Banks' report to Parliament, historic statements from the outset, were pitched at an audience. Cook plainly wanted it understood that he had found just the place he was sent to find. Having extolled the harbour, he indulged in a little Noble Savagery of his own.

From what I have said of the Natives of New-Holland they may appear to some to be the most wretched people upon the earth: but in reality they are far more happier than we Europeans; being wholy unacquainted not only with the superfluous but the necessary Conveniences so much sought after in Europe, they are happy in not knowing the use of them. They live in a Tranquillity which is not disturbed by the Inequality of Condition: The Earth and sea of their own accord furnishes them with all things necessary for life; they covet not Magnificent Houses, Household-stuff &cᵃ they live in a warm and fine Climate and enjoy a very wholsome Air: so that they have very little need of Clothing and this they seem to be fully sensible of for many to whome we gave Cloth &cᵃ to, left it carlessly upon the Sea beach and in the woods as a thing they had no manner of use for. In short they seem'd to set no value upon anything we gave them nor would they ever part with any thing of their own for any one article we could offer them. This in my opinion argues that they think themselves provided with all the necessarys of Life.

In fact a quite different reason was given by the Aborigines themselves when an oral history began to be recorded. Clothes and blankets thrown to them were a mystery.

. . . and they got a big long stick and they picked it up with the stick and they couldn't make out what that was. They thought this man was changing his skin. They said this man left his skin there. All the natives thought this man was taking his skin. They said this man has been peel himself like a snake and they got the stick and they picked it up with a stick and they looked and looked at this shirt and trousers . . . But when he took his shirt and he was white they thought he change his colour when he took his shirt off. They pick up that shirt with a stick because they was too frightened to pick it up with a hand because in our custom might be something very dangerous, witchcraft.

Detail of one of the earliest photographs taken in Australia: Murray Street, Hobart, 1848, showing the gaol and court buildings. *J. W. Newland, 1848*

TASMANIAN MUSEUM AND ART GALLERY

The botanist Joseph Banks, like Cook, presented his evidence on New Holland in a light calculated to interest the government. His slighting references to the natives made them appear too few and too timid to pose any obstacle to the annexation of their territory.

. . . In the Year 1770, he [Joseph Banks] saw very few [Natives], and did not think there were above Fifty in all the Neighbourhood, and had Reason to believe the Country was very thinly peopled; those he saw were naked, treacherous, and armed with Lances, but extremely cowardly, and constantly retired from our People when they made the least Appearance of Resistance . . .

Australia is a hot dry continent, the average rainfall over an area of almost eight million square kilometres is not more than 430 millimetres a year. This is made up of a variety of climates from tropical to Mediterranean to desert. Initially the newcomers occupied only tiny corners around the best deepwater harbours. And here the architects and engineers set about converting it to England. They built roads and bridges, they designed buildings imposed on the site without

William Lanne, reputed to be the last full-blood male Tasmanian Aborigine, photographed three years before his early death. *C. A. Woolley, 1866*

the least attempt to respond to this strange mystical terrain. Their ambition was to be as up to date as London and to echo when possible the elegance of Bath. The task of trying to reconcile the new towns with the landscape was left to the artists who did their best, painting pictures in which they planted horse-drawn gigs among the treeferns and busy clusters of rectangular houses washed by the same stone colour as the dry hills beyond.

Beyond the dry hills, the newcomers had to rely on words, on the reports brought back by the courageous few who set off in all directions to explore the interior. If there is a single image to show what this could be like, perhaps it is the failure of the Burke and Wills expedition. Having safely traversed the desert north to the Gulf of Carpentaria and half way back to Melbourne, they went missing. Public concern in the colonies was intense and four separate relief parties set out to find them, one heading north from South Australia, one heading west from Queensland, one aboard ship sailing to the Gulf of Carpentaria, and the fourth from Menindee in New South Wales led by the resourceful A. W. Howitt.

In September 1861, beyond Mount Hopeless, Howitt came upon some hoof marks and later a solitary horse lost in the desolate wilderness. However, it was not from Burke and Wills' team—amazingly enough it had escaped from the Charles Sturt expedition sixteen years before. Bernhard Grzimek commented, 'Every October for sixteen years it must have watched the black and white pelicans, the Brolga cranes and noisy flocks of rose-breasted cockatoos pass overhead on their spring journey from north to south. Every May, when the rains finally came with the advent of winter it must have seen them reappear and vanish northwards again in quest of warmer climes. For sixteen long years, or so it must be assumed, the lone horse saw neither a white man nor another member of its own species.'

When Howitt reached Cooper's Creek he found agitated groups of Aborigines there. Many of them turned and ran, but one man stood swaying, draped in rags and shreds of a hat, raised his hands, staggered and fell. It was John King, sole survivor of the missing expedition.

When the explorers found usable resources, pioneers followed and faced a life only marginally less lonely. This was what London expected of them. After all, the idea of the colony was to produce wealth for the greater glory of the Empire.

As New South Wales and Van Diemen's Land first took shape, whale oil and sealing brought revenue and the search continued for mast timber and hemp (as vital for transport then as oil is today); a landed squattocracy began demanding official support of their vested interests in competition with English mercantile companies at home. The wool clippers, like the tea clippers of the India trade, gilded commerce with the aura of romance. New money did battle against old, with disastrous results for those Governors who failed to use their autocratic power in the interests of certain lobby groups.

The Imperial habit of mind went much deeper than commerce. People's sensibilities were corrupted so they could no longer see what they were doing, even in such a seemingly blameless matter as the thirst for knowledge.

When William Lanne was the last surviving full-blood Tasmanian male, those two august academies The Royal Society and The Royal College of Surgeons were in rivalry for rights to his remains—the skull, the hands and the feet being the most prized parts. At thirty-four, Lanne was the butt of common contempt and habitually insulted on the Hobart waterfront as a drunk, but he was thought enough of a scientific curiosity to be introduced to HRH Prince Alfred, Queen Victoria's son, who was attending a regatta in 1868. One morning in February 1869 William Lanne collapsed while dressing and died.

Two distinguished medical men went into action in the interests of science and on behalf of their London colleagues: Dr W. L. Crowther for the Royal College of Surgeons and Dr Stokell for The Royal

Society. William Lanne's body had been taken to the morgue, the Dead House as it was then called. On the night of Friday 4 March Crowther and his son crept in by candlelight. They slit the skin down the back of the head and extracted the skull. Then opening an adjacent coffin they removed the skull from a white corpse, put it in the black skin, sewed it up and returned the bodies to their coffins.

The following day the Royal Society men, Dr Stokell, and Mr John Woodcock Graves (famous as composer of the song 'D'ye ken John Peel') arrived at the Dead House. They found the coffin bloodstained and the skull rolling loose in the skin. Stokell reported to a subsequent Board of Enquiry that when 'I got hold of the head in my hand the other dropped out and the face turned round, and at the back of the head the bones were sticking out through the nose and mouth.'

Furious at being tricked, the respected Dr Stokell was determined Dr Crowther wouldn't get all the prizes. He took the next best thing. He cut off William Lanne's hands and feet and gave them to Mr Graves who bore them away to be added to the Society's collection. At no stage in the resulting enquiry did either Dr Crowther or Dr Stokell emerge from the blindness of Imperial thinking—neither could see anything wrong in mutilating the corpse. Their outrage was against each other, the moral issue at stake was whether it was legal or gentlemanly to resort to underhand practices and break into a public building at night.

At the other end of the scale, wholesome changes were happening. The convicts were reinstated as human beings with rights and they bred a generation of healthy, independent 'currency lads and lasses'. Social outcasts found a new usefulness in farming. The rebellious spirit of the Irish nationalists gave edge to moves for representative government and the rights to education and trial by jury. At the height of the colonial phase, when government administrators still held the balance over moneyed speculators, the settlements were fully established—bustling and aggressive, inclined to be chauvinist, with a permanent population who had no intention of returning to their homelands. The working people had developed a particular style of laconic humour and a vigorous practicality which was uniquely Australian. By the 1840s society was settling to a stable, almost eighteenth-century pattern when gold was found and the camera arrived.

Photography presented the public with a window on the world where life was frozen and could be examined, and all its familiar details recognized in unfamiliar light. It was not intended as art. In composition what mattered most was the frame; and this frame could slice figures in half with impunity, it could even allow for the lopped-off hand of the photographer to appear at one side: the point was that its function as a window should be respected. Photographers were all amateurs and their passion was to record momentary flashes of what they saw. The ten-minute exposure needed for the improved Daguerreotype plates might seem painfully slow to our 1,000th-of-a-second mentality, but compared to the many hours required for painting a picture of the same scene, was hailed as instantaneous.

The enthusiast planning to photograph Murray Street, Hobart in 1848 accepted very different terms than those a painter might. He had no means of widening the angle of his frame to include a deeper perspective of buildings, he had no means of selecting or highlighting points of particular interest, and most significantly he couldn't leave out anything that was there. If he wanted people and vehicles in his photograph, he had to go and ask them to stand perfectly still for ten minutes. Of course this didn't give him control of the street—other people used it as they pleased, walking across his frame, leaving ghostly blurs on the plate. Yet we might guess this wouldn't have diminished his satisfaction with the result. His eye would surely have discounted any limitation of the medium, as listeners to shellac recordings a century later could hear past the hiss and crackle of the surface and not be distracted from the music. He had successfully produced a window on the world of Murray Street thanks to a marvel of technology. The immediate fascination of anybody who saw it would demonstrate he had achieved a living communication.

So general was this interest that within a few years photographic studios opened all over the country and another contrast with art became apparent. Portrait painters, as distinct from miniaturists, were almost exclusively concerned with rich clients who could afford their services and had a suitable wall for displaying the finished work. Photographs were nothing like the same tool of status. Among the middle classes they took over from the miniature and extended its possibilities to the group picture.

Sir Redmond Barry, of the State Library of Victoria, commissioned Barnett Johnstone to take an official photograph of the Queen's Reading Room in 1858. The Chief Librarian sat at the far end of the table, with his assistants and some workmen as library users, remaining perfectly still for the six-minute exposure. Afterwards, Johnstone had to process the negative (a wet collodion plate) in the library's cellar, surrounded by an audience of distinguished citizens, including a judge, an attorney-general and the mayor of the city, who all expressed delight and astonishment.

The camera was a new force. The world would never look quite the same again. Ill-prepared and unposed, life might at any moment be preserved as a fragment of history. And in this sense modern history begins with the photograph. Since its invention, the camera has provided a unique authenticity to our records. Owing to the mysterious operation of iconography, we feel a photograph puts us in direct touch with the past.

The first reading room, now Queen's Hall, of the State Library of Victoria. *Barnett Johnstone, 1858*

17

Home away from Home

Colonial life in the cities in the mid-nineteenth century was already comparable to England. And everything *was* compared to England, from the superior climate to the inferior fashions. Buildings, manners, newspapers, clothing, crimes and commerce all were reproductions of the familiar. The essence of the colony remained the motherland which was generally spoken of as 'home', even by those who had never been there and had no intention of going. London news was world news and the nerve centres of the colonies were its ports.

Even today it is remarkable how few inland towns have more than 50,000 inhabitants, while the coastal cities spawn their millions. As for the outback—it was the great unknown. Whether thought of as a challenge, a threat or a lure, the outback remained an optional extra for the settlers. The essential land was that narrow fringe along the coastline, the ports and their supporting farmlands.

The cities grew out around the sailing ship and its harbours. Powered by wind, these ships were engines of timber, hemp and canvas, navigated by the new sophisticated technology of the day; metal sextants and fine chronometers which, together with the new tables of Lunar Distances, allowed the officers to make numerous quick calculations of longitude. Ships carried everything needed for survival including the imposition of civilized order. Even more ponderous than emergency food supplies was the freight of laws; and among their livestock came new settlers. The quintessential colony was not so much at Government House (as many history books would have us believe) but at the docks. And even then, it is doubtful whether the squabbles of the early governors and the landed squatters left anything like so lasting a mark on the character of the place and its people as did the planners, the architects and the builders.

The very notion of a town built round a grid of streets puts the emphasis where it has remained ever since: on traffic and on the theatricality of vistas ending in public buildings—an environment expressing the underlying patterns of social power. The first determining factor in the plan was the town's relationship to its port. For Sydney, as for Hobart and Brisbane, the port *was* the town. However, something quite different happened in Melbourne, Perth and Adelaide. In each case, by founding the social centre away from the port there was a conscious attempt to segregate polite society from the riffraff of seamen and labourers. The great problem was transporting freight to the town. The spectacular growth of Melbourne in the 1850s was undoubtedly accelerated by the first rail link with the port and this in turn consolidated the new elitism of the financiers. Not long afterwards there were trains running to the goldfields at Ballarat and Bendigo. Within a couple of decades Melbourne became the money capital of the country, and has remained so ever since.

A similar attempt to build Parramatta as the fashionable settlement just inland of Sydney failed because it came too early and no such freight link could be established quickly enough. So Sydney grew

TSS *Vernon*: a statement of rest after the rigours and activity of the voyage. The figures create a tableau, formal as a dance. To establish the colony everything had to be brought by sea: people, plants, livestock and supplies. It all began with ships, the skill and courage of sailors, *NSWGP, 1876*

round the port. One of the oldest areas, known as the Rocks, developed into a sailors' district full of licensed and unlicensed grog shops, brothels and dives. Even the street names had characteristic gusto. While the politer thoroughfares of town were named to honour British Ministers and Prime Ministers, such as Castlereagh Street and Pitt Street, the Rocks boasted Cockroach Lane, Frog Hollow and Black Dog Lane, and the upper part of Essex Street was called Gallows Hill because from there you could look down at the hangings in the old gaol.

In those times of travel by foot or horse, the ideal of the hostelry always open and welcoming, was very much a necessity. The towns were full of inns built as family dwellings with accommodation for guests. And alcohol was an extraordinary force. From the outset spirits were the main currency among the poor and the gentlemen of the New South Wales Corps conducted an unscrupulous trade in rum.

In 1800 Philip Gidley King, the colony's third governor, decided to civilize Sydney by arranging for two Frenchmen, prisoners-of-war from Napoleon's new expansionist campaigns, to be brought from England to advise on a wine industry. Eighteen months later 12,000 vine cuttings were planted. The idea was eagerly taken up by landowners. By 1827 the Macarthur property Camden Park alone was producing 90,000 litres of wine annually. A red wine from Gregory Blaxland's farm at Parramatta won a medal in London in 1823.

The production of beer, the drink destined to become far and away the most popular in the colony, was also introduced by Governor King to break down the power of those who were trading in spirits. He arranged for two sets of brewing utensils and six bags of hops to be sent to New South Wales and in 1804 the first brewery began production in Parramatta. That wine and beer would soon become almost as great a problem as rum seems not to have occurred to him.

Administrative difficulties were already taking on a new aspect—conflict with vested interests. Colonial family dynasties were being founded and the ambitious laid out splendid gardens and mansions on vast estates which had mostly been granted free. Notable among these was Captain John Macarthur, famous for his tireless battle on behalf of self-interest. His wife, Elizabeth, was an important contributor to his success, and to her must go most of the credit for establishing Camden's merino wool industry while her husband pursued his litigations and lobbying in Sydney and London.

Among younger men, William Charles Wentworth emerged as leader of a new breed. Born on Norfolk Island in 1790, he became the first native-born Australian to hold public office in the colony when Governor Macquarie made him Acting Provost-Marshal in 1811. This was the beginning of a long and successful career as a man of affairs and as a sign of his status he bought Vaucluse House. This fine house was well known in the little town. It had been built by Sir Henry Browne Hayes, an Irishman who believed the only thing to 'circumvent the vipers' was a peat bog, and had five hundred barrels of it imported from Ireland to fill a trench two metres wide and a metre deep right around the house. Once Wentworth was installed in the house it became a meeting place and great issues were discussed there, such as an end to the convict system (which Wentworth was against), the setting up of partially representative government (which Wentworth was in favour of), and the right to trial by jury (to help reduce the autocratic power of the Judge-Advocate). And in later years it was here that the constitution of New South Wales was drafted. So much for circumventing the vipers.

As the colonies became financially strong, they pushed for self-government. The first legislative council in New South Wales was set up in 1825. Self-government was granted in 1856. The first Premier was S. A. Donaldson, son of a London merchant. As a young man he had been sent to the Mexican silver mines for his business training. Rachael Henning—author of a famous volume of letters—described Sir Stuart Donaldson later in his life as 'very stout, very bumptious

Shopkeepers were never far behind the settlers. This determined woman sold the essentials of life to the thousands who flocked to the goldfields of Gulgong, NSW. *A and A Photo Company, c. 1872*

and a great eater'. The explorer John Gilbert said he was 'an upstart and a coxcomb'. His Attorney-General, Judge Manning, came from a privileged Devonshire family. Educated at University College, London, he represented the better kind of Englishman to play a part in shaping the colonies. He is remembered chiefly for his championing of equal educational opportunities for women. Sir John Darvall, a sophisticated and witty Yorkshireman was Solicitor-General. The concepts and conduct of the law were still very much at the heart of the community and naturally, with so many convicts still around, continued to carry an unusually heavy connotation of crime and punishment.

With the flow of new immigrants, the free citizens of the colony came to outnumber the rest. A large proportion of the convicts had been assigned to the country as unpaid labour on estates anyway. So the tone of the towns changed. Even the gaols changed, and a new class of offender emerged—the delinquent. Policies were devised to reform him rather than just punish him. This was a long way from the lash. One of the most imaginative was the nautical rehabilitation scheme aboard the NSS *Sobraon*. Originally this Devitt & Moore ship plied the Melbourne–Sydney coastal trade, then the government acquired her and she was converted to a training vessel. The delinquents were offered an apprenticeship for a job.

The flow of wealth democratized, to some degree, the old poison of greed. Businesses and banks sprang up and demanded armed protection against attack, not just in Sydney and Hobart and Perth, or the other main centres, but out in the new frontier towns and especially on the goldfields: ordinary citizens had property and money to protect. And having taken the land itself by force, having already suffered sporadic resistance from the original owners, from escaped convicts and from bushrangers, nothing could be more predictable than a lively commitment to defence. A common feature of the colonies was the rifle club. Volunteer militia companies drilled in the bush, doubtless to the astonishment of the bell birds.

The soul of the Empire was expansion. And just as explorers had come from Europe to map and describe the coasts, so the young colonies sent their own explorers inland. Speculation on the unknown interior and what it might hold—from a land-locked sea to fabulous reefs of gold—became a passion. Expeditions led the way to grasslands, across mountains, and eventually the full length and breadth of the continent. Everywhere they went they were aware of being watched and followed by Aborigines. The colonists were beginning to think as Australians and soon it was not the British Government who financed these journeys, but local subscription.

The most lavishly equipped of these set out to cross Australia from south to north and back in 1860. The fifteen men took twenty-seven camels, which were to be cared for by three Indians, especially imported for the journey, six wagons, and copious supplies. They even carried shoes for the camels for rough ground and inflatable pillows to be strapped under the beasts' chins for fording rivers. One of the wagons had been constructed as a punt which could be taken off its wheelbase and used to ferry large loads across any rivers they might encounter. This was the Burke and Wills expedition.

So, one small settlement led to another and the invaders spread out over the country building huts and roads, felling trees and driving their livestock on to the grassy plains which had previously been the grazing land for kangaroos. However, even when a town was well-established in the eyes of its citizens, it was still no more than a huddle of shingle-roofed cottages, a diminutive pile of stone and timber in a clearing invisible from a couple of hours' walking distance. Hundreds of square kilometres of unmapped, wild country lay between one outpost and the next.

This was how they made a home away from home.

The native bush around Sydney Harbour provided a wide variety of building materials for the growing settlement. These shingle splitters worked in what is now known as Middle Harbour. *J. Paine, n.d.*

21

Above: One of the early Daguerreotypes taken in Australia in 1855 of Sir Charles Todd. Wooden with the determination to live up to his respectable profession, this is the Superintendent of Telegraphs to South Australia with his wife, Alice, after whom Alice Springs was named. Contact with the outside world was always important and ever since the first post receiving office was established in 1809 by Lieutenant-Governor Paterson, such official positions became highly respected and sought after.
Unknown, 1855

Right: Hobart from the Queen's Park, 1861. The print is one of a pair of stereoscopic pictures – a popular kind of photograph for many years, they were looked at through magnifying lenses mounted in an adjustable holder, the right eye seeing only the right-hand image, and the left eye only the left-hand image, each being taken from a slightly different angle, giving the impression of depth. As for the town, its Englishness is clear, with straight lines, fences and houses which provided shelter for marooned persons wishing the natives would show more inclination to emulate the exemplary Man Friday

and serve their interests. An unnamed society matron described it thus in the *Colonial Advocate* of 1 May 1828: 'To any one asking me about settling in Hobart Town, "alias Humdrumstadt" I should say, there were good salaries attached to the public officers, and little to do; and from all I can learn, the returns in business are very fair, and the commerce increasing; but if Settlers expect beyond that, unless to eat, drink, sleep, and mope, any thing requisite to render their lives endurable, let them not attempt it.' *Morton Allport, 1861*

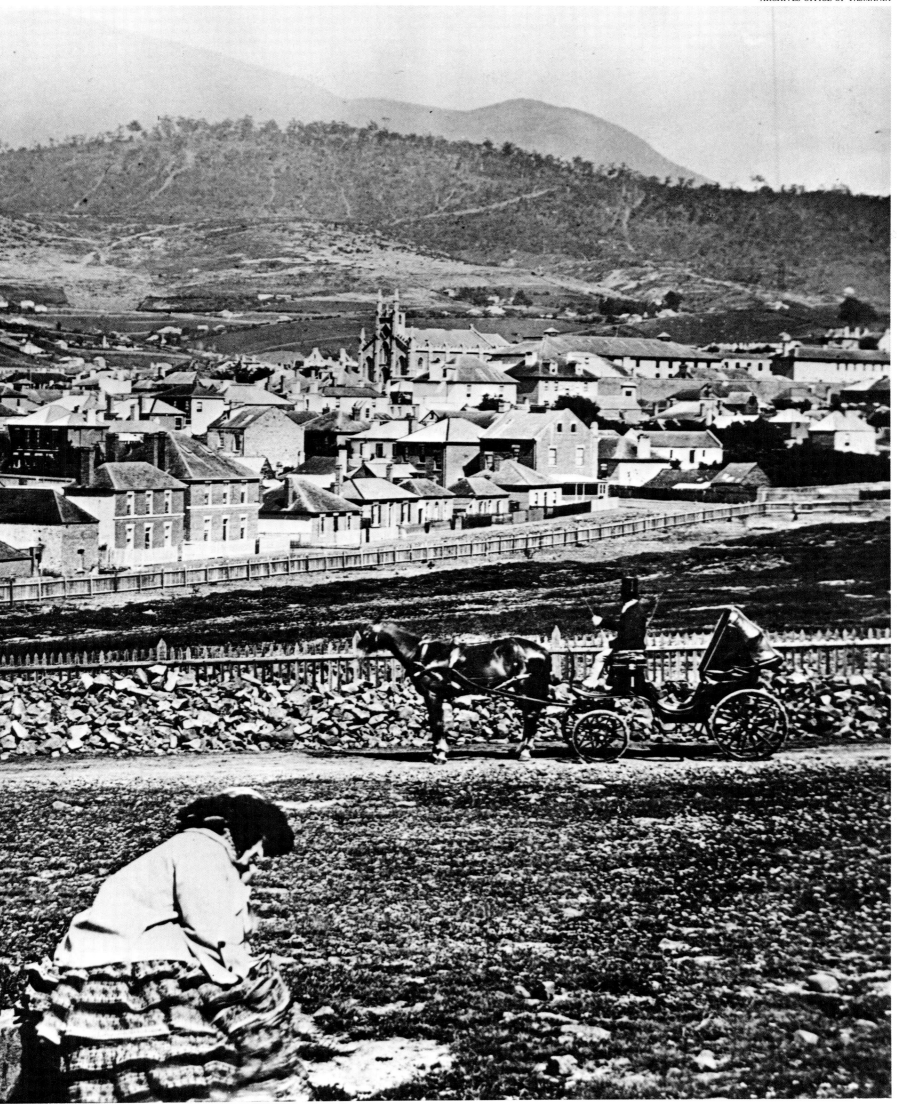

24

Splashing ashore into ragged, featureless bush must have been the way most white people saw Australia when they first ventured out of the immediate environs of Botany Bay. The picture shows the intrepid Sir Charles Todd (in a pith helmet, his right thumb tucked into his belt) and his expedition arriving in the Northern Territory to begin work on the Overland Telegraph Line. It captures the untouched feel of the land as it was first found. *S.W. Sweet*, c. *1870*

Above: 'G. I. Onslow Page 86' is pencilled under this picture, but whether they are the name and initials of the lovely woman is not known. Certainly she was one of the Macarthur family circle as this haunting photograph is from the family's album. *William Hetzer, 1857-79*

Opposite page
Above left: James Macarthur, son of Captain John Macarthur, seated on the porch of Camden Park with his wife and their daughter Elizabeth. The standing figure (centre) is Sir William Macarthur. The original caption names one other figure as Bowman, who succeeded W. C. Wentworth's father as Principal Surgeon of New South Wales and who married John Macarthur's second daughter, Mary. *William Hetzer, c. 1857*

Above right: W. C. Wentworth at Vaucluse House. Though Cambridge educated, he was colonial born and the son of transported parents, so he was definitely not the kind of person the Macarthurs would recognize socially. Indeed, he became their principal adversary among the settlers until, in 1837 he joined forces with James Macarthur to oppose official moves to stop the transportation of convicts. He was by this time a wealthy man who could see the value of free labour. *Unknown, n.d.*

Below: Sydney Cove. The atmosphere of an outpost of Empire is caught in this panorama of repetitions: the nine gables of Campbell's warehouse, the pattern of masts, the cannons lined up in the foreground at Dawe's Point (and pointing in towards Circular Quay!). All waiting for something to happen. *NSWGP c. 1870*

Above: Sir Henry Barkly, K. G. B., Governor of the Colony of Victoria 1856–63, looking like a remittance man, the awkward unwanted second son of a great family with his gauche bowtie, his rumpled lapels, his ridiculous curls, his easily frightened eyes anticipating something catastrophic or at least distasteful. In this, his appearance does him less than justice. He was a capable and tactful administrator who served the Crown ably in many parts of the world, including Jamaica, Mauritius, and Cape Colony. *Antoine Fauchery*, c. *1858*

Right: Many innovations were introduced during Barkly's term as Governor; responsible government in the colony, prison reform, permanent gas and water supplies for Melbourne, a new art gallery and museum. Also railway lines were built from Melbourne to Bendigo and from Geelong to Ballarat, but these were not the first to be constructed in Australia. That honour belongs to the little line opened in 1854 connecting Flinders Street with Hobson's Bay Pier, Sandridge, Port Melbourne, a distance of four kilometres. At this time huge numbers of people disembarked at the pier on their way to the Victorian goldfields. The peak had been reached in 1852 when up to 1,000 people a day landed here. *Charles Nettleton*, c. *1860*

The site of Perth was chosen in 1829, but the real expansion into a city did not happen until the goldrush of the 1890s. One of those who made the choice of site was Surveyor-General J. Septimus Roe, seen here with his family gathered like a bouquet to the success of the British ideal, with nothing indoors to suggest the vast hot land outside, many thousands of kilometres of which Septimus Roe had already travelled. *S. S. Evans (?) c. 1853*

Top: Alpha Cottage, with members of the Stone family: Maria Jemima, Fanny Annette, and Mrs Stone (nee Helms). The comfort of an English fence clarifies their territory. Unlike the Aborigines, theirs was not a sharing culture, but a possessing, exclusive culture. The roadway, St George's Terrace, Swan River Colony, is now the main thoroughfare of Perth. *Alfred H. Stone, c. 1868*

Above: The Roman Catholic Bishop's Palace is a palace indeed and larger than St Mary's Cathedral itself (seen on right). The photographer, Alfred Stone, who was the colony's first Crown Solicitor, has placed his wife, daughters and his sister-in-law, Miss Helms, in his picture to parade their finery on a street deep with dust and pocked by horse hoofs. *Alfred H. Stone, 1868*

31

Captain Charles Harvey Bagot, Royal India Fusiliers, an Irish veteran of British wars in Mahratta, India, and the East Indies. Spectacles pushed well up out of the way, he makes a short-sighted survey of the past from the security of the Empire. A capable pastoralist and copper miner of South Australia, he finally distinguished himself in the Legislative Council by opposing State aid to religion and demanding the imposition of a royalty on minerals. *Townsend Duryea, n.d.*

Left: The Williamstown Volunteer Rifle Company, SA, parade in front of their stone and timber houses, rifles at the port for inspection, bayonets fixed.
Unknown, 1886

Below: Clark Street, the main street of Hill End, one of the most famous of Australian goldmining towns, with its fashion houses boasting cosmopolitan names and reputations. A Berlin House sold fine, dyed knitting wools and similar wares and was often called a Fancy & Berlin Wool Depot. J. Baptiste was the local hairdresser. This area is now vacant land, the township having moved to a position outside the frame of this photograph, to the left.
B. O. Holtermann's Staff, c. 1872

In 1860 Robert O'Hara Burke (*opposite*), a district inspector of police, was chosen to lead a large expedition financed by public subscription. His lack of bushcraft led to his making tragically wrong decisions, besides which he proved a difficult man to travel with and provoked many quarrels. As the journey progressed and the party showed signs of splitting up, their astronomical and meteorological observer, William John Wills (*above*), accepted the position of second in command. In this ambrotype portrait the intelligence of the face is evident. *Both photographers unknown, c. 1860*

Below: John King was the only member of the party which went north from Cooper's Creek who survived. Both Burke and Wills had made the crossing from south to north and half way back when they died. Their bodies were eventually found and brought home to Melbourne for a public funeral. This block of granite was set up as a memorial. *Charles Nettleton, 1863*

Opposite page: The survey vessel HMS *Herald* made various voyages mapping Shark Bay on the north-west coast, Torres Strait to the north, and the Great Barrier Reef in the north-east, also visiting Java, Sumatra and Bali, 1857–60. The navigator was Lieutenant Arthur Onslow RN. He later married Elizabeth Macarthur, uniting two of the richest, most ambitious families in the colony. *William Hertzer, 1856*

Left: Navigation and sailing skills were the lifeblood of the colonies. This is Port Adelaide Dock. *S. W. Sweet, 1886*

Below: NSS *Sobraon*: the ship's schoolroom, with a sample exercise on the board waiting to be multiplied out in copperplate handwriting. And like a sample also, the two teachers present fullface and profile so alike as to seem the same man. The barefoot boys, wards of the State, show plainly that attention is compulsory. *NSWGP, 1898*

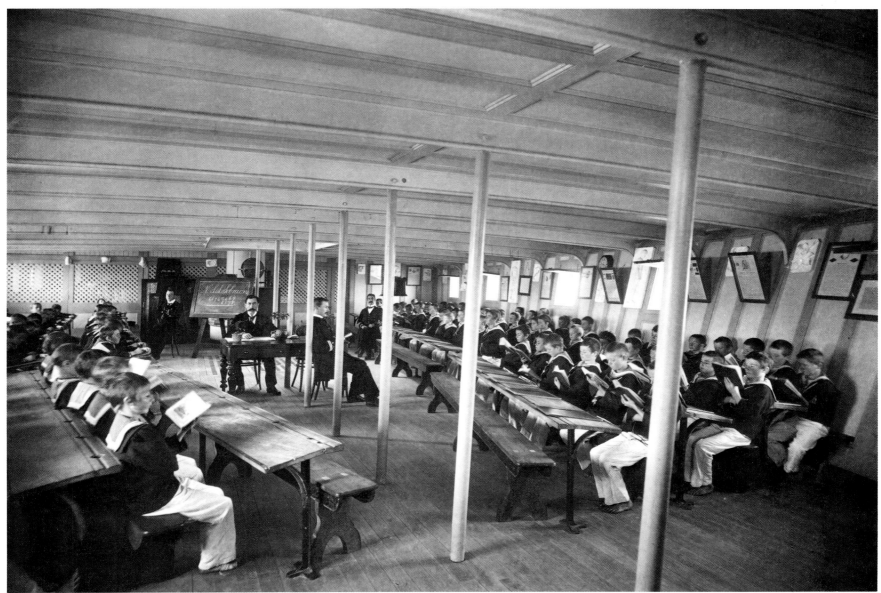

37

The berthing deck of the NSS *Sobraon* in a daytime simulation of the bunking arrangements for the delinquent boys, everything shipshape, and the sparseness and exactitude of information a delight in themselves. After a sister training ship NSS *Vernon* was destroyed by fire her bell was hung in this berthing deck. Even in 1945 hammocks were still used for ratings. They adjust comfortably to the motion of the ship and can be rolled and stowed away in the daytime when the sleeping quarters double as mess decks. *NSWGP, 1898*

Right: Members of the New South Wales Executive Council contemplating the satisfactions of office, 29 April 1856. They are the first Premier of New South Wales, Stuart Donaldson, with Judge W. M. Manning, and J. B. Darvall. *Unknown, 1856*

Below: The main port of Sydney developed around Circular Quay, shown here as a panorama in three sections. The district beyond, known as the Rocks, is still much the same and is one of the few areas of the city to escape the dead hand of air-conditioned commerce. On the left is the photographer's horse-drawn cab, and just right of centre a neat cluster of wool bales. *NSWGP, 1871*

Opposite page: The corner of Pitt and Park Streets, Sydney. By law all hotels had to keep an outside lamp burning from sunset to sunrise for guiding travellers. Before the availability of gas, the kerosene lamps had to be constantly attended. *Unknown, n.d.*

Men in Conflict

As the explorers mapped the way to new grasslands and fertile farming country, the colonists were quick to follow, claiming estates for themselves, 'squatting' as it was called. These were the rich and the military: the only free white men of New South Wales. With the essential provision of convict labour to do the work for them, they began fencing vast holdings. Later they were followed, when such a class came into being, by poor free men who selected small farms and struggled against the established squatters for ownership. Such squabbling among the greedy and desperate for the spoils of invasion preoccupied the administrations of the time, as well as historians later.

The deeper conflict was with the Aborigines, and this has not yet been honourably resolved. Only now, nearly two centuries after the war began (and war it has been from their point of view), is there any public movement to have a treaty drawn up and an official end to hostilities declared. Throughout the first half of the nineteenth century killing was only murder if black people were killing white. When whites killed blacks you could safely say it was settling a score, or protecting family and property, or sport. Judith Wright, in *The Cry for the Dead*, recreates the dispossession of the Aborigines:

It was the loss of the land which was worst . . . The land itself was now disfigured and desecrated, studded with huts, crossed by tracks and fences, eaten thin by strange animals, dirtied and spoiled, and guarded from its owners by irresistible and terrifying weapons. The all-embracing net of life and spirit which had held land, and people, and all things together was in tatters. The sustaining ceremonies could not be held, men and women could not visit their own birth-places or carry out their duties to the spirits. The exiled camps were racked by new sicknesses; pale unfamiliar babies were born to the women; deaths were now so frequent that proper burial became impossible and injustice had to be done to the rights of the dead.

Never was Robert Burns' plea more appropriate, 'O would some pow'r the giftie gie us, to see oursels as others see us.' The British saw themselves as rational, cultured, lawful and humane persons in conflict with ignorant savages much like those they had confronted in Africa, South America, India and Malaya. The respected and sober Captain Watkin Tench, in 1788, explained in *A Narrative of the Expedition to Botany Bay*: 'Notwithstanding the disregard they have invariably shewn for all the finery we could deck them with, they are fond of adorning themselves with scars, which increase their natural hideousness. It is hardly possible to see any thing in human shape more ugly, than one of these savages thus scarified, and farther ornamented with a fish bone stuck through the gristle of the nose.'

Unfortunately we have no record of how ugly the Aborigines thought the deathly white Tench and his roughnecks with their stumpy

The circumstances of this posed picture are not known but the meaning has been caught with ruthless clarity. The photograph was originally published as a post-card. *J. Harrington c. 1890*

limbs, bulging eyes, and vari-coloured skins that could be peeled off and put back on again, not to mention their tattoos.

In the quality of ignorance on both sides, one factor outweighs all others—acquiring an empire, the British arrived with long experience of battles against black people, but the Aborigines had never set eyes on white men before, and if they painted themselves with white mud it was to represent *gunjes* (spirits). The puzzle was, if these were the spirits of their own dead, why had they apparently forgotten their way round, their manners, their language, and even their relatives? Equally unaccountable were the ships swooping in like winged monsters, and cattle which were not only the largest land animals they had ever seen but dangerously armed with horns. Of all the consequences of contact with the white man, none was more frightening and mysterious than epidemics of diseases never experienced before, such as smallpox, from which countless Aborigines died in the early years of the nineteenth century. Such deaths and the deaths suffered by whites were doubtless interpreted as part of the conflict and a result of successful sorcery. Also it is more likely than not that they believed these enigmatic spirit visitors would one day collect their belongings and depart as unaccountably as they had come. This is a view still voiced by some older Aborigines. And, in the long term, who can tell?

Despite the cost, the ruthless occupation of the land proceeded and opposition was gradually suppressed. Tribe by tribe the native peoples were split up, chased off their traditional territory, shot or imprisoned. In Tasmania a race was almost wiped out, scarcely a trace remaining. In the final stages, when only a few of these Tasmanian people survived, the administrators decided on a humane protection order, rounded most of them up and exiled them to Flinders Island where they died, out of everyone's way, consoled by the sympathy of superintendents. The Black War of 1830–35 had been systematic genocide.

HERBERT CHARGOIS

The original caption reads ' "Cumjam" Murderer of Ferguson at Mentana, March 1894'. Perhaps he was more an avenger than a murderer, burning with hatred against the British moving into the Gulf Country which was his ancestral homeland. *Alphonse Chargois, 1894*

On the mainland, similar moves were afoot to herd Aborigines on to reserves for their own good. These reserves were tracts of land for which no colonist could yet find a use. There the unfortunate Aborigines were obliged to live with a mixture of people from different, often antagonistic, tribes, as if all of them were of a single kind. Their conversion was undertaken—not just to Christianity, but from lithe self-sufficiency, free of property, to lethargic submission and the true faith of consumerism. With kindly dedication, missionaries set out to strip them of everything that made life worth living, their religion, their language and their identity in the land of their forefathers.

They were taught to pray. They were taught to read and write. And best of all, they were taught to be ashamed of wearing no clothes. The reward was a guaranteed weekly hand-out of white flour, sugar and tobacco, for which they need do nothing but sit around and wait without causing trouble.

The alternative was to remain outside the protection of an incomprehensible law and risk the consequences. The worst that could happen sometimes did happen, as the people of Myall Creek in northern New South Wales discovered. They had been befriended by an assigned servant on Mr Dangar's station and invited to live near his hut. Early in June 1838 a party of horsemen (including the station superintendent and the servant) rode up, armed with pistols and swords. An eyewitness gave the following account:

They were taken out, and tied one by one to a long rope, used to catch cattle by the horns. Perceiving their fate, they began to weep and moan. The women, though tied, contrived to carry their infants in a net slung from their shoulders. Being all secured, men and boys, women, girls and sucklings, one of the horsemen led the way . . . The funeral procession then commenced its march, amid the tears and lamentations of the victims . . . Arrived at the place chosen for the catastrophe, the slaughter began. All, however, we can glean from the evidence is, that two shots were fired. The sword it should seem did the rest without noise, except the cries of the victims. Decapitation appears to have been considered the readiest way of despatching them, from the great number of skulls afterwards found.

What made this particular massacre unique was its consequences: eleven settlers responsible for the twenty-eight murders were brought to trial. It was the first time such a thing had happened. The jury took a quarter of an hour to decide to acquit them all, and the judge had to stop the public gallery cheering the verdict. But there was disquiet in the community, led by a courageous journalist, Edward Smith Hall, in his paper the *Sydney Monitor* and after a good deal of controversy a second trial was held twelve days later. Seven of the offenders were hanged on 18 December 1838.

So, fifty years after the war had begun, the law conceded that Aborigines were human beings after all.

Up to this time, it is possible that the tribal people had little idea an invasion had taken place. It's hard to believe they'd imagine such alien beings could intend staying—especially showing no proper respect for the sacred land—let alone simultaneously establishing identical patterns of settlement in many places widely scattered along the coastal plain and inland across the mountains. By the time the newcomers were feeling so much at home they could invite the Aborigines to stage mock ambushes for the amusement of a photograph, the Aborigines themselves had probably only just begun to see that the principal enemy was no longer the neighbouring tribe for whom they had an oral history of suspicion.

Prior to the 1860s there were more Aborigines in the country than whites. But the notion of combining tribes from all over the continent into a single fighting nation to defend their territory was wholly outside their experience and social code. And there is no reason to suppose they recognized the newcomers as one single people with a single language either. Certainly, though, they noticed straightaway that some of these strange beings had rights and some had none. Captain Tench, in 1791, taking a rest from his repugnance at their appearance and his condescension to their primitive lack of property, relates this incident:

A convict was at length taken in the act of stealing fishing-tackle from Dar-in-ga, the wife of Colbee. The governor ordered that he should be severely flogged, in the presence of as many natives as could be assembled, to whom the cause of punishment should be explained . . . There was not one of them that did not testify strong abhorrence of the punishment, and equal sympathy with the sufferer. The women were particularly affected; Daringa shed tears; and Barangaroo, kindling into anger, snatched a stick, and menaced the executioner.

Flogging was the most obvious of the daily means by which men were reduced to the lowest possible state. At Macquarie Harbour in 1822, for instance, 169 of the 182 prisoners received 2,000 lashes or more. But hardly less torturous were the working conditions. These outcasts were beasts of burden. Not only did they fell the tall timber but they had to toil in chain gangs bodily lifting the trees and carrying them on their shoulders to the mill. There were seven classes of convict in two main groupings: those wearing yellow stamped with the word FELON, a kind of clothing commonly called 'canaries', who were under complete detention; and those wearing ticket-of-leave grey, who could enjoy relative freedom. The most privileged lacked only social equality and liberty to travel at will. The recidivists at the other end of the scale were treated as caged animals too dangerous even for each other's society and liable for solitary confinement over years at a stretch. And this was the whole point of the system. The convicts, so mercilessly brutalized, were to become a permanent labour force. Once freed, they were frequently too poor to return to Britain even if they chose to. So they stayed and the stamp of defiance was on the first generation of white Australians.

Small wonder that the bushrangers came to be the folk heroes, outlaws, whose exploits were directed against the rich and respectable. Ben Hall, driven to action by police harassment, became the hero of folk ballads and an example to his kind: courageous, chivalrous to women, robbing coaches with panache, even holding up a whole town (Canowindra) for three days and turning the occasion into a kind of

festival. The most famous of all bushrangers, Ned Kelly, proved exceptionally difficult for the police to catch because the countryside was so full of sympathizers. When the gang was finally cornered in Jones' Hotel at Glenrowan, Kelly strode out in the bright moonlight clad in a helmet and armour made from the mouldboards of ploughs and weighing over 40 kilograms. In an extraordinary piece of theatre, he walked among his enemies for almost half an hour while ten of them fired bullets which merely dinted his impenetrable armour before they finally brought him down by wounding him in the legs.

The hostages held at the hotel were released by the gang only to find themselves fired upon by the police. During the trial Sergeant Steele, in particular, appeared in an ugly light. Mrs Reardon gave evidence on oath: 'I came into the yard and screamed for the police to have mercy on me, ''I am only a woman; allow me to escape with my children . . .'' A voice said, ''Put up your hands and come this way, or I will shoot you like b-----y dogs.'' It was Sergeant Steele. I put my baby under my arm and held up my hand, and my son let go one hand and held the other child by it. The man commenced firing, and he kept firing against us. I cannot say he was firing at us, but against us . . . My son was two yards from me. Just as I turned two shots went past me. I did not see my son shot.'

Ned Kelly conducted himself in court with impressive vigour and clarity of mind. When the judge passed the verdict of guilty, he responded with a fiery and challenging speech:

It is all very well to say we shot the police in cold blood. We had to do it in self-defence.

I don't say this out of flashness. I do not recognize myself as a great man; but it is quite possible for me to clear myself of this charge if I like to do so.

No; I declare before you and my God that my mind is as easy and clear as it can possibly be. (*sensation*)

I do not fear death, and I am the last man in the world to take a man's life away.

I dare say the day will come when we shall all have to go to a bigger court than this. Then we shall see who is right and who is wrong.

Ned Kelly was hanged in Melbourne Gaol on 11 November 1880, saying, as legend has it, 'Such is life.' He recognized that a conflict with authority is a conflict between man and man, not between man and a principle, let alone a divine right.

An unwary settler, 'taken by surprise' near Kalgoorlie, WA. *W. Roy Miller, c. 1895*

NATIONAL LIBRARY OF AUSTRALIA

46

Left: This noble figure – his face so strong, so filled with grief, his helmet of hair and square-shouldered cape – recalls a vision of warriors from Vikings to Tartars. He is from King George Sound, WA, and is dressed in kangaroo skin, pegged with a stick and worn fur inwards. A spear thrown by a man like this was a deadly weapon. Captain Tench recorded an attack on some convicts in 1788: 'A spear had passed entirely through the thickest part of the body of one of them, though a very robust man.' *Arthur Onslow, 1858*

Below: A policeman with Aboriginal prisoners in chains, at Wyndham Gaol, WA. Apart from the more obvious problems, there was undoubtedly a difficulty of communication here. Our society was as baffling to the Aborigines as theirs was to us. The idea of being chained together must have puzzled them: why immobilize an enemy rather than meet him in the open in honourable (and understandable) combat? How difficult they must have found it to grasp such a foreign concept as a gaol. *Andrew J. Campbell, 1902*

DAME MARY DURACK MILLER

47

On the back of the photograph is written 'The last of the Native Race of Tasmania all Dead': interesting evidence of the way people spoke of them. Obviously, when this picture was made officially for the Tasmanian Government they were not dead, nor were they dead when the *Illustrated London Journal* reprinted it on 7 January 1865, nor yet when it was subsequently put on display in the museum and Sir George Grey bought a copy to hang in the Auckland Art Gallery. Most notable is the contrast between those powerful women, Truganini (far left), Pattly (right), Bessy Clark (far right) and Lanne, the sad, beaten man.
H. A. Frith, 1864

Left: Truganini became known as the last surviving Tasmanian Aborigine. Though this was not true it made effective propaganda and many new settlers on the mainland said the same would happen there. Her electric rectitude contrasts with the indolent figure of John Woodcock Graves, author of the song 'D'ye ken John Peel', seeming still to be listening for the cry of the foxhounds. He is apparently unashamed at having carried off the hands and feet of her dead kinsman William Lanne for the Royal Society in London. In fact when she died in 1876 her bones were put on show in Hobart Museum and not for a hundred years did anyone think there was anything wrong in this. *Alfred Winter, 1870*

Below: 'Native "Aristocracy"' runs the original caption. Surely the celebrated Henry King of Sydney could not have foreseen how these humiliated faces, ragged clothes and bare feet would speak so eloquently across the years of his insensitivity as well as his skill. *Henry King, n.d.*

Opposite page
Above: Faceless under hats, the people of Barambah Aboriginal Settlement, Murgon, Qld, receive their hand-out of flour. The nutritional value of the food issued on missions and reserves was catastrophically below that of their native fare — kangaroos, lizards, fish, grubs, nuts, berries and seeds. This photograph is one from a series of thirty-five in the archives of the Commonwealth & Foreign Office, marked on the back: 'Department of Agriculture & Stock, Brisbane. SECRET. Not for PUBLIC VIEWING'. It was finally released in 1970. *Unknown, n.d.*

Below: Bethesda Mission Station, Killalpaninna, SA. The women, dressed like European peasants do not behave like them, they do not sit on logs or seats but directly on the earth, which they relate to with natural ease. The church itself, rising from the baked dirt, has cold-climate Christianity in every line. *Unknown*, c. *1900*

Left: This girl with six fingers and six toes was photographed for the Elder Scientific Exploration, 1891P92. Made to stand in a posture halfway between crucifixion and benediction, the white sheet intended to clearly display her deformity becomes a ceremonial shape, seeming to bear her up and ennoble her shame with the purity of a flag. *Dr Elliott, 1891-92*

Below: Children in north Queensland being initiated into arcane symbols. Slates ready, arms duly folded, the Western intellectual tradition already a stricture of straight lines. *Fred Hardie,* c. *1893*

Opposite page: The *Success* was built in Burma in 1840 and carried free emigrants from Britain. Later it was converted for use as a floating prison. Apparently no one thought to change its name—why not *Happiness* while they were at it? Though exhibited as a convict transport, it was never used as such. For ten years she was on display in Australian ports and then in England for a further 17 years. In 1912 she was bought by an American entrepreneur and made him a fortune as a travelling exhibit of colonial degradation. The Ned Kelly armour is a duplicate set made for the Melbourne Exhibition of 1881. *J. W. Beattie, n.d.*

Above: A dummy prisoner models gaol gear in the 'condemned cell' aboard the *Success*. In the early 1850s strong protests from the eastern colonies of Australia finally persuaded the British government to cease transporting offenders. They continued to be sent to Western Australia till 1868. Thousands of ex-convicts would have had the opportunity of visiting *Success*. *J. W. Beattie, n.d.*

INTERIOR CHAPEL, MODEL PRISON, PORT ARTHUR. 546 B . BEATTIE, HOBART.

Above left: Some survived the system, such as the confident David Howie, ex-convict and police constable of Bass Strait. *Unknown*, c. *1855*

Above right: Naturally the brutalization affected more than the convicts themselves. How clearly pity should also be felt for their persecutors is shown in this picture of James Boyd, Commandant of Port Arthur in the 1860s. Was it a convict-photographer who arranged the curtain and plaster bust with mock artistry and saw the effect of including so much of the jangling carpet and fussy furniture? *Unknown, n.d.*

Below: Port Arthur, Tas., during the time it was occupied by convicts. Palatial in size, the intensity of human suffering still hangs over the ruins a century later. Begun in 1850, the prison burnt down in 1877 while the population of the district cheered. *Adovarious H. Boyd*, c. *1873*

Left: The chapel of the Model Prison, Port Arthur. The sample convict, drained of human hope, gazes into God's house with a startled, knowing stoicism. The letters 'I F' are seen on the open doors of the pews. *J. W. Beattie, c.1880*

Below: The bestialities of the convict system lived on after it officially ended in the faces of those who had suffered: faces filled with knowledge of the lash. George Glassford was transported to Tasmania on the *Marquis of Hastings*. *Adovarious H. Boyd (?)*, c. *1873*

Left: Gaol building was a major part of the public works programme. As free immigrants arrived they voiced a concern that the convicts would corrupt all society if they weren't under the strictest restraint. In one instance the records detailing sentences to be served by convicts aboard the *Anne* were mislaid and arrived twenty years after the ship itself—meanwhile all the prisoners had been presumed convicted for life.

As settlement spread to the districts surrounding Sydney and Hobart a network of new prisons marked the landscape as surely as churches.

Buildings like this were designed with open areas for overseeing the movement of prisoners and staff, even to fretted stairways and catwalks, flanked by rows of cells. At the far end of the building, usually up on the first level, an area was reserved for whippings, tortures and official occasions, equipped with a gallows so executions need no longer be a public spectacle. *Unknown, n.d.*

Below: The Tasmanian bushranger Martin Cash in later, respectable years. An Irishman, he was transported in 1827 for seven years. After serving this term he lived a tempestuous life, frequently back in gaol. He escaped from Port Arthur with two others and they took to armed robbery as bushrangers. Captured, convicted and sentenced to Norfolk Island, he became a model prisoner and earned his pardon in 1853. For a while he worked as caretaker of Hobart Botanic Gardens and in 1870 published a boastful autobiography which made him famous. *J. W. Beattie (?), pre 1877*

Right: Ned Kelly, the most famous of our bushrangers and, next to Ben Hall, the most romantic figure among them. This picture was described as 'the latest yet taken' as Kelly left Pentridge Gaol, 1880, not long before his execution. The viewer, however, is left wondering why Kelly's head was superimposed on another man's image.
Charles Nettleton, 1880

Below left: Sergeant Steele, who took Ned Kelly after the gun battle. Damaging accusations were made against him by the citizens who had been held hostage in the Glenrowan Hotel. *John Wadeley or W. S. Barnes, 1880*

Below right: If Sergeant Steele carries with him the manner of a gamekeeper, his police, pictured here, might well be mistaken for poachers. The main force itself consisted of Superintendent Hare, Inspector O'Connor, constables Kelly, Barry, Gascoigne, Phillips and Arthur and five Queensland black trackers.
John Wadeley or W. S. Barnes, 1880

Opposite page
Above: When Ned Kelly was outlawed in 1878 he was 23, his brother Dan was 17, Steve Hart was 18 and Joe Byrne 21. After the police burnt the hotel down, two charred bodies were recovered and displayed at the feet of their enemies. This is the corpse of either Dan Kelly or Steve Hart; both were burnt beyond recognition. *John Wadeley (?), 1880*

Below: Joe Byrne, tallest and most handsome of the Kelly Gang, had already been shot dead when he was propped up for this photograph, providing the gentleman on the left with peace of mind and the satisfaction of the respectable; this, as it happens, is the painter Julian Ashton, with his sketch pad under his arm, demonstrating the inextricable connections between politics and art.
John William Lindt, 1880

The Land of Sacred Water

The British colonist with his passion for the exotic was offered a wealth of strange experience. The form of the landscape, even the green of the trees, was unfamiliar and intriguing. The animals were already a sensation throughout the world. The word *kangaroo* had a place in just about any language with a claim to sophistication. The parrots and budgerigars were exported for their resplendent plumage.

Yarn-spinners in England with no intention of ever seeing the place for themselves embellished the facts. Australia at that time was rather like the galactic empire of today's science fiction—and authors wove fantasies around this land which it pleased their naivety to joke about being upside-down.

The people who had come here to live, however, were not insensitive. They were intoxicated by the country, they recognized its beauty, they felt overawed in the presence of so much for which they had no names, and they accepted that they must learn to relate to it. With energy and a good deal of humour, they set about discovering the bounds of their alienation. They planted themselves boldly on hillsides where they didn't belong, amused at how strange they must look there. The size of the continent, the extent of the horizon and even the sky, challenged their whole sense of scale and within a single generation began working changes in them. These changes were so noticeable that in very few years 'new chums' were laughed at for their manners, their speech and their ignorance of the bush.

Explorers came back with tales of deserts of red sand, deserts of rounded stones, featureless plains flat as far as the eye could see, salt lakes filled with crystalline mirages of water, dense rainforests and snow-covered mountains. Perhaps the greatest effect of their journeys was not so much the opening up of new areas to the invading settlers, but furnishing the white Australian imagination with heroic identity.

The difficult thing to reconstruct is how little they knew of the land they had come to live in. Its size was more or less known from mariners' charts, also the fact that over a third of the landmass lay in the tropics. However, without aircraft or satellite photographs or any other means of seeing it whole or in large sections, a general geographic concept was hard to form. The information had to be built gradually and painstakingly by the explorers. It took almost a century for the picture to emerge clearly enough to say that the country could be described in four sections: a narrow coastal plain stretching the full length of the coastline, seldom more than 80 kilometres wide and often narrower than that; a broad sweep of eastern highlands, a rugged plateau extending from the northmost tip of Cape York Peninsula down to Victoria; a vast western plateau occupying more than half the continent, including Arnhem Land and reaching almost to Adelaide in the south and Perth in the west; and finally an immense sweep of desert, salt lakes and dried river courses extending from the Gulf of Carpentaria to the Great Australian Bight.

The fantasies of lush lands around an inland sea had to be forgotten.

The Lower Camp at the junction of Govett's Creek and the Grose River in the Blue Mountains, NSW. Typical of Australian landforms, this is not a mountain but a canyon. At the top lies a plateau. Explorers often found themselves thwarted by barriers like this. *NSWGP, 1876*

For the purposes of settlement, only the first and second of these four regions were at all hospitable—and even then, not in the hot north.

The Aborigines were nothing like so constricted—with their capacious languages they stored and communicated encyclopaedic knowledge of the land, how it came about, how to live in it, what it meant, interpretations of its bounty and barrenness, and most importantly the whereabouts of water.

As for what lay under the surface in the soil and rock, this didn't interest the colonists much at first. Coal was found both south and north of Sydney in 1797 and that was useful. In the same year Wilson's Promontory was discovered to be granite which was also an asset, while Bass and Flinders reported basalt on the south coast of New South Wales. Other minor outcrops of one kind or another were added to the known map. However, once gold was found, geological surveys suddenly became the key to heaven, experts were dispatched in all directions, and sent back detailed reports. This was the pattern of things to come: they believed the land was there to be exploited as they found a use for it, and never mind the consequences. One hundred and thirty years later the same attitude still rules most governmental decisions, with those in power contemplating the destruction of the Great Barrier Reef for the sake of oil and casting greedy eyes on Aboriginal sacred mountains now known to be composed of saleable minerals. The advertising industry grows fat on presenting dozens of such ravages to the public as development—when by definition mining can only be depletion.

The 'new' and the 'old', both dressed up for the photographer and displaying so plainly their relationship with the land. *Unknown, n.d.*

As for the indigenous animals, they were the first astounding delights to be carried back to Europe; egg-laying mammals, hopping animals the size of deer, little tree-climbing bears, prehistoric fish: 'a land of living fossils' as it was excitedly called. In 1840 the *British & Foreign Review* offered the following summary:

Everybody knows that the vast territory of Australia is distinguished by the most grotesque variations of the customary phaenomena of Nature; nettles and lilies grow to twenty feet in height, palm trees sprout like celery, trees are there with leaves twisted out of the ordinary position, but none of them bears eatable fruit; marsupial quadrupeds and birds without wings scour the plains; the swans are, of course, black; horned bats, vampires, or flying foxes, migrate across the Indian seas; the native dogs can neither bark nor swim, and no other species of animal found there is to be seen in any known part of the globe.

This enthusiasm for the exotic didn't prevent the colonists manifesting their interest by slaughtering the animals. The same with the plants. Down came the forests to make way for devastation by hard-hoofed sheep and cattle. The Queensland native cedar, for example, was entirely wiped out by a most efficient logging industry—efficient in the short term, in the long term it was blindly inefficient for not husbanding a valuable resource. Filled with nostalgia for 'home', the settlers planted familiar flowers and vegetables which they brought with them. Hundreds of foreign species were introduced, crops and weeds proliferated, choking rivers and taking over the local pastures.

Introduced animals ran wild. Feral carnivores, cats and dogs and foxes, preyed on Australian animals, nearly all of which were plant-eaters with no effective means of defending themselves. The domestic herds bred at calamitous speed, from the point of view of the damage they did.

So the effect of the relatively few people invading from Britain swiftly bloomed into a major catastrophe for this isolated country. The land changed. The Aborigines at last realized this was indeed an invasion. And, paradoxically, the newcomers began to voice a real affection for the place and a sense of belonging; the land must have seemed too big to be seriously spoiled, and plenty of them loved what they found here. One of the more attractive sides to the Anglo-Saxon mentality is a highly cultivated veneration for nature. The very vastness of the colony and the certainty that they had the right of conquest to possess it gave the settlers a profound pride. In 1823 W. C. Wentworth as a student at Cambridge University wrote:

. . . yon placid bay
Where Sydney's infant turrets proudly rise,
The new-born glory of the southern skies —
Dear Australasia, can I e'er forget
Thee, Mother Earth? Ah no, my heart e'en yet
With filial fondness loves to call to view
Scenes which, though oft remember'd, still are new.

Their possessiveness had a peculiar character; it really was as if most of them believed they were the first ever to live here. There was a similar division among explorers between the majority who named the features of the landscape they came upon using English words, and the minority who asked the tribespeople of the district how they spoke of the land—and gave it Aboriginal names.

When W. C. Wentworth was a mere youth, ten years before he wrote his homesick verse, he and two other pioneers credited themselves with finding the route across the Blue Mountains inland of Sydney. It now appears likely that the convicts who were in their party were the first white men to have seen over the pass known for countless centuries to the people who lived there before them. The area is thick with English place names including their own, Lawson, Blaxland and Wentworth. It should be mentioned that Lawson, at least, earned his reputation; he was a military man trained in surveying and his records while plotting their route are methodical and exact.

Places were often given more than one name, being found by separate parties, or had their names changed. The highest mountain in Australia first appeared on maps as Munyang. But in 1840 a Polish explorer, P. E. Strzelecki, renamed it in honour of one of his nation's freedom fighters, Tadeusz Kosciusko. At least he had the tact to feel his presumption required some justification: 'Although in a foreign country, on foreign ground, but amongst a people, who appreciate freedom and its votaries, I could not refrain from giving it the name Mount Kosciusko.'

The contrast between the ways in which our two cultures perceived the land could scarcely be more profound. The European-Australians named mountains and rivers in honour of the socially rich, the powerful and the heroic in Europe. The Aborigines named them for the significance they had in an anthropomorphic religion popularly called The Dreaming; and the names were celebrated, re-given again and again in rituals. The totem system, part of the foundation of every tribe, led to spectacular corroborees in which the painted dancer-singers became their totem ancestors among rocks and mountains which were also a fossilized history of animal-people whose spirits could still be called upon—and so man's bond with the rest of nature was reaffirmed. Even the desert wind blowing through old bones could be named as a member of the family in this song sung by Berak of the Mount Macedon district of Victoria in 1887:

We all go to the bones
all of them shining white in this Dulur country.
The noise of our father Bunjil
rushing down singing inside this breast of mine.

Australia is the driest of earth's continents and also the most evenly temperate— 40°C remains the highest average over practically the whole landmass, and the lowest extreme ever recorded, – 22°C is nowhere near the Siberian record of – 68°C in 1892. This combination has meant that though people have found it possible to range over the whole area since the dawn of human society, water has been a constant preoccupation. The most powerful spirit is the rainbow/water serpent representing the origin of life. Survival itself depends on knowledge of where water is to be found.

Likewise the convicts and their masters faced only two boundaries, the sea and the hot dry interior. This is still true today. The fact that our borders are not political, but are water and sun instead has had a notable effect on the development of an Australian mentality.

So, in the early stages, the invaders remained on the coastal fringe and the Aborigines retreated to the drier and hotter parts, taking with them their languages of traditional places. The pioneers improvised as well as they were able, labelling the features of this beautiful land for the things they were reminded of—table tops, sugarloafs, glasshouses—and for the regions they had come from. Poets writing about the bush from 1790 onwards took a long time to distil a language capable of conveying what they saw. During more than half a century they used English terms which simply wouldn't suffer transplantation: verdant dells, copses and brooks. The first breakthrough came with Charles Harpur in the 1850s.

He wrote of a creek that ran shaded

With boughs of the wild willow, hanging mixed
From either bank, or duskily befringed
With upward tapering, feathery swamp-oaks—
The sylvan eyelash always of remote
Australian waters . . .

The awkwardness of this description results from a genuine achievement at forcing English to do duty in a foreign landscape.

Photography, arriving in the 1840s, immediately succeeded where the poets were still struggling. With no words needed, the land and the light spoke for themselves.

The power of water to shape the land is just as magnificent underground as on the surface. These are probably the Timore Caves, NSW, which were used by the bushranger Frederick Ward, alias Thunderbolt, as a hideout. *Unknown, n.d.*

MITCHELL LIBRARY

Three generations in a place where they belong. A contemplative stand of men, the square of figures relates convincingly to both the water and the lines of the banks. The photographer's achievement is more exceptional than might at first appear. Despite having to set up his heavy camera on its tripod, put his head under the black cloth cover so he could focus the image, peering at it upside down, slide in the plate and open the shutter this has been achieved without a trace of ruffling the scene. There is no sense of his being an interference.
Fred Hardie, c. 1893

Right: This powerful figure sculpted with ritual scars is a woman of the Workii (Workia?) tribe. The tribal lands were north of Lake Nash in far western Queensland and included the present Avon Downs and Camooweal. *Charles Kerry, n.d.*

Below left: A north Queensland Aborigine from the Barron River, a district of spectacular gorges and waterfalls. The dramatic artistry of his headdress, nose ornament, necklace and armbands were apparently insufficient proof of barbarity: the photographer's negative has been crudely painted with an opaque medium masking the emulsion in broad bands across the young man's torso and upper arms, with a few blots and speckles here and there. *Charles Kerry, n.d.*

Below right: The man in the mask came from Prince of Wales Island in Torres Strait, from a tribe having connections with both Australia and New Guinea. However, the mask is not theatre of the type this photograph might suggest, with its clarity of detail displayed in an alien studio; at home in the forest it would blend with the landscape. *Charles Kerry, n.d.*

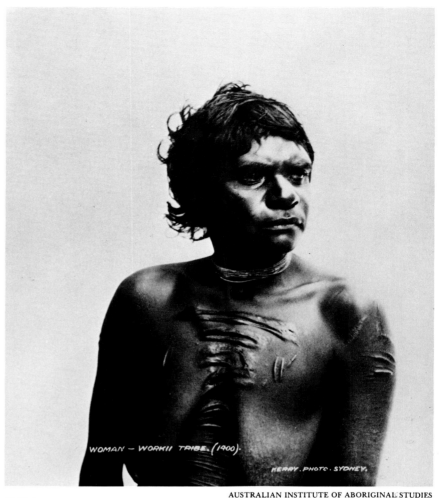

WOMAN — WORKII TRIBE. (1900).

KERRY. PHOTO. SYDNEY.

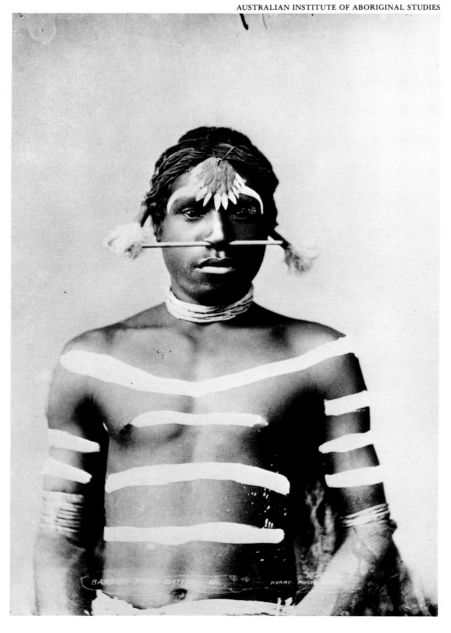

1364. "ABORIGINAL WITH MASK". Kerry. Sydney.

Left: Men fishing. This gentle harmony, men and trees blending, was to be shattered by the establishment of a convict gaol and the growth of the Port Macquarie township in the district. *T. Dick, n.d.*

Below: The Walls of Jerusalem, Lincoln County, Tas. This midland county lies very high and until recent times was not only scarcely populated but scarcely known, having no towns and no roads. The land, in which many rivers and creeks have their source, has been described as sterile and marshy. In the south-east corner of the county are some fine lakes, including Lake St Clair from which the Derwent River flows to Hobart. *Unknown, n.d.*

67

Right: Finding names for the land seems sometimes to have overtaxed the imaginative resources of explorers and settlers. Here a coven of photographers with their glass-plate cameras, members of the South Australian Amateur Photographic Society, have gathered at Waterfall Gully. *Unknown, 1889*

Below: Near Warrnambool, Vic., stands Tower Hill, an extinct volcano island in a huge crater. Seeming withdrawn within natural boundaries, this is one of the areas where relics of dinosaurs and the giant marsupial Diprotodon, have been found. *Unknown, c. 1900*

Opposite page: Queensland travellers in need of a drink, and the bottle they have found. The baobab tree is not only extraordinary to look at, it poses botanists with an enigma: there are two species to be found in the world, one is native to Australia, the other to Africa. The baobab is something of a camel among plants, the bulbous trunk being a reservoir of moisture and nutrition to help it withstand the hot harsh climate. The fruit is a small gourd, soft and edible inside, tasting a little like quince, and refreshing for the sweltering traveller. *J. S. Gotch, c. 1875*

Above: Buffalo Gorge, north-eastern Vic., from the top of the falls. This is an example of work that aspires to being art, to paint with light. The plastic forms of the rocks and the well of light call to mind the paintings of John Robert Cozens. The placement of the figure just within the mountain's shadow is almost too good to be true for a photograph where stage-management is far more difficult than the flick of a brush. *N. J. Caire, n.d.*

Opposite page: An artful picture of another kind. The people establish a scale for Ebor Falls, New England Tableland, and have been placed to comment on its width as well as its height. By having them dressed in dark clothes and using a long exposure, the photographer emphasizes the white water's special qualities of motion and luminosity. The falls are in the Dorrigo Range and their total height is 152 metres. *Charles Kerry*, c. *1900*

Right: 'The Way We Climb the Hills on the Buffalo Ranges, Victoria' reads the original caption: that is to say, with baskets, hampers, and snowshoes tucked under the arm, roped together and trying not to tip backwards at the angle of the trees. Perhaps this angle itself has been artificially increased to exaggerate the steepness of the climb.
George Rose, c. 1895

Below: This purports to be a ladies' toboggan race. An interloper peers out from cover. Although the snow doesn't stir the same passions in Australians as the beach, it has a great many devotees, principally among the wealthier classes. Sports and sporting facilities have the reputation of provoking more learned discussion and blind faith in the general community than all the religions put together. *Charles Kerry, 1900*

3227 LADIES TOBOGGAN RACE.

KERRY PHOTO SYDNEY

AUSTRALIAN CONSOLIDATED PRESS

Left: Australia's highest mountain, Mount Kosciusko is only 2,278 metres, but from June to October it is under heavy snow. Named by P. E. Strzelecki in 1840 after the Polish patriot Tadeusz Kosciusko, the mountain lies in one of Australia's largest national parks. *NSWGP, 1908*

Below: Mt Feathertop. Because of the dense surrounding forest, this mountain was regarded as almost inaccessible for a hundred years. Expeditions which did go there were usually serious about their climbing. Rising to 1,922 metres, it stands in the southernmost outcrop of the Australian Alps, in Victoria. *V. C. Scott O'Connor, n.d.*

Right: Sunrise at Tasman's Arch, Eagle Hawk Neck, Tas. The whole land was a sacred presence to the original inhabitants. Loss of a place like this must have been as hard to bear as loss of their cathedral would be to the citizens of Chartres. Eagle Hawk Neck is a narrow isthmus, a mere 182 metres wide at one point, connecting the Tasman Peninsula to the rest of Tasmania. Because this narrow neck was strategically easy to patrol, Port Arthur at the end of the peninsula, was chosen as the site for a convict gaol in 1830. *J. W. Beattie, n.d.*

Below: During much of the last century huge areas were forested. The trees, never interfered with—because the Aborigines built no buildings and had no use for logs—grew to a great age. This massive specimen on the Great Dividing Range was nicknamed Big Ben and measured over 9 metres in girth. Once Western civilization arrived timber was cleared for pasture and had the additional misfortune of being among the most immediately marketable resources available. Eucalypts are hardwood, some species being noteworthy for their perfect straightness, clean grain and lack of side branches. *C. Rudd (?) c. 1885*

Opposite page: The Lizard's Head, Chillagoe, Qld. The region is noted for its limestone deposits which have weathered into fantastic shapes. There are extensive caves with stalactites and stalagmites, but at the time this picture was taken they were seldom visited owing to the remoteness of the area 1,900 kilometres north of Brisbane and 225 kilometres inland from the coast. *Unknown, n.d.*

THE LIZARD'S HEAD
CHILLAGOE

Opposite page: Visitors at a blowhole, known as the Remarkable Cave. Even the present tame moment is given a touch of danger by knowing that during high seas massive forces of water rush through this opening. It was near this place that Abel Tasman, usually credited with being the first European to explore the Tasmanian coast, came ashore and set up the Dutch flag in December 1642. *Unknown, n.d.*

Left: Sandstone formation near Katherine Telegraph Station, NT. The Overland Telegraph Line crossed the rich river flats of the Katherine River 320 kilometres south-west of Darwin. The Station was set up in January 1871 despite the difficulties encountered during the heavy rains of the wet season. *Unknown, c. 1890*

Below: Timer Rock, Warrumbungle Mountains, NSW. At considerable labour, colonists conformed to the patterns they had grown up with. What you did when you took possession of a piece of land was put a fence around it, call it yours, shut your livestock in and keep other people out. *Unknown, n.d.*

Right: Among trees burnt by bushfires, tourists take possession of the vista at Wentworth Falls, Blue Mountains, NSW. The Blue Mountains are really the eastern edge of a broad plateau where the rock has fallen away along a fault line to form cliffs. Approached from the coast these cliffs appear to be mountains. They were named by Arthur Phillip, the first governor, the Carmarthen Hills after a mountainous region in south Wales. However, owing to a special quality of light (and each country has its own) they became popularly known as the Blue Mountains. *Henry King, 1894*

Below: 'The Three Sisters', Blue Mountains, NSW, viewed across a chasm and the teacup's infinite futures by three sisters.
NSWGP, 1887

Opposite page: Water had sacred significance for the original inhabitants, and might well have again unless our wasteful society learns to conserve and respect it better. Even so, creeks and waterfalls always hold a fascination, and for a long time past picnic parties have travelled considerable distances to spots like Blackheath for their social outings—this is up on the plateau seen in the Govett's Creek photograph on page 60. *Unknown*, c. *1900*

Overleaf: Far outback, the country presents a harsh contrast to the lush coastal plain. It is so dry that camels became essential beasts of burden. Originally imported from India and then Afghanistan, accompanied by Afghan handlers, they flourished. Australia soon came to have—and still has—the world's largest camel population. Locally bred camels can carry an average load of 270 kilograms 40 kilometres a day for two months. *E. O. Hoppé*, c. *1930*

STREAM K'HEATH

Life in the Backblocks

Settlers moved across the ranges out into the grasslands beyond, unaware that the Aborigines had created much of this pasture by regular and selective burning off, or that the herds of kangaroos attracted to this open country were their principal food supply. The newcomers drove livestock there and claimed the land, killing off or fencing out the kangaroos. Travel was slow and hazardous. Many of them pushed hundreds of kilometres from civilization. Food depots and base camps were set up which remained to become small towns. In some cases their own local port developed so that at least part of the journey could be made by sea. Twofold Bay was a typical case of this kind. Goods, mail and passengers came by the 'packet' (as such coastal shipping was called). From there they travelled inland by coach to a supply centre, and so on to their final destination at a farming or wool-growing property. This advertisement appeared regularly in the Sydney press in the 1840s:

The Settlers in the District of Maneroo are informed that they can be furnished with all necessary shearing supplies at the Store, Boyd Town, Twofold Bay, at moderate prices—

Tea	Earthenware
Sugar	McManus' Parramatta Drays
Flour	Woolpacks
Tobacco	Sheep shears
Salt	Seaming twine
Soap	Boots and shoes
Soda	Blankets and rugs
Corrosive sublimate	Slops* of every description
Hardware	

N.B. Every facility for the shipment of wool and produce by regular packets to Sydney.

* Ready-made working clothes.

Soon, a distinctive style of life had developed. The treasure people sought and claimed was independence; the chance to be self-reliant and create their own code of values. This was what industrial society had taken away from so many working people in Britain. Here, privilege and property, strong as they were, were nothing like so entrenched. And the labouring class opposed them more openly, they made a virtue of their sympathy for the under-dog. Outlaws were popular heroes. The growth of a folk balladry showed this clearly with its rigid code of ethics and consistent presentation of bushrangers as victims of repressive authority. The ballad 'Bold Jack Donahue' begins

There was a valiant highwayman of courage and renown,
Who scorned to live in slavery or humble to the Crown

Railway construction gang, central Qld. Fettlers like these laboured in hot, exhausting conditions. The bowyangs strapped around their trousers gave the leg more freedom to flex by bagging the material at the knee. New chums were told it was done to keep out poisonous snakes. *Unknown, c. 1886*

'The Wild Colonial Boy' behaved exactly as a bushranger should

> In sixty-one this daring youth commenced his wild career
> With a heart that knew no danger, no foeman did he fear.
> He held the Beechworth mail-coach up, and robbed Judge
>   McEvoy,
> Who trembled and gave up his gold to the wild colonial boy.
>
> He bade the Judge good-morning, and told him to beware
> For he'd never rob a decent judge that acted on the square;
> But not to rob a mother of her son and only joy
> Or you'll breed a race of outlaws like the wild colonial boy.

The ballads were news, they were declarations of sympathy, of identity, and they spread throughout the backblocks with tremendous rapidity. Everybody knew it was at Goobang Creek that Ben Hall met his fate and died with the dignity he had shown in life. The names of the Kelly Gang were household words—the villains of the piece were troopers Scanlon and Johnson, just as the villains of the Hall ballads were Sir Frederick Pottinger and 'cowardly-hearted Condell, the Sergeant of police'.

By comparison, the people of Sydney, Melbourne and the other big centres remained far more English and at least somewhat more respectful of authority. To enjoy common aspirations, people had to be in touch, they had to be able to meet and communicate. They also had to have the means of transporting their produce for their stake in freedom to be economically possible. So road making was essential. No sooner were the roads there, simple dirt tracks as they were, than carts and drays and sulkies were on them. The horse emerged as

indispensable in this huge country. Horse breeders, horse breakers, saddlers and blacksmiths were to be found at the heart of every settled area. And horse racing in Australia, far from being the sport of kings, was the passion of the common man. Bullocks were yoked up for the heavy plodding jobs and camels soon proved marvellously versatile work animals—even for the police. The *Australian Encyclopaedia* as recently as 1927 assured its readers that a camel will cover 160 kilometres a day for a week and that 'an offender on horseback has no chance against a constable on a dromedary'.

Many pioneer families lived in the harshest conditions. They had no knowledge of how to live off the land until their own crops bore fruit. More often than not their only rations for months at a time were a bag of flour, a tea chest and a sugar bag. Given one bushfire, they were ruined. In their fight for contact they were up against a press hostile to the spending of public money on roads and bridges. However, time was on their side and their productivity was needed. The hazards of bushfires and floods were a measure of the new resilience these folk discovered in themselves; the stories of how they lived through trials and crises grew into an oral tradition. A new, laconic manner of speech became the preferred style. Casual humour was cultivated in the face of hardship. Survival depended on mutual help. You had to be able to rely on your friends. Itinerant workers teamed up and roamed the bush in pairs. The code of mateship developed till it assumed the position of a central ethical ideal.

Stories and pictures often show the lonely pioneer and his even more lonely wife. But the essence of winning through was, as it always has been, social. Even pioneers living far apart kept a sense of community with each other and looked forward to gathering together whenever

No settlement, however remote or small, would be complete without its pub. This is the Westralia Hotel, Kalgoorlie, WA. *E. O. Hoppé, c. 1930*

MANSALL COLLECTION, LONDON

possible. Between times, there were visiting seasonal workers, swagmen, the mailman, also health and education services, infrequent though these were, to bring and carry news and to share the district gossip.

In a camera history of pioneer life, while we have no photograph of people in the act of dropping from exhaustion, we can see in the hands and faces of these composed subjects enough to tell us what they lived through. And we find women not just parading their Sunday best, but parading it out on harsh baked earth in front of slab huts. The perfection of their dresses, so beautifully ironed, would not be noteworthy or even noticeable at the parish church of St James in Macquarie Street Sydney, but in the scrub or on the goldfields it acquires a touch of heroism.

The townships these people built in the bush began to show a particular character in common. Far from the Italian Renaissance model of enclosed vistas, arcaded streets leading to key buildings, with the tamed landscape peeping over the top, the Australian backblocks town was typically a straight, wide stretch of country serving as a road and flanked by two lines of low buildings facing each other. Looking through town, the eye was led endless distances beyond. Space invaded the townscape to be its dominant feature. People liked space. It was no use joining the academic architects deploring the larrikin lack of sophistication. People didn't think design and good taste were any sort of priorities at all, they had too much sense for that, and too much tact—they put up their buildings where the buildings seemed to fit.

The average house had from two to four rooms either side of a central corridor. The kitchen was out the back in a separate hut, as a precaution against fire. The lavatory, if the family went in for such luxuries, would be a large pit dug in the ground well away from the home with a lid of boards on which a wooden outhouse stood, complete with a seat inside. In the first half of the nineteenth century people used mainly bark for roofing, but then the brilliant invention of corrugated iron became available and Australia made positive moves to become the world capital of its use. Light and strong, it was the perfect material for roofs and, once it could be bent, rainwater tanks. It was easy to transport in stacks, simple to use in building, suitably light for a timber frame and walls to support, and durable. Elsewhere in the world people were welcome to despise corrugated iron as an inferior building material, in Australia no such snobbery prevented people recognizing it as ideal.

In many respects it was a makeshift life, but a good one. And then gold miners came by the thousand. Unwanted as they were, they populated districts previously very quiet. Following the gold, the banks arrived, opening branch offices in rough wooden shacks. This meant the roads had to be improved so the coach and the gold escort could get through to the city quickly and safely. Also of course the banks were eager to seize whatever business opportunities came their way. Farmers began to find themselves out-maneouvred and caught in a tangle of mortgages. The backblocks were becoming civilized, slow as the process was.

Then mail services started reaching remote parts. Private contractors, usually an individual with a reliable horse and cart, brought regular deliveries along backblocks tracks. Families nailed their mailboxes to posts out on the track and came from the house, maybe several kilometres away, to clear them.

For many pioneers the absolute isolation of the early days was past.

Mail services brought isolated settlers news of family, friends and the world beyond their boundary fences. *CIO, n.d.*

85

A men's fashion-plate of Crimean shirts, leather boots, wide belts, patriarchal beards and various hats from the pith helmet to the velvet smoking cap. In fact, these flash fellows are far from civilization. They are engineers on the Overland Telegraph Line: J. A. G. Little, R. C. Patterson and A. J. Mitchell. The older man, second from right, is the superintendent, Sir Charles Todd. The photograph was taken at the Roper River, NT, 1872, at the end of a three-month wait while the wet season ended and the flooded river went down.
S.W. Sweet, 1872

Right: Afghan traders and their camels, Chillagoe, Qld. The trader in European rig is wearing the outward sign of his expertise in the foreign language of the country. He is the one who will conduct all business transactions. The unfortunate camels are muzzled to limit their natural ability at self-expression, being well known as biters and spitters. *Unknown, c. 1895*

Below: If the resplendent Miss Bridget Darmody's composure seems unassailable, so does the camel's. Taken at Parachilna, SA, looking east towards the Flinders Rangers. The rein is connected to a peg through the camel's nose. The formation and tenderness of a camel's mouth make it impossible to use a bit to guide it, as with a horse. *S. W. Sweet, c. 1886*

Left: Survey work on the Transcontinental Railway link from Port Pirie, SA, to Kalgoorlie, WA, a distance of 1,783 kilometres. Most of this line crosses a dead flat desert and one stretch of track is the longest straight in the world, 478.3 kilometres. This is the Western Australian team at the terminal peg and cairn marking the border of South Australia.
Unknown, 1909

Below: Many explorers used camels. Michael Terry's riding camel, Dick, was capable of covering 96 kilometres a day.
Unknown, 1933

Right: A bank building at St George, Qld, with the roof held down by a timber frame. A range of male St Georgians has been conscripted to serve in the picture. And with security the way it seems to be, no wonder one of them is a policeman. The town grew up as a stopping place for drovers taking stock on the long journey from central Queensland to southern markets.
J. S. Gotch (?), n.d.

Below: On 19 October 1872 in the Star of Hope gold mine, Hill End, NSW, the world's largest piece of reef gold was hauled to the surface. It weighed 235,143 grams, of which over 93,300 were pure gold. Partners in the mine, Bernard Otto Holtermann and Louis Beyers, are seen here at left and right of the doorway laying hands on smaller samples from the Star of Hope.
B. O. Holtermann's Staff, 1872

Holtermann's claim, Hill End, NSW.
The circular and octagonal roofs
sheltered the horses plodding round in
circles driving the whim, the other roofs
house shafts along the western slope of
Hawkins Hill. These bark huts have
been built with the miners' unerring eye
for landforms, the pitch parallel with
the hillside; each appears isolated,
relating only to its own slope,
communication between them being by
foot. *B. O. Holtermann's Staff, c. 1872*

Right: Thought to be the first oast house in the Gippsland area, Vic. at Bairnsdale. The owner of this beautiful kiln for drying hops was A. W. Howitt. Already well known as an explorer, magistrate and translator of Aboriginal legends, he came to the forefront of public attention as leader of the expedition to central Australia to bring back the remains of Burke and Wills.
F. Cornell, 1872

Below: Humour is a great part of survival in adversity. Here on the Western Australian goldfields a young blade takes an elegant al fresco breakfast, with his morning paper, unperturbed by his chimney being so perilously close to that inflammable roof. The chair he's sitting on carries the name H. H. De Bool and one wooden case reads 'Haricots-Verts Coupés', which tells something about the diet of the diggers.
Unknown, c. 1900

Left: Tree-stump house at Wynstay, south Gippsland, Vic. The fairytale world of the house in the woods and *of* the woods is created by this lovely place; the image reinforced by those magical hats, the male and the female, communicating over some simple task of survival. *N. J. Caire, n.d.*

Below: Coalminer's house. Lithgow Valley, NSW, about 160 kilometres west of Sydney. The oven is built in the usual place, separate from the house as a precaution against fire; it is made of packed clay with a simple hole for the smoke. The chimney on the right of the house is also a standard construction, an independent unit outside the building with the fireplace opening into the room through a hole in the wall. *NSWGP, 1879*

Right: Station employees in a bush hut at Lake Poppii discovered sweeping up, drinking tea, darning, and hypnotizing the dog. The society of men without women was a common feature of pioneer days in the backblocks. It is plain to see that mutual tolerance and an easygoing lifestyle were the most desirable of virtues. *Unknown, n.d.*

Below: Mr Stock's selection in the 1880s, tucked away in a remote corner of the Groajingolong district of Gippsland, Vic. This is backblocks living indeed. The pioneers have brought the necessary tools with them, Nature has provided materials for the rough bark slab shelter and the fish for the next meal. *N. J. Caire, c. 1885*

Opposite page: A mixture of skins—koala, possum, echidna—tacked on the wall to dry out. These bushmen seem well pleased with their catch which will bring them some extra income. They probably never gave more than a passing thought to their contribution to the destruction of the unique animals they have killed. *Unknown, n.d.*

RETURNED FROM M^c RAGGED RUSH

1000 MILES TRIP IN THE BUSH

Opposite page: Posed in front of a badly painted, badly observed bush scene on a false grass mat, the incongruous realities of this prospector's 1,500-kilometre trip to the goldrush come touchingly alive. 'Returned from the Mt Ragged rush.' Mt Ragged is in the arid desert in the south of Western Australia, near the Great Australian Bight. The journey was across a wilderness with very few towns or settlements on the way.
Unknown, c. 1900

Left: Northern Territory Railways. Where the line wasn't fenced, locomotives often faced messy problems with wandering cattle. Some engines were small enough for this to lead to disaster. The 'Sandfly' suffers the consequences of colliding, with a cow.
Foelsche, c. 1901

Below: The kind of settlement being connected by huge lengths of railway in the early days hardly warranted expenditure on comfort, The upkeep, both on roads and rail, in remote areas was a tremendous burden on tiny communities such as Condon, WA. Flat, two-dimensional landscape like this must have baffled the British settlers, being so foreign to their own.
L. Gray Williams and Co., 1897

Right: The Aborigines were not to know what ideas of towns and pavements filled the heads of the early white settlers. At first the structures they put up were not very different from their own gunyahs. This particular hut might have been abandoned to fall down—on the other hand it might have become the nucleus of a town with stone buildings and thousands of inhabitants. We cannot tell. *N. J. Caire, c. 1880*

Below: Pioneer farmers methodically set about their huge task of eliminating hundreds of square kilometres of forest. Each stage of this clearing process can be seen here. Like amputated elephants' feet the treestumps stand round the new house. Behind, rise the simple skeleton trunks of ringbarked trees. The wind has thinned the foliage in the next line of forest where the canopy has been broken. Then the untouched bush, with all it holds, covers the hill-line at the back. The stove in the kitchen hut is alight and there is evidently no shortage of fuel. *Unknown, n.d.*

Opposite page: In the vastness of the bush a touching female figure at a cross of fallen logs. A small holding carved out of surrounding bush, at Cobham near Gilderoy, Vic. *N. J. Caire, n.d.*

Overleaf: The pioneer's wife works with her husband clearing land and burning stumps where the corner of their block fronts on to the main road. The initial labour of cultivating virgin land was indeed daunting. *George Bell, Kerry and Co., c. 1900*

ARCHIVES OFFICE OF TASMANIA

THE
PIONEER'S
WIFE

930. Kerry
Sydney.

Right: Three young men of Bermagui, a fishing comunity on the far south coast of New South Wales: Charles Ferguson, William (Wallaga) Mead, and an unidentified friend. The town became headline news in 1880 with the Bermagui mystery. In October of that year a government geologist who had arrived to look over the new gold diggings disappeared. And so did several other men and a fishing boat. The boat was found a few kilometres north, apparently deliberately wrecked. No trace of the men was ever discovered, despite intercession by Queen Victoria. *W. H. Corkhill, c. 1900*

Below: Woolabrah bore, Moree District, NSW: depth 600 metres, flow over 2 million litres a day, temperature 32°C. The name Moree is derived from an Aboriginal word meaning 'long spring'. The artesian water, with its heavy mineral content, was soon found to have curative uses and baths were built for rheumatic patients. This is the centre of a rich pastoral district raising sheep and fat cattle, growing corn and wheat. *NSWGP, 1898*

Opposite page: The photographer's family at Central Tilba, NSW: Frances Corkhill with her son Norman, and in the foreground her daughters Pearl and Edith. This is from a large and valuable collection presented by Pearl, Sister Corkhill, to the National Library of Australia in 1975. Living in a tiny gold town perched on the side of a mountain on the coast, these children lived an ideally free, healthy life in surroundings of great beauty. Their forthright directness has been admirably caught by their father. *W. H. Corkhill, c. 1900*

NSW GOVERNMENT PRINTING OFFICE

Right: The scourges of the settlers were bushfires, drought, floods and loneliness. A home at Crafers, SA, beyond saving. In all probability the owner refused to give in to his misfortune and rebuilt on the same site.
Krischock, 1939

Below: The February floods of 1893 in southern Queensland were the most devastating on record. In Brisbane two immense storms struck in less than a fortnight; seventy inches (nearly two metres) of rain were recorded until further registration was impossible on the equipment. A journalist wrote, 'The hush over the doomed city was like that before an impending siege.' Nearby, Ipswich was also flooded. The locals smile in the face of adversity and declare a Sunday afternoon for the photographer, lounging in boats and sheltering under umbrellas, and seeing everything from a novel perspective.
Francis Whitehead, 1893

Left: The 1926 Gippsland bushfires raged for six weeks, easing off and then flaring up again. There were many stories of loss, suffering and courage from the worst hit areas, Warburton, Powelltown and Noojee. The one that all Australia knew about was how 15-year-old Florence Hidges saved the lives of her three younger sisters by crouching over them as the fire swept past. She was severely burned but survived. The town of Noojee was gutted, huge areas of valuable mountain ash forest were left as charcoal, sawmills were wiped out and timber getters' families died, trapped in their huts. *Unknown, 1926*

Below: The 1890 flood in West Maitland, NSW. The scene has been arranged by the photographer with everyone instructed to remain still for the exposure. The phantom horseman in the foreground is the unexpected element, the delight of photography. The weak shadows show that the sun is coming out, but often with floods the worst might still be to come as the headwaters continue to flow down from higher land. A practical advantage of timber buildings set up on stumps is that once the floodwaters go down they dry out remarkably quickly. *M. Moss, 1890*

Yandilla Street, Pittsworth, Qld. The town was named after the Pitt family who founded the pastoral property of Goombungee in 1854. The marble players have chosen the middle of the road for their game. It is incidental that they are watched over by the *Pittsworth Sentinel* on the left and other buildings—the great presence in the town is the road. Traffic is evidently infrequent. Time and decay frame the picture with bold marbling of their own. *J. H. Pardey, c. 1908*

Left: Yenda, NSW, in the Murrumbidgee Irrigation Area, only three months old and already idiosyncratic. The citizens have obliged with a display of transport, a beautifully placed bicycle, a car, three sulkies and a cart, plus the last two carriages of a train disappearing off left. The iron roofs bouncing the light cast deep Australian shadows. The lack of a firmly defined approach road has led to independent decisions on how to drive in. The photograph was taken for the Department of Immigration, evidence of impressive optimism if it was to lure prospective settlers. *CIO, 1922*

Below: Three brothers of the pipe in the 1920s. Two of them are wearing ex-servicemen's badges, which continued to be more common than not, until the late 1960s when war and war service suffered a massive reversal of public respect as a result of the undeclared war in Vietnam. *W. J. Mildenhall, 1926*

AUSTRALIAN ARCHIVES

SOUTH AUSTRALIAN ARCHIVES

Above: A vigorous bridge-building programme was urgently needed to keep communications open during flood seasons, although one can hardly imagine a flood in the drought-stricken conditions expressed by this photograph, the men with faces sheltered from the blistering wind. This is the opening of the Victoria Bridge, Laura, SA. *Unknown, 1936*

Right: The swagman was an itinerant bushworker who carried his swag on his back. This bedroll was known as a 'matilda,' the origin of the word is obscure but the phrase 'waltzing matilda' might well derive from the matilda being rolled (German: *walzung*). This swagman was no doubt looking for work. Anyone who thinks men tramped the roads for fun, or as tourists, or for the greater glory of the National Image, need only look at his face, his hands and his feet to know the truth of the matter. *E. Gall, 1901*

Opposite page

Above: The black soil plains of northern NSW are rich agricultural land but can pose problems for travellers in the wet. The chances of extricating this car before the land dries out are minimal. *W. E. Pheagan, n.d.*

Below: If conditions are not tiresomely wet, the chances are they're desperately dry. Narrandera, one of the oldest towns in the wheat-farming Riverina district of NSW, prepares for the onslaught of a dust storm. Afterwards there will remain the labour of cleaning up, inside as well as outside—and this was before the invention of the vacuum cleaner! *C. T. Dugdale, 1903*

God made them High or Lowly

All things bright and beautiful,
All creatures great and small,
All things wise and wonderful,
The Lord God made them all.

The rich man in his castle,
The poor man at his gate,
God made them, high or lowly,
And order'd their estate.

This cheerful Protestant hymn is ruthlessly frank in its social teaching, a teaching which colonial society emphatically endorsed. New South Wales began with a fixed caste system. At the top were the naval or military governors and their confidential staff. At the next level were the army officers and wealthy traders. Below them came the private soldiers and the working people. Then there were the convicts. And lastly the Aborigines.

The convict-based towns built on the mainland and Van Diemen's Land immediately reflected this pattern. The governors' favourites were granted seigneurial estates in the surrounding rural districts and became what was sarcastically dubbed the 'bunyip aristocracy'. Those with prestige announced it to the world with the imposing buildings they lived and worked in. Government House was characteristically Georgian in style, aiming at simple, solid elegance, set in spacious gardens of curvilinear lawns, gravel driveways and pleasing vistas. The business sector of town crowded round the port, lining the old footpaths and bullock tracks. The newer parts were planned with streets set out in a grid of right angles imposed on the site irrespective of where the land rose or fell or where it was crossed by creeks. It was a well-known truth that shops had to be glassed in with, preferably, a window fronting on to the footpath. This is how they were built in Europe, so this is how they were built in the Antipodes, even in the heat of Brisbane and Perth. The assumption that you needed a role in life went undisputed, a grocer was not also a clerk or a fisherman.

Gradually a mood of independence seeped in from the battlers in the backblocks and the social rigidities relaxed. The tight little terracehouses of the English model gave way to sprawling places shaded by verandahs—an Indian device the British had already found suitable for the hotter outposts of empire. The labouring classes lived in slab timber huts roofed with bark. A few, but very few, Aborigines hung around the fringes of these towns for the patronage of discarded clothes and food hand-outs, living off the excitement of a new kind of society, one which promised many of them an unimagined independence from the rule of old men and timeless, unchanging ritual. However, it is harder to forgive those we injure than those who injure us. The words of Andrew Bent, an ex-convict, voiced the sentiments of many when he wrote in his newspaper *The Colonial*

The ideal of colonial spaciousness: Government House Brisbane, whose splendid gardens stretched right down to the river. In recent times it has been used as a conservatorium of music and later as an administration block for the Queensland Institute of Technology. *J. P. Thompson, 1894*

Advocate, 'Unless the blacks are *exterminated* or *removed*, it is plainly proved, by fatal and sanguinary experience, that all hope of their ceasing in their aggressions, is the height of absurdity.' (Hobart Town, 1 May 1828.) White people grew to resent them and indoctrinated their children with attitudes to support their own self-esteem. If the Aborigines were not shown as vicious, cannibals even, they were sneered at as feckless. *The Young Australian Alphabet* of 1871 carried this verse,

B is for blackfellow
We can all see
Lazily sleeping
Under a tree.

From the 1790s onward, it was recognized that children would be the mainstay of any permanent colony. The older the immigrants, homesick, less resilient, proved not so willing to make do without familiar comforts and discomforts. Much thought and discussion was given to the welfare of children and how they might blot out the stigma of having convict parents or ancestors. For those who could afford it, sons and daughters were put through a polite education. A typical school was Mrs Marr's which she advertised in the Sydney press throughout the 1840s.

DAME MARY DURACK MILLER

Reg and Mary, children of the wealthy Durack family of Western Australia. *Unknown, 1915*

Mrs Alexander Marr begs respectfully to inform her Friends and the Public that she continues to instruct Young Ladies in the usual routine of English Education, including Reading, Writing, Arithmetic, Grammar, Geography, Plain and Fancy Needlework, Music, French, Drawing &c, on moderate terms.

From her long experience, Mrs A. M. feels confident that those Ladies who may honor her with their patronage, will be highly satisfied with the improvement of those Pupils they may intrust to her care.

Respectable references, as to character and ability, can be produced.

Hours from 9 a.m. till 4 p.m., with one hour's intermission.

In the case of most schools, such hours applied six days a week from Monday to Saturday. Shops and banks, likewise, were open on Saturdays. Those who grew up without an education knew that respectability could be bought. Money became the measure of the new gentility just as had happened in America and well before it was general in England. Successful men who had been deprived of schooling pressed for a change in the system. Free education was introduced in Australia for the first time in Queensland in 1870. Other initiatives were taken to bring the classroom to the outback children. Right up to the present day there are unique programmes devised specifically for local conditions; the most important breakthrough came with radio and the 'School of the Air'.

Moral education was the preserve of the churches, which wielded considerable power, especially in the early days, and offered weekly assurances that the injustices of society were, in general, divinely ordained, and any restitution earned would be made good in heaven. The establishment of the churches was helped by generous grants of land and exemption from taxes.

If you wanted rights, you had to be a success first and then you could demand them. Workers' movements such as the Luddites of 1811–16 who smashed factory machinery in the English midlands had no immediate counterpart here, because for a long time to come Australia would remain an eighteenth-century rural society, virtually untouched by the Industrial Revolution. Agitation to improve the conditions of the poor came mainly from well-intentioned philanthropists. In 1844, for example, the Mayor of Sydney chaired a meeting of notable citizens to discuss a limit to the hours of business, 'closing the shops in the City at a reasonable hour, so the young men and women employed there, whose animal spirits have been destroyed, whose physical energies impaired, and whose mental faculties weakened by work, work, work, will now have instilled into them a knowledge of the value of leisure as a source of enjoyment through life.' (The *Atlas*, 21 December 1844)

The company town to end them all was set up by a Scots adventurer Ben Boyd at Twofold Bay. A man of great energy, he housed his own community of workers and built a town for them in an almost mediaeval attempt at feudalism. By 1844 he ran a bank and owned 727,200 hectares, including fourteen stations in the Maneroo (now called Monaro) district inland. At Boyd Town he built a large jetty and a lighthouse and ran a whaling fleet. In 1847 he joined the scramble, shipping Pacific Islanders to the colony for the sugar plantations, always with an eye to the possibility of cheap labour for himself. Within a year, however, his financial speculations collapsed and he was ruined. A traveller visiting Twofold Bay in 1848 described the town as 'the seediest place on this terrestrial ball'.

At all times since the first eleven free settlers arrived in 1793, immigration has been a basic factor in the growth of population. By 1850 146,000 convicts had been brought here and 187,000 free immigrants had come. Probably for the first time in history there were more whites in the country than Aborigines. For the colonists, never again was there any question of security of tenure. They were here to stay: the new Australia had begun.

Then the goldrush led to a further enormous influx. In the ten years from 1851 to 1860 the non-Aboriginal population rose from 405,400 to 1,145,600, and they were not just British subjects as before, but Chinese, Germans, Poles and many other nationalities. The Europeans tended to live in their own communities but they were tolerated and even liked. The Chinese, however, provoked a new wave of racism.

So many Chinese flooded in that in 1855 the Victorian authorities imposed a tax on them per head as they landed. An eyewitness, J. Chandler, recalled one way this was avoided. 'John soon found a back door. I met between six and seven hundred coming overland from Adelaide. They had four wagons carrying their sick, lame, and provisions. They were all walking single file, each one with a pole and two baskets. They stretched for over two miles in procession.' At £10 a head poll tax, this caravan represented a £7,000 loss of revenue to their European rivals for the riches of Aboriginal land. By 1860 there were an estimated 42,000 Chinese in Victoria alone.

Violence broke out, culminating in the riot at Lambing Flat, New South Wales. In December 1860 a party of white miners attacked some Chinese, cutting off their pigtails—and in some cases their scalps with them. Further mob violence occurred in March, June and July 1861.

In the cities, life went on as usual. Money was made, power changed hands, buildings were put up. Tennis was played and, of course, cricket. Picnics provided another source of exercise. Music was the prerogative of the wealthy who laid great store by their pianofortes and their acquaintance with Schubert. Literary societies went through the motions of poetry. Polite art flourished with landscapes, and with portraits as undistinguished as their subjects.

When the camera arrived to takes its place in this society, photographers soon found other subjects than the middle-class patrons of the miniaturist painters, whom they put out of business, and showed the poor in their windows on the world. The poor were a subject they could call their own, the faces of working folk and the humble streets they lived in.

The ordinary people responded with spirit, acting, clowning, posturing for the camera, understanding and accepting what it would show, thoroughly enjoying the novel limelight as principals in their own drama of life. Brides and bridegrooms discovered their one day of luxury could be perpetuated—photographic plates proliferated with couples decked out in awkward splendour; labourers lined up for tableaux beside industrial machinery; axemen posed ready to deliver their final stroke, the tree tottering, while a fanatic recorded the moment for posterity. And here was another gift. The photograph gave ordinary people that which had previously been the sole prerogative of the rich: semblances to the life of the generations of their family. They had photographs taken for posterity, they were founding dynasties of likenesses, their portraits were not just self-indulgence but a legacy for grandchildren and great-grandchildren. The photograph promised them a touch of immortality and their loyalty to it was absolute.

The society shown by this new medium was a society of the fit and normal. Such emphasis was laid on strength, endurance, being self-sufficient and capable with the hands, little room was left for the infirm and handicapped. Those suffering malformation or dwarfism found the best they could hope for was parading their abnormality as entertainers.

MERCURY NEWSPAPER LIBRARY

Members of the cast of 'Snow White and the Seven Dwarfs' at Hobart Railway Station during their first Tasmanian season. *Michael Sharland, n.d.*

Right: Charles Monds has photographed his children with their roles already clearly defined, minimizing the chances of either of these two upsetting the even tenor of society when they grow up. *Charles Monds, c. 1895*

Below: Sir Henry Loch, (with flowing beard and top hat) a veteran of the Crimean War, was sent as a diplomat to China and helped negotiate an English concession in Tientsin, after which he was taken prisoner by the Chinese and exhibited in a cage with a correspondent of *The Times*. He is seen here in less turbulent later years as Governor of Victoria, enjoying the company of their Excellencies the Governors of Tasmania and South Australia who were visiting for the Melbourne Cup. *Unknown, 1888*

Mr Josiah Boothby of Adelaide, impressive in his rumpled evening suit and medals. Born in England in 1837, he arrived in South Australia in 1853. Boothby was a distinguished civil servant and received the Cross of the Legion of Honour from the French government and was made a Companion of the Order of St Michael and St George. *Unknown, n.d.*

SOUTH AUSTRALIAN ARCHIVES

When Sir John Langdon Bonython died at the age of 91 in 1936, his estate, worth £4,000,000, was the largest ever left by an Australian. Yet in the course of his life he had given away huge sums to public institutions: an unknown amount to save the chemical and metallurgy laboratories of the School of Mines and Industries from closure, £50,000 to Adelaide University for building the Great Hall and a further £20,000 to endow a Chair of Law, also £100,000 to the South Australian State for the completion of Parliament House. This is the most vivid image: the newspaper owner who buys the government its home. While the politicians were in office (and he tried it out as an occupation himself in mid-career), he was in power. His influence through the Adelaide Advertiser was as enormous as the wealth this advertising brought him. *Unknown, c. 1929*

SOUTH AUSTRALIAN ARCHIVES

Right: From the 1850s to 1900 the small photograph called a *carte de visite* became very popular. Measuring 10 × 6 cm, they were mounted on card which was usually printed with decorative advertising for the photographer's studio. If this *carte de visite* were for a publican in fancy dress we might only be astounded at the costume. In fact what is astounding is that the subject is His Grace Archbishop Polding of Sydney, taken on 29 April 1870. An Englishman from Liverpool he was consecrated first Titular Bishop of Hiero-Caesarea and first Vicar Apostolic of New Holland and Van Diemen's Land. When he arrived in 1835 with three priests, his diocese was the whole of Australia, in which five priests were serving. He was made first Catholic Archbishop of Sydney in 1842 and by the time he died in 1877 there were 12 dioceses and 135 priests.
Alexander McDonald, 1870

Below: Reverend George Mackie, *carte de visite*. He was a vigorous campaigner for temperance societies. A typical item in *The Public Weal, A Temperance Handbill* of 5 September 1868, records the opening of the Hope of Brunswick Female Tent, 'the first female tent in connection with our honourable order (Rechabites) . . . opened by warrant from the Albert District, SA, at Brunswick by the Rev. G. Mackie'.
Patterson Brothers, c. 1860

Left: This Presbyterian church served the mining community of Stanthorpe, Qld, in 1872. The cheerful congregation pose outside their lightless house of God. Love and care have gone into the squaring and trimming of the finest bark sheets for the building. *William Boag, 1872*

Below: Remote from the simple needs of bush folk in bark churches, Daniel Murphy, first Catholic Archbishop of Hobart, turning aside from the sobrieties of his secretary Father Gilleran, stares from the blanketed comfort of his landau with all the security of being both powerful and right. *Unknown, n.d.*

Right: William Barnet founded The
Bunyip in Gawler, SA. Later this
newspaper came to incorporate The
Gawler Times and *Gawler Standard*,
advertising itself as 'The oldest
Provincial Newspaper in South Australia
and has the LARGEST
CIRCULATION out of the City. Price:
One Penny.' The company also ran
'The Bunyip' Stationery Establishment.
'This Department is thoroughly up-to-
date with every requisite required by
School-Masters, Scholars, and the live
Business Man. In this department will
also be found Photo Frames, Glove and
Handkerchief Boxes, Pictures to
brighten the home, Workboxes, Desks,
Fancy Blotters, Lovely Purses, &c...'
William Barnet and his wife celebrated
their diamond wedding anniversary in
1884 with a portrait. From the look of
Mrs Barnet, the photographer had
better get the picture right this time.
She has undoubtedly dressed for the
occasion. The posy of flowers is
suffering a bit of punishment.
Unknown, 1884

Opposite page
Above: Encampment of volunteers for
the Sudan contingent. For two weeks
they gathered in Centennial Park ready
for a heroes' departure as the whole city
of Sydney flocked to the Quay to
farewell them. The sole recruit in this
group is adequately supported in his
fervour to avenge the death of General
Gordon at Khartoum. *NSWGP (?), 1885*

Below: The uniform maketh the man.
Imperial army officers who
accompanied the Duke of York and
Cornwall on his visit to Australia in
1901. Left to right: Lieut Chichester
(Somerset Light Infantry), Lieut
Chichester (Royal Fusiliers), Lieut
Davies (Middlesex Volunteers), Owen
Smyth (Supt Public Buildings), Lieut
Dougall (79th Cameron Highlanders),
Lieut Bernard (Rifle Brigade), Capt.
Powell (Royal Engineers),——Oliphant
(SA Militia), Lieut-Col Hampson
(SA Militia), Hon. R. W. Foster
(Commissioner of Public Works), Lieut
McLean (Army Service Corps), Lieut
Baring (Coldstream Guards), Lieut
Collins (King's Dragoon Guards), Lieut
Hyde (Royal Army Medical Corps),
Lieut Sutherland (Norfolk Militia), Mr
Calder (reporter with cigar).
J. Gazard, 1901

SOUTH AUSTRALIAN ARCHIVES

Right: Erskine House group, Lorne, Vic., February 1898. A walking party liberally equipped with sticks, possibly Victorian National Gallery students and teachers, with offspring and an unexplained motto. Erskine House had originally been the Mountjoy homestead around which Lorne was founded. Later it was converted into a guest house boasting 'a large dancing and concert hall, with a small stage for tableaux and amateur theatricals, plus the hot sea baths and salt swimming bath, which give pretty well all the advantages that a tourist can desire... In the height of the season the evening dance at Erskine House is one of the attractions of Lorne.' The district boasts many picnic spots, such as Corra Lynn, a succession of cascades and pools, and The Phantom Falls (so called because for years after it was first reported, no one could find it again in the densely timbered country). *Unknown, 1898*

Below: Sons of the Prince of Wales (later Edward VII)—Prince Albert Victor Christian Edward (Eddie, *left*) and Prince George Frederick Ernest Albert (George), at Ballarat, Victoria. They are not, in fact, dressed for a steeplechase, the sport of kings, but in clothes deemed appropriate for meeting miners—the shaft cable of the Band of Hope & Albion Consols Gold Mine may be seen behind them. The pirate in the striped shirt is the commander of the visiting British squadron, Vice-Admiral Clanwilliam. After this, the princes survived a voyage to Sydney in the HMS *Inconstant* (only the British would have the sense of humour). Eddie died in 1892. George returned twenty years later as Duke of York and Cornwall to perform the ceremony of Federation. Eventually he was crowned King George V. *Willetts, 1881*

Right: The Duke and Duchess of York and Cornwall, visiting Victoria in 1901 to perform the hat-and-rabbit trick of Federation without independence, were welcomed by various sectors of the community. This arch was erected in Swanston Street, Melbourne, by Chinese citizens. The British Imperialists were no strangers to exotic flamboyance of this kind though a mild eyebrow might have been raised at seeing it here in Australia. The Duke had visited China itself on his previous voyage to the South Seas. *Unknown, 1901*

Below: Among those whose sweat helped the rich get richer, the Chinese were particularly unfortunate. Their clannishness assured them of a hostile reception, so did their colour, their speech and the way they wore their hair. Most of all their capacity for hard work was bitterly resented. Survivors of the T'ai Ping massacres in China, these gentlemen face the disturbances on the goldfields at Weldborough, Tas. with equanimity, plus whatever background research the local newspapers can offer. *ABRA, n.d.*

Left: Proud and serene, Chang the Chinese giant towers over a fellow citizen in Ballarat. To get sufficient space, even the urn on which he leans has been pushed off-centre.
Bardwell's Studio, c. 1860

Overleaf: Lord Brassey (after whom the dance tune 'Lord Brassey's Hornpipe' was named) was Governor of Victoria 1895–1900. In 1890 he visited most parts of the world in his yacht *Sunbeam*, collecting this photograph of a Chinese funeral at Cooktown, north Qld, during the voyage. There was often intense ill feeling towards the Chinese in gold mining areas which resulted in riots, looting and killing.
Lord Brassey (?), 1890

Above: Fruit shop in the main street of Brisbane, 1871 — and a family group as striking in their assurance as their boldly lettered name. At the time fruit and vegetables were available on a purely seasonal basis. Not until the 1880s with the introduction of irrigation, cool storage and refrigeration was there any means of extending the natural growth, harvesting and distribution pattern of the different varieties. The unidentified shop next door is offering something neatly done. *William Boag, 1871*

Opposite page
Above: Daniel Corcoran's grocery, 33 George Street, Launceston, Tas., with its splendid gaslight. *Unknown, pre 1908*

Below: Inside Corcoran's, the grocers are surrounded by their moveable fresco in praise of orderliness. The shop is filled with nostalgic detail, from Arnott's biscuits and Silver Star Starch, to those plain bags in which shopkeepers packed the flour, sugar and rice they bought by the sack. *Unknown, pre 1908*

Above: English immigrants, bringing
their uncertainties with them to
Western Australia and, in one case at
least, their certainties. *C. E. Farr, 1910*

Right: A Scottish family, newly arrived
in New South Wales in ill-fitting clothes
and with so much defeat already in
their faces, only the eldest boy seeming
to have much confidence left.
NSWGP, 1908

NSW GOVERNMENT PRINTING OFFICE

Left: Children from Dr Barnardo's Home arriving to settle. The percentage of these orphans expected to return to Britain permanently was minimal compared to the percentage of adults. Like those social orphans, the ex-convicts, they were regarded as permanent settlers, with good reason. Migration of Barnardo children began in 1921 and by 1950 some 2,000 had arrived under the scheme, supported entirely by voluntary contributions. Barnardo's ran two suburban homes in Sydney and a farm at Picton, NSW.
Unknown, 1924

Below: The *Royal Tar*, on 17 July 1893, about to sail for South America with a very special party on board—the first Australians to emigrate elsewhere. They were leaving for the very reason others came here: to find land they could live on freely and as they chose. This was the New Australia Movement, off to Paraguay under the leadership of William Lane, because they foresaw no possibility of 'socialism in our time' otherwise. The Depression was still afflicting the country and their departure was a public statement that marked the end of a dream. Utopia was abandoned in Australia: the wrong turning had already been taken and there was no going back. In its place people lowered their expectations and hoped only for work. The consuming passion to be average, which afflicted the nation for the next seventy years, began at this time. Of the fascinating details in this magnificent picture, none is more curious than the figure beside the stern lifeboat apparently pointing a pistol ashore. Although most of the Utopians came home eventually, disillusioned, some stayed and a group of their sons and daughters arrived back in old age for a visit in 1981.
Unknown, 1893

ROYAL TAR PORT ADELAIDE DEC 25 93,

131

Below: Although the ideal of universal literacy had its opponents as well as its supporters, literacy for the middle class was fervently believed in. In the cities, schools with pretensions to gentility flourished from the very early days. It took a hundred years for a network of free public schools to be built all over the country. Many outback centres had very small one-teacher schools. Here, pupils of the Scottsdale Public School, Tas., pose with their awards and certificates at Presentation Night. A touch of sexual discrimination does appear to have intruded. And it is not clear what the girl on the left is doing with her hand in the basket. *Unknown, c. 1900*

Right: A child at the blackboard is demonstrating the efficacy of the Montessori system of education. Dr Maria Montessori achieved remarkable success with retarded children, then in 1907 she opened her first school for normal children in Rome. The method was greatly admired and Montessori schools were set up in America and other parts of Europe. Although some private schools in Australia are run on Montessori lines, the system is still not thought acceptable for the State schools; its ideals of self-motivation, self-discipline and freedom with responsibility are still considered avant-garde. *NSWGP, 1914*

ARCHIVES OFFICE OF TASMANIA

Right: A cheerful couple from the Clermont district of Queensland. For many Aborigines, white society was an exotic and exciting charade, offering change and variety and the theatrical character of a costume drama. *Gordon Cumming Pullar, c. 1910*

Below: Mrs Fanny Cochrane Smith, whose claim to be the last full-blood Tasmanian Aborigine was recognized by the Tasmanian Parliament in 1884. She is singing native songs into an Edison phonograph recording machine operated by Mr H. Walison of Sandy Bay, Hobart. The cylinders are now in the Tasmanian Museum. *Howard and Rollings, 1903*

For a long time Daisy Bates was thought of as an example to the community's conscience. Born in Ireland in 1851, she came to Australia when 23, returning to England ten years later. In 1899 she was commissioned by *The Times* to investigate allegations of cruelty to Aborigines in Western Australia. Her report was a whitewash, acknowledging poor administration but turning a blind eye to the merciless persecution which was rife, and which continued for a further fifty years. She bought a 74,000-hectare cattle property in the central north of Western Australia and for twenty-five years she lived, on and off, with Aboriginal people. Her book *The Passing of the Aborigines* (1938), though outspoken against church missionaries, supported the propaganda that Aborigines were a dying race best left to fade away in peace. A remarkable woman, she obviously was, but serious questions are now being asked about what she did and what her motives were. *Moore's Studio, 1936*

Opposite page: Landowners came to hold huge properties, running many thousands of sheep or cattle on a single station. They dealt ruthlessly with the challenge of small farmers and in some cases continued to acquire more land until their stations were as big as the whole county they had come from in the UK. No rural success story was more sensational than that of Sir Sidney Kidman (1857–1935). Although he came from a comfortable Adelaide family, the story is told that at the age of 13 he bought a one-eyed horse and set out for Sydney with five shillings in his pocket. At 15 he was working for £1 a week and saved enough from this to buy a bullock team. At 21 he inherited £400 from his grandfather's estate, with this he traded in horses, invested in mines and in 1880 purchased Owen Springs cattle station. By irresistible drive he came to control huge areas of central Australia. His holdings extended from South Australia into parts of western New South Wales and Queensland, an estimated 260,000 square kilometres—the size of Great Britain. *Crown Studios, 1907*

Left: A group of drovers, Charleville, Qld. Charleville is the centre of a large sheep raising area. Before the railway was put through in 1888, some 500 bullock teams were hauling wool in the district to the railhead at Roma. For the purposes of droving, sheep are limited to flocks of about 300 and by law they have to move a minimum of 10 kilometres a day or they are no longer considered to be on the road. Cattle droving is done on a different basis and a bigger scale: usually a contractor who has the plant (horses, saddles and cooking equipment etc) hires a team of men such as these to work for him and they drive other people's livestock. *H. J. Walton, c. 1906*

Below: Broome, WA, was the terminus of the Eastern Extension Cable Company's alternative cable from Banjoewangie, East Java and their property included extensive buildings for the accommodation of staff, including this residence. From left to right, Mrs Fountain, Mr Fountain (Manager of Cable House), Mrs Fountain (snr) and Bishop Frewer (Anglican Bishop of the North-West). Needless to say, it would be no more polite to insist on having the names of the seven plant tubs than the seven standing men. The eye is expected to slip discreetly past and simply register a tremor of interest that they are apparently of several racial types, Japanese, Malay, Indian; also that the two junior men in suits might have to remain anonymous because they are servants as well, or clerks, or too young to matter. Like so many fine households in the sweltering north, this one is built of termite-proof material—corrugated iron sheeting with cast-iron columns and stairs. Life here appears to have had more in common with the Indian Raj than the larrikin egalitarianism of Sydney or Melbourne. *Unknown, 1913*

137

Top: Wallerawang, NSW, a winter panorama of four photographs. The town and its railway station, which achieved a famous reference in Henry Lawson's story 'Drifting Apart', epitomizes the individuality and flavour of the poor man's Australia.
Everingham, 1928

Above: While working people revelled in the freedoms of the colony and developed a distinctive accent and lifestyle, those at the top lavished money and effort on remaining English and protecting themselves from these satisfactions. A far remove from the bush, these immaculate lawns of Cranbrook House, invited the ladies and gentlemen to do nothing to their hearts' content, providing the brolgas with a diversion. *Unknown, 1914*

The warm climate and fine beaches
soon led to a national passion for
bathing in the surf. To counteract the
inherent dangers, Mrs Biddel offered a
life-saving class. Methods such as this
one which 'effected a release from the
clutch of a victim' were used in water
rescue. During the following fourteen
years young men formed clubs for
patrolling the Sydney beaches, and since
there were no other such clubs in the
world, they had to evolve their own
techniques for saving people. From
1907, when the Bondi club introduced
the reel and line, surf clubs formed an
association and set new standards in
drill, equipment and life-saving
procedures. The most dramatic crises
were shark attacks, though those were
not as frequent as people imagined.
Sharks came to exert a hypnotic,
malignant power over the popular
imagination, vying with snakes and
poisonous spiders as symbols for fear. In
fact only 79 deaths from shark attack
were recorded from 1788 to 1950, an
average of one every two years.
Charles Kerry, c. 1900

AUSTRALIAN CONSOLIDATED PRESS

The straitlaced moralism of Victorian times was probably, in part, the creation of the following generation anxious to seem modern and liberated. This photographer's intrusion suggests all was not quite as it is usually presented. It was taken at Fern Tree near Hobart. *Unknown*, c. *1895*

Left: Clermont in the central west of Queensland is in the tropics, 360 kilometres west of the nearest port, Rockhampton. Surrounded by forests, the district was first known for its copper mine in the 1860s. Then gold was found. By the time this picture was taken in 1912 the gold had almost given out. Clermont had become a pastoral area. These ladies of the Lamont family in their Edwardian look and dainty tea table in faithful replica of London are doubtless suffering from the heat. They are being visited by Mr and Mrs Gordon Pullar. (Mrs Pullar is centre foreground, Mr Pullar is taking the photograph.) *Gordon Cumming Pullar, c. 1912*

Below: For the gentlemen, a serious game of cards—preferably of a kind not too intellectually taxing, which would be *infra dig*. Here a whist club meets on Mr Finlayson's back terrace in Stanley Street, North Adelaide. As usual with men's activities, they are free of the hampering presence of children, but the dog is permitted the luxury of the leather armchair. *Unknown, 1895*

Right: A 'Suitcase Parade'. Opponents of the Hotel Hours Bill assemble outside Parliament House, Adelaide. Guardians of the family, these women protest against longer hotel hours, galvanized by the experience of keeping their menfolk in order and maintaining contact between them and the children.
Unknown, 1938

Below: Undoubtedly alcohol had become a serious social problem within a couple of years of the colony's founding. It remained so. By 1950 the average consumption of intoxicating liquor had reached over 95 litres a year per head of population. For most of the period covered in this book public bars were solely for men, and no food was allowed them while they drank. The majority of States enforced 6 p.m. closing: so after work the rush for the pub was a swill, while as many men as possible guzzled as much beer as possible in the limited time available. 'All's Well when Dad is Sober' is a montage picture with a certain drunkenness of its own. The inserted horseman is, apparently, the Rev. G. Mackie of kind memory—a more detailed portrait is to be found on page 118. The crude application of the texts makes the necessary point about the use to which the boy is being put by persons unknown. He may well have been a member of the Sons of Temperance Benefit Society which, according to sectarian news sheets of the day, met weekly in country and city centres.
Patterson Brothers, c. 1872

ALL IS RIGHT WHEN DAD IS SOBER.

IN KIND REMEMBRANCE OF THE REV. G. MACKIE

Getting Through— and Answering Back

Transport always seemed as much at the heart of Australian culture as settlement. So much settlement over the past two hundred years has proved impermanent: whole towns dead, farms taken over by the dusty desert they have created, and few of the very early buildings still standing. Old timber structures rot back into the soil. A history of construction, occupation, abandonment and decay can occur within a single lifespan.

While settlement has fluctuated, the river routes, the roads and railways remain—crowded by a populace among the most restless and itinerant in the world.

Two hundred years would be scarcely enough for regions to have developed distinctive social characteristics even if people lived their lifetime in one place. Given the constant movement from city to bush and back, from State to State, from the coast inland and back to the coast, regional variations are even less marked than might be expected. Naturally there is a contrast between Cooktown in the hot north and Launceston in the cold south, there is even a slight difference in the accent of the inhabitants. But considering the 3,000 kilometres between them, these differences are far less remarkable than the likenesses.

The most idiosyncratically national figure of all white Australians was the swagman. He had no home. He carried his possessions in a bedroll on his back and tramped the roads, living in the open and seeking occasional work.

Teams of bushworkers spent large parts of each year on the road travelling from one job to the next; shearers, cane cutters, fruit pickers. Gold prospectors followed the rush from New South Wales to Victoria to Tasmania to Western Australia to Queensland. And most celebrated of all, the drovers established overland routes, driving thousands of head of cattle at a time across enormous distances to the ports where they would be sold, slaughtered and marketed—journeys in some cases taking six or seven months and traversing the continent from north to south.

In the early colonial times the major highways were the rivers. Transport bases were set up all along great systems such as the Murray-Darling, the Murrumbidgee, the Hawkesbury and the Hunter. Paddle steamers plied the navigable reaches and where goods and passengers had to be brought across the river to the wharves, ferry services were set up. In the case of Echuca on the confluence of the Murray and Campaspe Rivers the town was founded because Isaac White ran a punt service there in 1847. Five years later Henry Hopwood operated the ferry and built a pontoon bridge to float across the Murray. Over this bridge drovers brought flocks of sheep and herds of cattle from the New South Wales side to feed the gold miners on the Victorian diggings. By 1864 Echuca had become the second port of Victoria, connected to the goldmining centre of Bendigo by

The coastal country is a network of gullies and ridges. State governments providing railway services faced high costs in bridge and cutting constructions. This gully at Mitcham on the Adelaide/Melbourne line is bridged with an imaginative sweep. *Unknown, n.d.*

railway. It was the main inland supply route. Long afterwards Echuca remained important as a transport centre for the agricultural industry.

Movement overland was far more strenuous and difficult than movement by water. Heavy loads were pulled by bullocks. The first working bullocks were brought from India in the *Endeavour* in 1795 and for the next hundred years they were absolutely essential to the establishment of the colony. The great bullock teams used hauling timber and wool developed from the carts pulled by one or two beasts.

In the towns light horse-drawn vehicles became a common sight and then came the public coach on which you could purchase a seat for a journey. The first public conveyance by land was advertised as a Common Stage Cart and offered seats from Sydney to Richmond via Parramatta and Windsor, a distance of 72 kilometres. This service was soon superseded by the first coach, which began operations on 10 March 1821 carrying six passengers inside, six outside, a postman with his satchel of Her Majesty's Mail and, according to the *Sydney Gazette* of the day, 'the bugles in the basket sounding all the way'.

During the 1820s most services ran from Sydney within a radius of 65 kilometres, then referred to as 'the interior'. In the next decade the main route was extended to Bathurst, a journey of 112 kilometres which took thirteen hours, leaving at 6 a.m. and arriving at 7 p.m. By the 1850s there were coaches travelling regularly from Sydney to Melbourne, over 900 kilometres. This was also the period of the gold escort. These horse-drawn coaches were used to carry gold from the diggings under the protection of mounted troopers.

It was gold that brought Freeman Cobb to Victoria. He arrived with three other Americans who had all worked for the Wells Fargo coaching company. The roads were crowded with thousands of diggers on their way to the fields. Seeing a business opportunity, they imported several coaches from America and in 1853 Cobb & Co. was founded. The firm was a tremendous success and was soon operating in New South Wales and Queensland, right up to Port Douglas north of Cairns, west to Normanton on the Gulf of Carpentaria and in a complete network south to Adelaide. The team used for a coach was normally eight horses, sometimes ten.

The first Australian railway was opened thirty years after its English counterpart. The pattern of railways then followed the distribution of population. Beginning with a rail link from the port to the city of Melbourne, each colony in turn began independently owned systems which developed, fanning out from the main cities. Then a subsidiary fan of lines centred on the secondary ports, such as Port Pirie, Newcastle, Rockhampton and Cairns. As these clusters of lines spread further, they were linked up round the coast, and that became the basis of all future rail services. Cobb & Co. supplemented many of these connections, running coaches between railheads, especially in the far inland. Coastal shipping suffered a blow from which it never recovered. During the next hundred years the wharves and warehouses of the river ports began dwindling and standing empty. The great days of inter-city travel by sea were over.

With the coming of the twentieth century, the railways themselves were due to suffer a couple of massive blows. In 1900 the first petrol-powered car, a Benz, was imported to Melbourne. In the same year Thompson's Australian-made steam car excited extraordinary interest at the Royal Show in Sydney and three other makers were offering self-powered vehicles for sale. Big money was poured into the industry, the huge American oil cartels, rubber tyre manufacturers, engine and coach-building companies began amassing corporate fortunes. As early as 1905 the Dunlop Rubber Company sponsored two Motor Car Reliability Trials. In February twenty-three cars took part in a drive from Sydney to Melbourne, to Ballarat and back to Sydney. The public went wild with excitement. And then in November, they sponsored another rally from Melbourne to Sydney; twenty-eight cars and ten motorcycles started. Five days later, nineteen of the cars had reached Sydney but the organizers could not pick a winner, so they sent the contestants up the Blue Mountains and back (a further 112 kilometres) and there were still six cars with a chance. The newspapers filled pages of each edition with detailed information: it was a national event. The remaining contestants agreed to fight it out on a return journey to Melbourne, making a total of over 2,042 kilometres, 1,339 of which were run in conditions where engines could not be stopped nor running repairs carried out. The fastest time for the round trip was recorded by a Mr Hobbs, 49 hours, 12 minutes' driving time. The Sydney *Daily Telegraph* editorial commented, 'The keen interest taken in the motor contest is something more than a sporting interest. It is the recognition that in the development of the motor lies the solution of many transit problems of the future and among these the problems of our great ''dry'' spaces west and south-west.' Of course, the proliferation of the car led to pressure on local shires to provide roads and, once provided, to improve them.

Even today, long after the three-rut horse tracks (the centre rut made by the horse, the outer ruts by wagon wheels) have given way to the two-rut motor vehicle tracks, many country roads are still unsealed, deep in dust through the dry weather and quagmires during the wet. The new car enthusiasts soon accepted that when travelling far outback the main thing was to get through alive. The traveller could not afford the luxury of worrying about comfort, as his European or American counterpart might.

These earnest gentlemen are official 'letter carriers' of the New South Wales government. *NSWGP, 1890*

Mrs Thompson crossing Paddy's Ford in the first motor car reliability trial from Sydney to Melbourne, 21–25 February 1905. She is driving a 6HP Wolseley, entering the water at a spanking pace, with no show of nerves. *Unknown, 1905*

In some ways Australians are the least materialistic people in the industrial world. This could have been learnt from the Aborigines, but more likely we are being taught independently by the same land. And transport provides as clear an example as any. You can't afford to cosset your vehicle for its own sake in the bush, the vehicle has a function and that's that. It gets knocked about, it is expected to give service and its worth is measured in toughness and functional practicality. Europe, by contrast, is crammed with objects, precious and revered, from heirlooms and furniture to cathedrals and whole towns. A typical Australian phenomenon is the rusted wreck of a car standing on a remote plain, with a motorist hunting its skeleton for a bolt or some wire he can use to patch up his own truck, broken down a kilometre away to the west, to see him through the next stage.

This is a society that loves consumer goods, but treats them with a fine carelessness.

The motor car had taken passengers away from the railways and given people an intoxicating freedom of movement and independence. During this same period another blow to the railways was being hatched by inventors. Lawrence Hargrave, born in England, arrived in Australia at the age of sixteen. In 1884, when he was in his thirties, he began successful experiments with aerodynamics, making and flying superbly built models. His experiments were of the greatest importance and were studied in Britain and France. Ten years later he developed kite design to a pitch of sophistication sufficient for lifting him off the ground. Flight had begun.

The honour of having made the first powered flight in the country went to Colin Defries at Victoria Park Racecourse, Sydney. He flew 105 metres in five and a half seconds, at a height varying from just under a metre to over four metres. So swift was development that only two years later W. E. Hart, who held Australian pilot's licence No.1, reached the staggering altitude of 914 metres when he flew from Penrith to Parramatta in 1912. In the interests of war, aircraft design and pilot training received massive government encouragement from 1914 to 1918. From then on the idea of commercial flights became a reality.

If the public had been wildly excited by car rallies, they became hysterical about air races. The aviators were the new explorers. All the glamour of hero-worship was lavished on them. Bert Hinkler flew from London to Darwin in fifteen days in 1928, the longest solo flight ever made. He was called 'the brilliant bird man of Bundaberg'. From Darwin he flew to his hometown in Queensland, setting the style for hometown welcomes which became such an emotional feature of flying. A tremendous welcome was arranged with landlines from Bundaberg to Brisbane, Sydney and Melbourne for carrying direct radio broadcasts, also an experimental short-wave broadcast was made in the hope that it might be picked up by English listeners.

In the same year Charles Kingsford Smith and his crew in the 'Southern Cross' made the first flight across the Pacific Ocean. Ten thousand people flocked to Eagle Farm aerodrome in Brisbane for the landing and five thousand motor vehicles sounded their horns as the crowd cheered and the three-engined Fokker monoplane touched down. One can only imagine how thrilled they were as they circled over the landing strip and saw that massive welcome awaiting them. Kingsford Smith's hometown was Brisbane, so it had a special meaning for him. He had been a stunt man in the infant Australian film industry, walking on the wings of planes among other tricks. When a senior American flyer, Bert Balchen, addressed a Sydney audience and berated them for not treating Kingsford Smith as a celebrity, saying, 'Don't you know he's the greatest pilot in the world,' Smithy smiled with embarrassment and replied, 'Mine's a beer.' He was lost over the Bay of Bengal in 1935. Bert Hinkler before him had crashed in Italy in 1933. It was the danger of aviation, and the speed, that gave it such appeal, but the hold it had on the public imagination was, of course, the timeless dream of flying known at least as far back as the Greek myth of Icarus.

It is small wonder that Australians were among the pioneer aviators.

Not only are distances such a challenge, but flying conditions are ideal, this being the world's flattest landmass with a most stable climate of fine clear skies most of the year. The first commercial airline, the Queensland and Northern Territory Aerial Services (QANTAS) did not fly the Sydney-Melbourne route, but from Longreach to Winton in central Queensland. And that fact tells its own story. The people who operated the outback transport services were a special breed. For courage and resourcefulness they would be hard to beat.

One form of travel was faster than flight, though: the projection of the human voice over huge distances. Radio changed the life of the nation, from the cities to the bush. Well before this time telecommunications had been set up bringing the marvel of two-way communication, people could not only hear voices but answer back. By 1872 submarine cables had been laid around the world, a vast telegraphic system was in operation and there was some urgency for Australia to be linked to it. Charles Todd, Postmaster-General in Adelaide, won the contract for South Australia. Using the route north across the continent explored by John McDouall Stuart, he successfully negotiated for the cable to be connected from Java to Darwin and from there by overland telegraph line to Adelaide. For the first time Australians were no longer reliant on ships to bring and take information.

The vital importance of communications is emphasized by its fragility and by the dangers of handling electricity. The ladder, the cross, the naked man—all powerful symbols—are viewed here with a humorous eye. The original caption claims that the workman has swum a flooded river but does not explain the clothed figures. *Unknown, 1943*

149

In the late nineteenth century, with the harnessing of electricity, telecommunications came into being. And Britain, among other nations, began a vigorous programme of laying submarine cables to connect all parts of her Empire. Here, during February 1876 in Botany Bay, the cable laying ship *Hibernia* stands off the La Perouse monument. The blurred spars show the ship is rocking even on so calm a sea. Most of the men are sailors who 'enlivened the proceedings by chanting lively sea songs' said the *Evening News* wholly misconstruing the shanty's purpose: to keep up a regular rhythm so everybody would pull together. The cable systems put Australia instantly in touch with the rest of the world. The familiar, inescapable sense of being the most remote and isolated continent, vanished overnight. *NSWGP, 1876*

Left: By contrast with the smooth comforts possible on the river, road travel was rough and even more vulnerable to bad weather. Even so, it was appreciated by country folk. Aborigines off to Lake Tyers Reserve, Vic., on a damp winter day, taking advantage of a transport system not available to them before their continent shrank to a peppering of reserved dots on the map. *N. J. Caire*, c. *1880*

Below: The first road built from Sydney to Bathurst over the Blue Mountains was completed in 1815 in the impressively short space of six months. In 1822 the western descent was rebuilt closer to Mount Victoria. The third road, the one shown in this photograph, also built by convicts, was completed in 1832. It is still in use. *NSWGP, 1887*

NSW GOVERNMENT PRINTING OFFICE

Right: As roads and towns grew more sophisticated, so did vehicles, such as this horse-drawn ambulance owned by the Department of Public Health, Coast Hospital, NSW, with its perfectly clinical elegance and appropriate nurse. *Unknown, n.d.*

Below: Wheels came to be a universal passion. A cyclist on his Otto in the Domain, Sydney. The problem with the Otto was not the problem of overbalancing sideways as on a bicycle, but of tipping over forwards or backwards. The small trailing wheel was not very efficient, and the steering was made clumsy by the twin front wheels. Fortunately the Otto remained a slow machine at the best of times. *Unknown, n.d.*

Opposite page: In the safe lane beside the skirting-board, this unknown velocipede enthusiast balances on his wooden wheels with quite remarkable aplomb during a slow, studio exposure. Invented in 1869, this style of machine came to be popularly known as a 'boneshaker'. *Unknown, c. 1865*

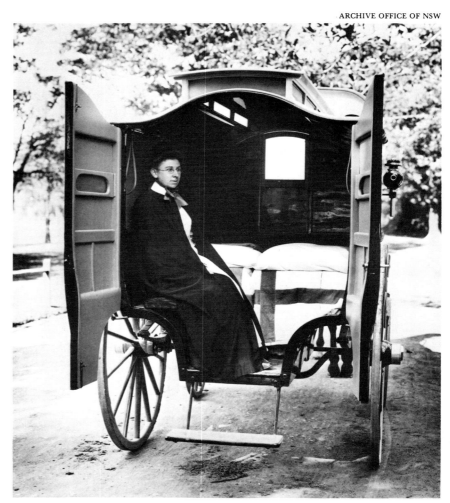

Above: In competition with steam, the last and greatest of the sailing ships were built, huge clippers with four masts capable of mounting a vast spread of sail. Packed with wool, tea or wheat, they raced each other across the oceans in a spectacular and glamorous club of the élite. The record was set by *Thermopylae* in 1870—from London to Melbourne in sixty days. So fast and efficient were they that the last one in service, the *Pamir*, didn't make her farewell voyage until 1948.
Peter Brierley, 1947

Opposite page: The wake for the *Hereward*, aground at Maroubra Beach, Sydney. At one stage of the salvage she was momentarily afloat, but the watchman on deck panicked and escaped ashore instead of winching her clear. November 1898. Remains of the wreck are still at Maroubra. Inshore manoeuvrability was one quality not guaranteed on sailing ships. At the mercy of adverse winds and currents, they frequently came to grief on our wild shores, at a rate of forty a year.
Unknown, 1898

Right: Standing on the afterdeck of his splendid clipper *Rodney*, Captain Corner shows off the ultimate wet weather gear. The blinds and curtains suggest this might be that haven of civilization—his own cabin. His Norman face is straight off the Bayeux tapestry, with a touch of humour. The steep camber of the deck may be judged by the angle at which the doors are cut. The *Rodney*, 1,447 tons, sailed under the houseflag of Devitt and Moore.
Unknown, 1898

Right: The Viaduct over Stonequarry Creek, Picton, NSW. Travellers by road could expect to ford creek crossings at their own risk, or cross on ferries or punts. Once a public railway system was planned, among the first and most expensive jobs was the construction of viaducts. In areas close to the cities or serving well-populated districts these were designed for permanence. *NSWGP, 1879*

Below: The Taradale Viaduct near Castlemaine, Vic. Situated 127 kilometres from Melbourne, this viaduct was part of a line which served a prosperous goldmining community, crossing the type of creek that can become a raging torrent in flood times. *A. Morris and Co., c. 1863*

Opposite page
Above: The railway became a pivot on which the future balanced. Here, on the Jerilderie Plains, Vic., is the 415-mile post from Sydney. Travelling such a route, it is hard to resist wondering if the line has been finished at the other end. *NSWGP, 1899*

Below: In some cities the cheapest and most convenient system was to bring the trains along the main street, stopping frequently for the passengers, rather like a tram service. This one was in Adelaide, the Glenelg train in King William Street. While shop awnings announce food, and telephone wires carry the voices of those not travelling today, the train is a dark uncertain magnet for the waiting crowd. Steam offered the photographer a romantic chiaroscuro combined with the powerful imagery of big machines. *Unknown, c. 1900*

Above: A B55 class locomotive, 4 April 1901, on the Lithgow Zigzag. The Zigzag line was an engineering solution to moving trains up and down a mountain face when there was not enough money for tunnelling through. The Lithgow Zigzag descended over 167 metres from Clarence in the Blue Mountains and despite the sharp hairpin bends, it was intended that locomotives remain on the tracks.
Unknown, 1901

Opposite page
Above: Derailment at Coal Mine Bend, between Jerusalem and Flat Top, Tas., 24 April 1877. Almost 60 kilometres from Hobart, the coal mine itself was right beside the line. At this time Jerusalem was a town of 350 people with two hotels and two churches in mountainous ironstone country not far from Jericho.
Samuel Clifford, 1877

Below: This B110 at Seymour, Vic., having unceremoniously off-loaded its freight of coal and sleepers, came to an unscheduled stop on 13 April (apparently a fateful month for derailments). The bunker the coal was intended for is seen on the right. The inevitable youngsters are there to assess the damage. At left a blurred figure balances on one clear leg.
Unknown, 1904

Right: Henry Hopwood with the punt and pontoon bridge around which the town of Echuca developed to become the main port on the River Murray. The cable punt has just drawn in, a wool wagon is ready to rumble off; a queue of customers waits on the far side. *Thomas Foster Chuck, c. 1860*

Below: The main highways into the interior were the rivers, most of them slow and silted, their water opaque and the reflections cloudy. Here the passenger steamer *Nellie* plies the Murray. *Alfred Withers, c. 1908*

Opposite page
Above: There was not much glamour attached to the river steamers in their day. However, this huddle of moored boats tied in against a muddy shore at Morgan, SA, by no means represents the average working scene—they were held up for nine months owing to the low water in that year of disasters, 1915, while the nation was mourning its young men butchered at Gallipoli. This photograph was originally produced as a postcard. *Unknown, 1915*

Below: A steamer with wool barge in tow arrives at the wharf at Echuca. The barge is carrying approximately 600 bales. *Grimwood Studios, c. 1920*

Below: One of the benefits of a weatherboard house was that it could be loaded on to a dray and set up on a new foundation of piles somewhere else. Or, if the whole house were too large, it could be taken in halves. Nevertheless the sight was unusual enough to create a sense of occasion. Here a family, with the aid of a bullock team, is shifting house from the rich goldfield of Boulder (near Kalgoorlie), WA, to Collie Burn. *Unknown, c. 1900*

Bottom: The Derby 'Express', Tas. Steam traction engines took the place of bullock teams in moving heavy loads. Though they could move great weights they were extremely clumsy and slow, hence the nickname given to this one by the tin mining community at Derby. *H. C. Webster, c. 1900*

Opposite page
Above: A Hackney tram, Adelaide, SA, has been turned into a superb gallery of framed portraits, firmly anchored at each end by conductors with their feet on the ground. Actually, this toast-rack tram has been assembled backwards for the sake of the picture—the long bar which is lowered to prevent people boarding from the right should be down on this side of the tram not the other, and so should the striped canvas blinds for weather protection. *Unknown, 1909*

Below: Before such niceties of traffic regulation had been formulated there was only one rule—drive on the left-hand side of the road. The passion for precise codes of road use eventually led to the painting of white lines down the middle of the footpaths so that pedestrians should also be encouraged to stick to the left! This Brisbane tram is connecting the Treasury—the corner of which is in the photograph—with the gaol at Boggo Road. Seating the ladies and children at the front with the aged and disabled was the standard custom for another half century, while men and youths lounged in a fog of smoke at the back. Not long after this picture was taken in 1912 it would not have been possible to catch passengers entering from the wrong side, in the path of any tram belting along the return line from the gaol to the Treasury. The lady inside about to alight is going the correct way. The moment catches a wonderfully alive gesture of the effort required to manage the high step in voluminous skirts. *Unknown, c. 1912*

BATTYE LIBRARY

ARCHIVES OFFICE OF TASMANIA

Right: This apparently new vehicle was photographed at Lady Macquarie's Seat, Sydney. It is possible that the lads were taking it for a spin before delivering it for service in Cooma, NSW. *NSWGP 1909*

Below: Loaded vehicle at Pittsworth, Qld, 1911. The passion for cars has grown more and more obsessive with the years. The mobility they gave bush people led to a revolution of lifestyle in the outback. *J. H. Pardey, c. 1911*

Roberts' Car Sales, Ipswich, Qld, with new models on display. The photographer who took this shot could not have known that the great Walker Evans would raise this same genre to such an art in America in the following decade. Ipswich is a coalmining, industrial town near Brisbane. It began as a convict camp where they burnt lime in kilns for cement and transported it down the river for building Brisbane. It grew into a river port and then the first railway in Queensland connected it with Grand chester. At this time it looked possible that Ipswich would be the principal city and capital of the new colony. A railway workshop was set up to service the line and expanded into making rolling stock. The Queensland Railway Workshops are still there. *Whitehead Studios, c. 1920*

Above: Lawrence Hargrave with box kites at Stanwell Park, NSW, on 12 November 1894. The kites are marked with letters for cross-reference with a report on this important experiment which was published in the London magazine *Engineering* the following February. Four of these box kites lifted him almost 5 metres above the ground. It was a breakthrough in the history of flight. *Charles Bayliss, 1894*

Right: The tension of control—J. R. Duigan of Mia Mia, Vic., in his home-made aircraft, built in a shed at his sheep station Spring Plains. He made one of the earliest powered flights on 16 July 1910. The two-bladed pusher propeller is seen diagonally behind the motor, a twenty-horsepower engine made by a Melbourne engineer, T. E. Tilley. *Unknown, 1910*

Above: A visiting Frenchman, Maurice Guillaux, demonstrating his Bleriot monoplane at Victoria Park Racecourse, Sydney. He flew the first air mail from Melbourne to Sydney, July 1914. Written on the cover of the package was, 'Kindly let us know if same arrives safely.' People knew by this time that here was the shape of things to come. *Harold Cazneaux, 1914*

Below: Blunt landing technique. A bi-plane at Kalgoorlie, WA. At this stage all pilots were amateurs and experimenters. *Unknown*, c. *1915*

171

Opposite page
Above: Queensland and Northern Territory Aerial Services BE2E landing at Winton in central Queensland on the way to Darwin, December 1919. The company eventually became known as QANTAS. In the heat, the excitement of an outback landing in the swirl of skirts, the dust flying and the propeller still whirling around. The flurry is also personal, the people rush up to the plane to touch it, they are not kept back by fear or regulations.
Unknown, 1919

Below: Composure in the face of things to come. This photograph was taken in an open plane at 1,828 metres by Frank Hurley. The three masks—calling up a wealth of ancient symbolism—are Ross Smith, Keith Smith, and W. A. Holman. This was the year when the Smiths made the first flight from England to Australia, winning the Commonwealth Government's huge prize of £10,000. *Frank Hurley, 1919*

Left: Amy Johnson arrives in triumph in Darwin, 24 May 1930. Born in Hull in 1904, she was the first woman to make this flight from England. She bought a second-hand De Havilland Moth for £700 and set aside £100 for petrol; at the time she took off, she had never remained longer than two hours in the air at a stretch. Her worst experiences were landing in the desert in a sandstorm, and flying through a storm at sea off Java during which she had to fly so low her chief fear was being washed away by one of the giant waves. At the outbreak of the Second World War she joined the Air Transport Auxiliary. A veteran of flights over the world's great oceans, both solo and with her husband James Mollison, it was her fate to die on 5 January 1941, lost in an aircraft crossing the River Thames estuary. *Unknown, 1930*

Right: RMS *Himalaya* departing from Sydney. In the post-war boom years a generation of young Australians caught the travel fever and sailed for Europe. Overseas air fares were still too expensive for most and the four-week journey by sea offered the attraction of a carefree holiday. There was something of a quest in this too because, for most, London was the objective—as if they had to conquer the colonial past.
David Moore, 1950

Below: Relatives seeing off a liner leaving for London. The departure of the great ships carried the air of adventure; the slowness, ritual and sheer size made it a splendid occasion.
David Moore, 1950

By the Sweat of their Brows

For the first years of near-starvation, the convicts and their masters had no time for anything beyond providing basic necessities and maintaining the system of authority. They built shelters and gaols, caught fish, grew crops, bred animals for meat, and gazed longingly out to sea in the desperate hope that help would come from their homeland. It scarcely ever did.

Once the farms succeeded and there was enough food an immediate change came over the settlement; people began to think of other interests, there was music, they made long-term plans, they tried experimental farming. In 1797 Captain Waterhouse and Lieutenant Kent returned from The Cape of Good Hope with a small flock of merino sheep. These were eagerly bought by several of the land holders. And so began Australia's wool industry. Ten years later the first consignment was shipped to England—111 kilograms. Vines were sown under official patronage and wine produced.

Seal skin and seal oil had already been established as the colony's first export. One ship alone, the thirty-ton schooner *Martha* carried 1,300 sealskins and 30 tierces (190 litres) of oil for export in 1799. The sealers lived their harsh life scouring the rocky islands of Bass Strait for prey, but it was a life that many enjoyed. Governor King complained in 1805 at the shortage of agricultural labour because so many men had gone sealing, enticed away from Sydney by American skippers.

Scientists tramped the countryside cataloguing the marvellous world of unfamiliar plants and animals, others of the community wrote poems and fashioned furniture. Coopers and wheelwrights were in demand. The trades began to flourish. By 1840 that wonderful burgeoning of a complex society was well under way, offering a vast variety of jobs people could do to earn enough to survive, from boiling whale blubber to lamplighting, from Mounted Constable Bates registering dogs, births and deaths, to Jack Doolan the bushranger robbing Judge McEvoy.

Farm labour was feeling the effects of mechanization. Until this time everything had been done by hand, but now the harvesters arrived, a new model every couple of years, reaping, threshing, binding and even winnowing the crop. At first they were drawn by horses, then steam traction engines. Before long the farm would be transformed by tractors and self-powered agricultural machines.

Timber getters attacked the ancient forests with cross-cut saws, axes and adzes. So many other trades depended on the supply of wood, they were the principal suppliers of raw materials in the early days. And though the forests lacked softwoods, the hardwoods were of stunning size and quality. The peppermint gum, tallest of them all, is rivalled only by the *Wellingtonia gigantea* of California. The German botanist Baron von Mueller reported finding a specimen in Victoria 128 metres high. Visitors to the London Exhibition of 1851 were shown a eucalypt plank 152 mm thick, over 500 mm broad, and

In the manner of August Sander this photograph of a blacksmith and his son in Tasmania has faith in the resonance of real life. The figures are simply assembled in the doorway without adjustments to their appearance, every detail contributing to the portrait of their lives and trade. *Charles Monds, c. 1890*

44 metres long. Nine years later another was sent to London measuring 3 metres broad and 23 metres long.

In the nineteenth century the altered face of Australia was almost entirely due to manual labour, a large percentage of which was involved in mining. The Kapunda copper mine was described in 1848 as being set 'among some gentle undulating ranges, lightly timbered . . . the situation most pretty and picturesque but the land at poor Kapunda has been caught up by speculators squatting all round, digging, and delving, bursting with envy, hatred, and uncharitableness'. Mining companies became big property owners, not only holding a lease on the land but running whole transport systems as well. When the Ebenezer Coal Mine was up for sale in December 1844 a full column of newspaper print was needed to detail the inventory of lots to be auctioned. The summary explained it as: 'Coal mine, wharfs, sailing vessels, barges, boats, shipping depot, residence, milking cows, cattle, horses, carts, drays and implements.' The miners, of course, also went with the mine. However, a few years later the new management found themselves severely short-staffed, the coal miners had gone off to become gold miners.

The gold diggings were soon converted to densely populated wildernesses, every shred of undergrowth stripped, the trees felled, the bare land pocked with shafts and eroding with every downpour of rain. The tents, the spruiking trades-people selling meat and ale, the hubbub of excitement gave the field a carnival air. And though it was often rough, there were plentiful accounts of how basically cheerful the miners remained. In 1851 the Rev. D. MacKenzie reported from Hill End, 'It is like a fair, or what you might suppose to be a gipsy encampment on a large scale . . . at dusk, the barking of dogs, the shouting of men, and the incessant firing of guns, are a great source of annoyance to people of weak nerves. Some scores of youngsters amuse themselves by firing guns and pistols without having any rational object to serve . . .'

Accidents and individual tragedies were common. The painter Arthur Streeton, wrote to his friend Tom Roberts about the experience of going to paint a mining scene among small pits with the occasional dynamite charge being set off:

Mounted Constable Bates, Koroonda, SA. *Ruskin Studio, c. 1915*

I look up and down at my subject; is it worth painting? Why, of course, damn it all! that is providing I'm capable of translating my impression to the canvas—all is serene as I work and peg away, retiring under the rock a bit when they light any shots, then, 'Up with that b— waggon, Bill.' 11.30: The fish train struggles over the hill and round to Glenbrook. 12 o'clock: The next shift comes toddling down the hot track with their billies, and I commence to discuss my lunch and tea (of which I consume over a quart every lunch), and now I hear 'Fire, fire's on,' from the gang close by; rest my billy on the rock, take out my pipe, and listen for the shots, with my eye watching the bright red-gum yonder. BOOM! and then rumbling of rock, the navvy under the rock with me, and watching, says, 'Man killed.' He runs down the sheltered side, and cries, 'Man killed!' Another takes it up, and now it has run through the camp. More shots and crashing rock, and we peep over; he lies all hidden bar his legs. All the shots are now gone except one, and all wait, not daring to go near; then men, nippers, and a woman hurry down, the woman with a bottle and rags. Then someone says the last hole was not lit, and they raise the rock and lift him on to the stretcher, fold his arms over his chest, and slowly six of them carry him past me. Oh, how full of dread is the grey, mysterious expression of death—'tis like a whirlpool for the eyes. Blown to death twenty yards from me, and, as a navvy said, it was an ''orrible sight'. By Jove! a passing corpse does chain your eyes, and indeed all your senses, just as strongly as love. All the men followed slowly up the hill, and now all are gone but me and the fatal rocks. I don't feel up to my lunch, so have a smoke and peg away at my canvas, but the poor chap, whom I was speaking to only yesterday, haunted me so that I put my canvas away, and came away, too, and had a shower and smoke, and thought of him all the while.

This letter was dated 17 December 1891. The painting Streeton was working on he called 'Fire's On!', one of his best-known pictures, now in the Art Gallery of New South Wales. He was also a man at work that day.

The unsung heroes of the workforce have always been the women. Whether left at home to manage with the children as best they could, or slaving in the outback beside their husbands, women were the solid foundation of society, the strongest force for settling down. And, of course, there were many paid jobs women did right from the first, perhaps none more surprising than the women pearl divers of Broome. The pearl fishing industry, while under white management and control, used mainly Malay, Filipino and Japanese divers, and Aboriginal women. The divers worked naked. Once this piece of intelligence was made public in Perth, there was an outcry against such horrors and improprieties being allowed. The government took prompt action and in 1868 female diving was forbidden.

Since the generation after Shakespeare, at least, women have had a place in entertainments. One possible reason for the decline in quality of plays during the nineteenth century was that though the public came to demand heroines rather than heroes, the plays were still being written by men. Then, when photography began to invade the advertising world actresses were freely used. Some of the early film makers were women. And the stars were by no means simply exploited as sex objects; quite the reverse. One of the first major film projects made in Australia was a Salvation Army epic called 'Soldiers of the Cross', 1900. A compilation of slides, film clips, music and narration, it was toured around to drum up support for the Army's work among the needy. The other army was quite a different matter.

The most impregnable fortresses of male exclusiveness were the services: the army, the navy, the police and the fire brigade. The fire brigade as a public service was a recent innovation, created by act of parliament in 1884. However, within a couple of years it was thoroughly militarized and that's where its efficiency lay. 'The training of the men is so perfect,' a commentator explained, 'that within ten or twelve seconds of the call being received the superintendent has the motor chemical engine outside the station and travelling at twenty miles an hour to the place of danger.'

When trade unions were established, they became an active agent for keeping women out of the workforce. Women were seen as a threat to wage levels of members because throughout the spectrum of jobs lower rates of pay were set for them and for this reason employers might be tempted to replace men with women.

The trade union movement began in 1822 when some convicts attempted to organize for better rations and higher nominal rates of pay. It was dealt with by the upholders of rational humanitarian civilization—they were severely beaten up and the leader put to the lash. Half a century was to pass before unions were established as acceptable and effective organizations, to face the test in the great Depression of the 1890s.

Attitudes to work are impossible to summarize. The work itself is not always the cliché of routine boredom sold in exchange for a pay packet. The pioneer days are too recent a memory for that. Work as a survival skill has given all work a special quality. Versatility in work has come to be regarded as a virtue. Men and women have felt remarkably free to switch jobs, not just between different employers in similar business, but to take work entirely new to them. Workers developed a worldly ability to turn their hand to anything and make a go of it. The bookie, the cook, and the schoolteacher are not immediately recognizable by their appearance, nor by their accent. In England you would not expect the street sweeper and your bank manager to speak anything alike. In Australia they might well have exactly the same accent. This absence of social strata in speech has had a profound effect on social mobility.

There is a sense in which photography of people at work shares this spirit. Seeming to show possibilities rather than rigid categories, the photographer looks at his fellow workers with the interest of someone who might well be joining them soon. And in this way the viewer is also drawn into the picture. Even in the nightmare world of underground mining we are invited to enter rather than stand aside and look in from a safe distance.

The frame of the photograph of people working is often defined by the workspace, which also comments on the nature of their task. So, the ploughman with his team of horses is a shaping force in the landscape of free horizons. For the factory worker, by contrast, the workspace is the shaping force; he is cramped and limited, deprived of daylight, and doubtless battered by noise that persists throughout the day on a damaging scale. Similarly, the intimacy the gold miner enjoys blowing dust off a few grains of precious metal in his dish can hardly be thought of in the category of employees of the Broken Hill Silver Mine dwarfed by an industrial landscape.

The optimism of the worker can be explained by his knowing that he could be in all these photographs, the same man shifting his lifestyle and horizons. Even those who never change their job know that it is possible, if they ever want to try it. In times of financial depression the restriction of this freedom is one of the first signs of trouble and is resented by those in safe jobs as well as those unemployed.

The image of Australia so long promoted abroad is a land rich in resources awaiting energetic people to convert it into wealth. Although the promoters seldom make clear for whom the wealth, beyond question it is there. For a while, at the end of the nineteenth century, Victoria was the richest State in the world. The workforce was enlivened with adventurers prepared to face any hardship and eager to take risks. They were not so hampered by the niceties of social decorum as people in the British Isles. The use made of the country was haphazard and competitive. They showed little imaginative vision when it came to creating a society with its own ethics and priorities— the differences emerged without being planned.

By the 1920s advertising had become a powerful medium of commercial communication. Campaigns promoting everything from bathing suits to biscuits proved a boon to photographers. *Unknown* c. 1927

179

The feed floor, Mount Lyell smelters, Queenstown, Tas. At the time they were the largest smelters in the world. The mine started by producing gold and iron, the smelting of copper began later, in 1896. The air over the whole town was heavy with sulphur from these smelters and the surrounding landscape showed its corrosive effects.
Stephen Spurling, n.d.

181

Opposite page: Until the 1860s, Cremorne Point in Sydney was a pleasure garden, patrons arriving by ferry from across the harbour to hear the bands and to dance in the pavilion. The wharf was decorated with Chinese lanterns at night. When coal was found and mined at various locations around the harbour, these men worked the diamond drill here at Cremorne Point. They drilled a long way down and they did find coal, but it was never mined owing to the difficulty of getting at it. A decade later the pleasure gardens were closed, subdivided and sold off for housing. *NSWGP, 1893*

Above: Flensing a whale at Twofold Bay, NSW, 10 November 1870. The intense stench carried for great distances around whaling stations. In an extraordinary partnership that lasted many years here at Twofold Bay, a pack of killer whales would drive the big humpbacked whales inshore for the whalers to harpoon them, and be fed with all the parts man could not use. This is one of a pair of stereo images. *Charles Walter, 1870*

Below: 'Brother Payne', knife grinder, a classic nineteenth-century figure plying his trade in the bitter streets of Hobart. *Unknown, n.d.*

Right: For all the discomforts, the dangers and low wages, workmen had a pride in their trade. The second half of last century saw the growth of unions and a new declaration of identity as 'working class'. When the Hawkesbury River Bridge was completed in 1889, on the day of the tests, engineers and workers posed for their photograph to be taken, while above them hung a blaze of light like collective satisfaction. Built by the Union Bridge Company, New York, USA, the bridge totalled 887 metres in length, had seven 126.7-metre spans, and five of the piers were sunk to depths of 46-48 metres below high-water level, which at the time was a record. *NSWGP(?), 1889*

Below: At the railway workshops, Chullora, NSW, the workers and management parade with the job they have finished. *Unknown*, c. *1886*

Opposite page: Goldmining, New England, NSW. The rails here at this private claim are more modest and wooden. The entrance to the shaft is eloquent of the dangers in a small mine, dug and propped by amateurs, and subject to government supervision only in respect to their miners' licences. No safety controls were required and few taken. *Charles Kerry*, c. *1900*

STATE RAIL AUTHORITY OF NSW

GOLD
MINING.
NEW
ENGLAND.

330. Kerry.
Photo.
Sydney.

Below: A gang of miners on their way to the workplace, Moonta Mines, SA, on 23 August 1895. A large number of miners at Moonta and at the neighbouring Wallaroo Mines were Cornish migrants. They were known as Cousin Jacks. *Unknown, 1895*

Bottom: As recently as 1913 child labour was still used in the mines, here the 'pickers' watch the conveyor belt, picking out stones and rubbish from the ore at Moonta Mines. It is interesting to note that South Australia set up the first childrens' courts in the world in 1899 for child offenders. Adult offenders exploiting the children were apparently still able to operate. *Unknown, 1913*

Right: Lighting the open pan of flash powder with a match was a dangerous risk to capture these leeched forms and staring eyes in the dark, the wet clothes and skin shining like bronze. The men are preparing a place to fix a timber support in the main level, Wallaroo Mines, SA. Though they are at the workface, and have a pneumatic drill, they are not wearing helmets and so have neither head protection nor helmet lights. *Unknown, c. 1916*

SOUTH AUSTRALIAN ARCHIVES

Where sufficient water was available, gold prospectors could use the comparatively simple method of sluicing the dirt away from the granules of gold. Where there was not enough water the painstaking dry-blowing process had to be used. Working with two dishes, the prospector holds up one full of pulverized dirt, tipping the lip of the dish towards the wind. As the earth falls gradually to the dish on the ground, the dust is blown away. The dishes are then exchanged, and he goes through the routine again. This is repeated until he has only a small amount of heavier material left. He then sorts through the stones and gravel, picking them out and throwing them away. The final stage is the intimacy the photograph shows, the fossicker blows the little heap across the bottom of the dish while he peers in for any trace of gold dust. *J. J. Dwyer*, c. *1896*

Opposite page
Above: 'Crowd listening to Father Long announcing locality of famous Sacred Nugget, Kanowna, 1898, Kalgoorlie, WA', reads the caption on the print. A great assembly of attentive hats: stetsons, caps, felt puddings, military caps, homburgs, bowlers, and 'wide-awakes' (a low-crowned hat in straw or felt). A man's society. *J. J. Dwyer, 1898*

Below: Broken Hill Proprietory Limited, silver mines in the arid far west of NSW. BHP, as the company became known, grew to be the largest of all Australian industrial empires, expanding into many mining and manufacturing areas, notably steel. This building contains the first smelters at Broken Hill; the smooth wall with its drama of repeated arches dominates the dark curves of the barrels, the bright pattern of silver ingots on display, and the dwarfed men. *NSWGP, 1892*

189

Right: This is clearly a demonstration photograph. The table, the same one used by the folder in the picture below, has been propped up to be a workable height, though obviously not a large enough space to be used in the normal run of his trade. No job appears too big for this craftsman binder.
NSWGP, 1892

Below: Lighter industries were employing women well before the turn of the century. Here at the New South Wales Government Printing Office, Sydney, a young woman folds pages ready for binding, with a temporary screen stretched behind to display what she does. *NSWGP, 1892*

Opposite page: Some kinds of work have always been hard to differentiate from pleasure. The antiquarian bookseller is often a hobbyist and enthusiast. Mr Legrand's face and figure speak for him. The painting on the easel is almost of a scale where it might be a window on the past, with sailing ships in Hobart harbour.
J. W. Beattie, n.d.

The precious resource of tall timber was exploited with impressive energy and no long-term planning. Axemen developed their skill to a high degree of specialization, knowing just where to cut which kind of tree and how to be sure it would fall as planned. In the great virgin forests the task often looked daunting. But these were men not accustomed to giving in lightly... as the Commonwealth Government found out in 1929. Once the Depression was well under way, the courts reduced all wages by 10% and increased the working week from forty-four to forty-eight hours. While other unions protested, the timber workers struck. And despite heavy fines they voted overwhelmingly to stay on strike. *Unknown, n.d.*

Top: Log hauling with bullock teams in south-west Western Australia. The log on the right is ready to be winched up on to its wheeled frame like the other. At the feet of the man leaning against the wheel is a model of it about 200 millimetres high. In his right hand he has the long-handled bullock whip for driving the beasts. The karri forests have since been depleted to a critical level. *WAGP*, c. *1920*

Below: The drama of this sawmill at Dorrigo, NSW, is the stark repetition of inert forms, here highlighted by low-blowing smoke and the tree skeletons beyond. Timber men cut a rich variety of hardwoods — twenty-eight principal eucalypts and twenty-two non-eucalypts (such as Silver Ash and Turpentine). They were used for building, for fuel, for cabinet-making, pit props and railway sleepers. *NSWGP, 1905*

Right: The sheep population rose from a few thousand in 1800 to 100 million in 1900. So instead of the sheep owner with a couple of convict labourers cutting the fleeces off, trained teams of professional shearers were employed. These teams, highly competitive and proud of their skill, travelled the land as nomads, generally on foot, visiting one property after another and moving on as soon as the sheep had been shorn. Each fleece would be spread on a special slatted table and examined for sorting into different classes of fineness. Then the wool was pressed into bales ready for transporting. Once it reached the docks, most of it was shipped to England to be milled, and then some was bought back in the form of knitting wool for garments. This is the shearing shed at Burrawong, NSW. *NSWGP, 1899*

Below: The sheep station, rather like a mediaeval castle, was a complete community supplying the needs of the workers as well as the owners — even to shearing the shearers. No sweeping up problem here. *Charles Kerry, c. 1900*

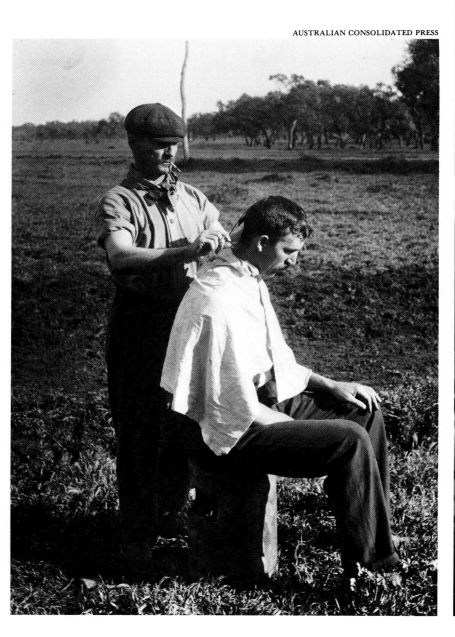

WOOLSORTING & CLASSING AT THE SHEARING SHEDS BURRAWONG N.S. WALES

A majestic sight in the outback: bullock drays hauling bales of wool – in this case from Belltrees Station, Scone, NSW. Meanwhile the penalties of captivity are observed by a rogue bull on the bank. As for the bullockies, they became a brotherhood of track, with a rich folklore and distinctive tradition. Their usual dress was a red shirt, moleskin trousers and a woven cabbage-tree hat. Their language was often more colourful than their clothing. Furnley Maurice caught their character in a few lines.

Within him there's a spirit careless, free;
Slow to condemn he is and slow to praise,
Profuse in grumbling generosity,
And drenched at heart with the light of burning days.

With the development of synthetic fibres, many woolgrowers switched to beef production. Belltrees itself is now a cattle station. *Charles Kerry,* c. *1900*

AUSTRALIAN CONSOLIDATED PRESS

Right: With his tea-strainer moustache, his tree-like neck and kindly eyes, this man is the very figure of the Australian rural worker. Atherton Tableland, Qld.
E. O. Hoppé, c. 1930

Below: Harvest time at Colebrook, Tas. Three generations of a family stook the sheaves. Even after a hundred years, the farms and farming methods still looked very English and the work was as slow as it had been for a thousand years; one man with a scythe could reap about half a hectare a day at most. With even the simplest of reaping machines the workload was transformed, that same man, with a brace of horses, could do double the work previously expected of a team of eight men.
J. W. Beattie, c. 1923

Opposite page
Above: Ploughing with a traction engine, Tamworth district, NSW. Already the big machine has introduced the blight of mass-production; the land utterly uniform, the men bringing the weight of their boredom to bear on the disc ploughs, the art of ploughing an individual furrow a thing of the past. Along the skyline stand ghosts of the bush that once grew in this soil.
Unknown, c. 1910

Below: Several teams of horses, setting out with loads of wheat. For the benefit of a British audience, the picture bears the caption, 'Kicking up a dust — a scene from sunny Australia'. Once the wheat was winnowed and bagged it was carried in carts to the nearest railhead, often the beginning of a journey halfway around the world. Then, as now, the country enjoyed a huge export trade in wheat.
E. O. Hoppé (?), c. 1930

Harvesting wheat, Mount Templeton, SA. The dark line of the land itself links the horses with the farmer's hand. Wheat was planted in 1788 soon after the First Fleet arrived, but the areas around Sydney were not well suited to the crop and soon Tasmania became the main producer, followed by South Australia. In 1843 an Adelaide miller, John Ridley, produced the first mechanical stripper which not only stripped the heads of the wheat but also thrashed the grain with rotating beaters. Machines such as this made possible the planting of huge acreages. The so-called Wheat Belt developed in two vast tracts of land, one in the south-west of Western Australia and the other in the south and south-east of Australia. This Wheat Belt fluctuates between 160–320 kilometres in width. The average family farm may be from 200–400 hectares, depending on the rainfall — larger properties were needed to reap sufficient yield in lower rainfall districts. Harvesting begins in November in the north of the Wheat Belt and ends in January in the south. *Unknown, n.d.*

Opposite page

Above: In the sub-tropical sugarcane growing areas of Queensland, Pacific Islanders were brought in as labourers. The conditions of their contracts were often scurrilously dishonest and they worked in conditions indistinguishable from slavery. In some cases—such as the notorious ship *Carl* run by James Patrick Murray—Islanders were imprisoned under the hatches and even murdered by their captors. Only after Federation in 1901 was any legislative move made to prevent this practice continuing. Here Kanaka workers are seen in the young cane, Bundaberg district, Qld, beside an irrigation channel. *Unknown, c. 1896*

Below: The meat export industry began in earnest when refrigerated compartments on ships had been developed by Thomas Mort. This was another Australian invention, spurred by the problems of remoteness from the market. Afterwards, beef, mutton and rabbits were exported to England, the first cargo leaving in 1879. The rabbit plague wreaked almost as much devastation on the land as sheep and is still with us. Rabbits returned only a small income compared with the huge wealth of the wool industry. This is why we never hear of a sheep plague. In 1907 a fence, 1,610 kilometres long, was built from north to south to prevent rabbits from invading Western Australia. *Unknown, n.d.*

Left: In northern parts of the country, indentured labour was common. Japanese pearl divers and crew aboard a lugger at Broome, WA, posing with self-conscious unapproachability that contrasts with the pudgy casualness of the skipper—possibly the outcome of the photographer's own nationality. *Unknown, n.d.*

Below: Wharf labourers were an essential and powerful sector of the workforce. Shipping accounted for a huge amount of inter-city cargo as well as imports and exports. On the rail tracks of Darwin docks, wharf lumpers take a 'smoke-oh', lounging in the sweltering heat, learning to be tolerant of criticism from those who never did a hand's turn of hard work in their lives. *Unknown, n.d.*

Right: During the past century Tasmania has been converted more and more obsessively into one vast hydro-electric scheme, disproportionate political power passing into the hands of the electricity authority. Dams of many kinds and sizes are found throughout the State. This is Duck Reach Power Station. Launceston, nearby, was one of the first cities to light its streets with electricity. *Unknown, n.d.*

Opposite above: Immense public projects provided work for large numbers of men prepared to live on the job for months at a time. In so dry a continent, the conservation of water was an early priority. The Burrinjuck Dam (originally Barren Jack) was begun in 1909 and completed in 1927, as part of the Murrumbidgee River Irrigation Scheme, providing water for pastures, orchards, vineyards, rice fields and other crops. The total length of the wall is 219 metres and the height 80 metres. *Howard and Shearsby, 1910*

Left: In May 1925 the Burrinjuck Dam flooded. This exciting view of the torrent was photographed in two sections. At the centre of the wall, a large tree can be seen about to be washed over. *Unknown, 1925*

The more complex society became, the more specialized people's jobs needed to be. Some, like this railway signalman, bore responsibility for the safety of thousands each day. *Unknown, c. 1910*

Below: Others were trapped with the isolation of a single function in a production line. This is the fitting shop of Meadowbank Engineering Co. NSW. Small plants like this could be run on a single steam motor—noisy and thumping its maddening rhythm all day. No safety shields were installed and it was not until the mid-1880s that the union movement was strong enough to begin turning its attention to the need for legislation governing safety standards in factories. And for many years after that workers still operated dangerous machinery without protective guards. *NSWGP, 1922*

NSW GOVERNMENT PRINTING OFFICE

Among the more glamorous jobs in heavy industry was train driving. Certainly it was taken to be the standard ambition for small boys. But the real subject of this photograph is the blast furnace. Harold Cazneaux was commissioned to take pictures of the BHP Steel Works at Newcastle for the company's jubilee book, and the management put the workforce to cleaning and polishing up these huge structures for the event. The scuptural, romantic quality of the Cazneaux photograph was obviously just the kind of result they wanted. The Newcastle Iron and Steel Works opened in 1915 and transformed the character of industrial Australia. Although iron foundries had been in operation since 1850, when Broken Hill Proprietory decided to move into steel production this was the first integrated iron and steel industry, with the raw materials shipped direct from Iron Knob and Iron Monarch, SA. It was a turning point for heavy industry. *Harold Cazneaux, 1935*

Left: Most glamorous of all were the filmstars. But, of course, they also had to work and face the uncertainties of living by freelance contracts and frequent lapses in income. George Wallace, the actor in this still photograph (taken by an independent photographer while the film was being made) earned every penny of his pay for the perfection of that straight back. The film called *Let George Do It*, was made in 1938, one of the many comedies directed by Ken G. Hall for Cinesound. Wallace spent his later years as a vaudeville actor at the Theatre Royal, Brisbane. *Unknown, 1938*

Above: The work closest of all to pleasure in the public view is the entertainment industry, perhaps film expecially. The world's first full length feature film was *The Story of the Kelly Gang* made in Australia in 1906, a brief fragment of which is all that survives. This young cameraman is Arthur Higgins, filming *The Sentimental Bloke*, a classic directed by Raymond Longford in 1919. He is using a Prevost movie camera. He and his brothers Ernest and Tasman worked as cameramen throughout the period 1900–50. *Unknown, 1919*

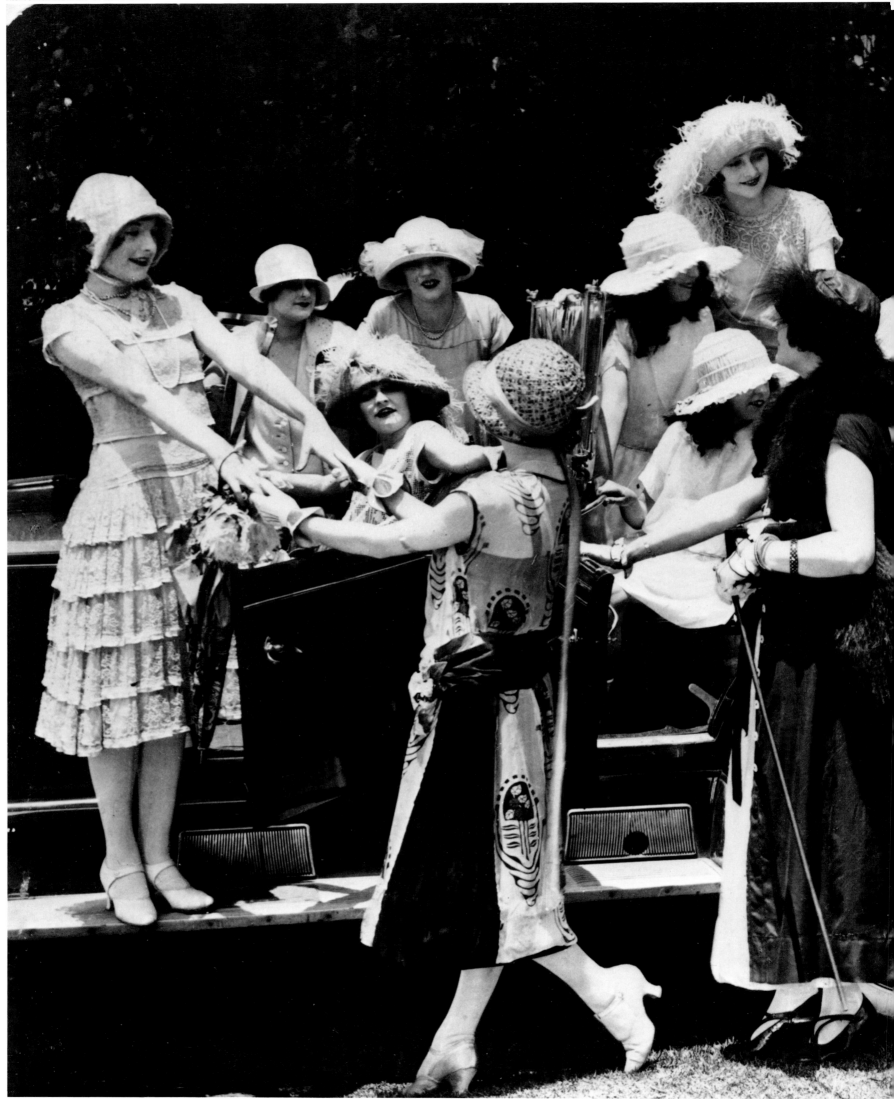

In Pursuit of Happiness

In July 1885 Mr T. D. Jennings, aged sixty-one, landed at Sydney and found himself instantly a celebrity. People stopped him in the street, the government granted him a complimentary pass for all railway and tram travel. The reason for this attention was Mr Jennings' size: 177 cm (5'10") tall, chest 172 cm (68"), waist 208 cm (82"), calf 52 cm (20½") and weight a grand 206 kg (455 lbs).

He was the perfect jolly fat man, his huge laugh ringing out over Circular Quay the moment he was safely delivered ashore. Until his recent retirement he had been a ferryman who loved his work. He loved hard labour at the oars, he loved his passengers, he loved his food and drink. Mr Jennings had only been persuaded to retire from his business five years previously because the harder he worked the fatter he grew and he felt he was carrying enough weight as it was, apart from the practical consideration that if he worked much more his clothes would no longer fit. He could sit perfectly comfortably on two chairs, and pronounced the Sydney trams satisfactory even though one journey ended in the embarrassment of the step disintegrating under him. So, by his corpulent ebullient presence, Mr Jennings advertised to the world his success in the pursuit of happiness.

Others reserved their outbursts for the privacy of the family parlour, where they played the piano and sang. Everybody sang. Music-making was important socially, though piano accompaniment was generally thought a female task. Among the middle class, men didn't regard instrumental skills as quite in their line. By contrast, the strong tradition of bush songs and folk music among the working class depended mainly on male accordionists, violinists and bones-players. In professional music, also, the roles of the sexes were the reverse of parlour ballads: the ladies were the star singers (in Nellie Melba, Ada Crossley and Florence Austral, Australia had singers of world renown) whereas the orchestras were made up exclusively of men. By the 1850s musical societies flourished in all the main centres, organizing concerts and celebrity tours. The popular music was unquestionably the drawingroom ballad; the piano occupied a place of honour, and the strains of 'When I was a King in Babylon' and 'The Inchcape Rock' haunted the suburbs on summer evenings when the windows were open.

Local halls—often flimsy weatherboard structures—pulsed to the stamp and slide of a multitude of feet. Young ladies breathlessly awaited their coming-out, their official entry into society, which is to say into the competition for a suitable marriage. And once this goal was attained it was sealed for life, marriages were accepted as being made in heaven. At every ball the debutantes filed up on stage to be presented; the following Sunday saw them displaying themselves at church. Not till the Great Depression of 1929 were the churches shaken by public scepticism and public anger. Australia was a church-minded nation, Sundays being spent earning stores of happiness in the afterlife through prayer, hymn singing, the confessional, dutiful

The plot of F. Stuart-Whyte's 1925 film, *Painted Daughters*, was set in the world of the theatre and high fashion, high fashion being its usual slavish imitation of European models. This still shot shows the arrival of a car-load of debutantes. Unfortunately the film has since been lost. *Unknown, 1925*

boredom and the ritual avoidance of entertainments. For this one day a week the pubs stood empty and the pool tables unused. A theatrical performance on a Sunday would have been unthinkable. For the other six days, however, they flourished. A wide choice of amusements was offered in most cities, from music hall to oratorio. The 1856 Melbourne opera season, as an example, included *Der Freischütz*, *La Sonnambula*, *Norma*, *L'elisir d'amour*, and *Martha*. Not only were these major works, but recent too. Weber's *Der Freischütz* had its premiere

in Berlin in 1821, Bellini's *La Sonnambula* in Milan, 1831, also his *Norma* was shown in the same city later that year, Donizetti's *L'elisir d'amour* in Milan, 1832, and Flotow's *Martha* in Paris, 1844 and then in Vienna, 1847. So Melbourne in 1856 was thoroughly up to date with these ambitious productions, all of which were staged without any subsidies or state patronage.

The theatres themselves made handsome profits, a fact which is underlined not only by the continual growth in the number of them,

With suitably grandiose studio background Mr T. D. Jennings poses for his portrait. The *Mercury, 1885*

but the promptness with which they were rebuilt when they burnt down. And theatres seem to have been particularly prone to burning down: in Sydney the Royal burnt in 1840 despite the combined efforts of 200 soldiers and 300 convicts plus all the combined private firefighting brigades, The Victoria Theatre in George St in 1844, in 1860 The Prince of Wales Theatre burnt to the ground and again in 1872. In 1892 it was the Theatre Royal, in 1899 the Tivoli and in 1902 His Majesty's Theatre. Australia's second oldest city, Hobart, is unique in never having lost a theatre by fire.

Among the adventurous drama seasons offered, none was more surprising than the tour by Janet Achurch and her husband Charles Carrington. They had been performing Henrik Ibsen's *A Doll's House* in London when the entrepreneur J. C. Williamson contracted them to tour Australia. The play achieved a *succès de scandale* in Sydney in 1890, eleven years after its original Norwegian production, and again in Melbourne the following year. Williamson's began advertising the company as the latest in avant-garde drama. The audiences responded more favourably to *Camille* which was also in their repertoire, but generally the reception verged on puzzlement. However, this was nothing compared to the total incomprehension that greeted their next production. The Archer translation of *Hedda Gabler* (written in 1890) was sent to Janet Achurch and the company first showed this play in the provinces, in Brisbane, in 1892, before it had been performed anywhere else in the English-speaking world. Ibsen's themes attacking such social institutions as the law, the family and religion, aroused passionate opposition from respectable persons who made sure their outrage was publicly known.

Books were immensely important as a source of entertainment, from the mushy romances of Ouida to great Dickens novels issued in serial form as monthly booklets. While for those who required something applicable to practical use there were floods of trade manuals and handbooks on anything down to the rules of card games. One desirable volume, entitled *Jerks in from Short Leg*, by Quid, offered valuable advice on all aspects of cricket, including confidence, temper, cricket nurseries, and the ladies.

By the end of the century, competition sports emerged as one arena in which we could aim for championship class and have the world take notice. We already knew all about cricket and rugby, then the Olympic Games were revived in 1896. A new age of sportsmen and sportswomen (including racing car drivers and aviators) claimed the laurels monopolized for so long by the explorers. These were the new public heroes, and only the belated treks into the icy wildernesses of Antarctica were to fire the public fascination with exploration again.

When the All-England Cricket Team visited the colonies in 1861–62, twenty-one years before the legendary burning of 'The Ashes', enthusiastic crowds turned out to watch them play. Cobb & Co. assigned to them their famous driver, Edward Devine, known as Cabbage-tree Ned, with the Great Coach drawn by twelve matched grey horses. Spectators often combined the long day at the cricket oval with a picnic on the boundary.

Picnics of all sorts were a passion. Pleasure-seekers delighted in carting their cumbersome hampers and folding furniture into the bush, braving the flies and mosquitoes, to endure the discomfort of a meal which might have been eaten at home with a fraction of the bother. After devouring gritty tidbits, the young were set such traditional enjoyments as tracking bees to their hollow logs and gathering wild honey while the angry swarm did its best to get the honey back, or collecting birds eggs for the pleasure of blowing them hollow and mounting them on cardboard displays. This was the great outdoors, and little else mattered.

Naturally, in a colony founded by sailors, sailing and rowing were for a long time the dominant sports. A Sydney regatta on 31 January 1845 comprised 'matches for yachts under five tons, watermen's skiffs, sailing boats, gigs rowed by amateurs, and yachts under eight tons', according to The *Atlas* the following morning. The events became more distinctively colonial with 'Whale boats, five oars, with gear complete for sperm whaling; all gigs pulling four oars; first class yachts of eight tons and upwards; licensed Watermen's skiffs pulling two oars; Gig and dingy, the Gig not under twenty feet, the race to be decided in twenty minutes, the man in the dingy must be caught by the bowman of the gig [this kind of match being a novelty in the colonial regattas, it gave universal satisfaction]. Owing to the dingy fouling another boat she was caught by the gig, but the sculler jumped overboard and swam ashore, and thus gained the prize. There was a similar match, but the prize is yet pending, owing to some dispute. This closed the aquatic sports of the day, which passed off without accident of any kind, except the sinking of the *Prince of Wales*.'

From the gentle dreaminess of gathering wild flowers to madcap escapades in motor cars, people found release from the pressures of life. They crowded into tents to watch performing dwarfs and into theatres for Russian ballet. Associations for lost causes and ratbag commitments enjoyed a bonanza, everybody joined. Bicycle clubs and camera clubs vied for members. Citizens spent the latter half of the century learning to paint watercolours and resuscitate the asphyxiated. The hobby was democratized. And a new figure appeared judge-like in stature and incorruptibility—the umpire.

Amusement continued to be sought in dalliance, and happiness found itself pursued out into the bush by families with hampers of provisions and a determination to learn the lessons of Wordsworth.

In the main, leisure activities were much like those enjoyed in England, except that the country was wilder, the facilities fewer, the risks more exciting, and the constraints of gentility less strangling. People took things easy and relished the relaxed pace of life.

For some, however, happiness had little to do with frivolous pastimes: the drive to achieve, to be first, best was to escape the inferiority complex of being colonial and provincial. This applied throughout all pursuits, from Nellie Melba polishing her top E flats to Douglas Mawson charting 1,600 kilometres of previously unknown Antarctic coast and claiming 5,762,750 square kilometres of frozen territory for an astonished Australia.

Antarctic explorer Douglas Mawson, photographed in Adelaide after his first expedition with Ernest Shackleton and Edgeworth David. *Unknown, 1910*

Right: The first All-England Cricket Eleven sailed for Australia aboard the SS *Great Britain* in 1861. The records are almost as unclear about the team's names as for the Aborigines' tour of England (*opposite*). The team has been identified as follows:
Standing (left to right): R. Iddison, G. Griffith, G. Mudie, H. H. Stephenson (Captain, centre without cap), G. Wells (holding a ball). E. Stephenson (holding a bat), T. Hearne.
Sitting (left to right): W. Caffyn, G. Bennett (behind Caffyn), T. Sewell (holding a ball).
Sitting on the deck: C. Lawrence, W. Mortlock.
Charles Nettleton, 1861

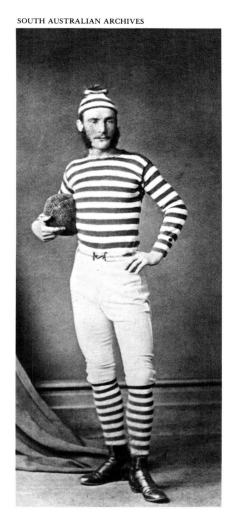

Opposite page
Below: Ten years before the first white Australian cricket team appeared at Lord's an Aboriginal team played there, in 1868. In the several published versions of this photograph the names given the players vary, yet they tell their own story. The standing figures, left to right, would seem to be Bullocky, Tiger (or Tarpot), T. W. Wills (an Englishman and captain), Johnny Mullagh and Red Cap. The seated figures being Dick-a-Dick, Cuzens Mosquito (or Peter Rose), Twopenny, Jim Crow and King Cole. Sports historians have suggested that most of the team were weak players; but the scoresheets show that the Englishmen who played against them couldn't have been much better. Contemporary descriptions of the matches gave the impression that they offered good, exciting value. No Aborigine has represented Australia in world cricket since. *C. Hewitt(?), 1868*

Left: Among other British sports enthusiastically pursued were football (soccer) and rugby football. James Smith Pearce was a third-row forward, right wing, in the Kapunda Football Club, 1879. Kapunda was a famous copper mine in South Australia till it closed in 1888. From cap to boots this sportsman is an example to his kind. *James Uren, 1879*

Below: The hunt assembles outside the New Norfolk Hotel, Tas. In the eithteenth century hunting had become enormously popular as the new dangerous sport, those who rode to hounds were intoxicated by speed. Not surprisingly then, foxes were introduced to the colony before long. Otherwise what would the hunters hunt? The question of the harm these predators might do was entirely extraneous. The importance of the horse can be gauged by the fact that in 1861 in New South Wales alone there were 230,000 horses, to 350,000 white people. *Unknown, c. 1865*

Overleaf: The *Namoi* with passengers about to set out on a Federal Convention picnic along the Hawkesbury River just north of Sydney. From the earliest days the flats along the Hawkesbury were valuable farming land. The river itself was soon thought of as a recreational retreat, and to this day is still almost free from invasion by commerce. Tidal and salty in its lower reaches, the Hawkesbury is navigable by small steamers up to Windsor, a town established by convict labour in 1794 as Green Hills. *NSWGP, 1897*

Right: Improved technology in camera
design and emulsions allowed for faster
shutter speeds and action photographs,
such as the flurry and dust seen at the
Mowbray Hurdle, Launceston, Tas. The
Mowbray Racecourse Company was
founded in 1876, but interest declined
soon after this, a contemporary account
explaining that racing had 'lost much of
its charm now the bookie has gone and
the betting is done by means of that
cold-blooded machine the "tote".' The
separate Australian colonies were
dogged in their determination to be
different from each other, even in the
matter of racing. In Tasmania, South
Australia and Western Australia races
were run anti-clockwise, elsewhere
clockwise. *Unknown, 1897*

Below: Bicycle manufacture had made
swift developments before the turn of
the century and already a recognizable
racing cycle had evolved by 1897 when
this action photograph was taken of the
First Class Handicap at Launceston.
Unknown, 1897

Left: Showing his form at rowing the foot-stool through sylvan bush at the San Francisco Palace of Art, 250–252 George Street, a Sydney sculler. *Thomas H. Boyd, n.d.*

Below: Making use of a flood, these organized 'fours' in team uniform line up prior to a race. The two single scullers have a larrikin disregard for appearances, in one case, not only with a pipe stuck in his mouth but a dog as cox. Since all Australian colonies were founded on rivers and safe harbours, water sports were popular right from the outset. Organized rowing events date from the first regatta of 1818. *Charles Bayliss, n.d.*

Right: Complete with teapot, folding chairs and table, a family party shelters in a giant hollow tree. The land itself had begun to modify the traditions they brought with them. But such genteel practices as sitting on chairs or spreading cloths to cover the ground have persisted to the present day. *N. J. Caire, n.d.*

Below: Gathering wildflowers in Western Australia. Reminiscent of a mediaeval tapestry, the abundance of flowers over the entire surface holds all the other elements together. This picture is from the album of an unknown traveller, his ticket, also enclosed in the album, was for a world tour begun on the *Orotava* leaving London on 5 April 1895 for Albany, WA. The mallee-scrub, gimlet and salmon-gum woodlands of the West are particularly rich in wildflowers during spring and summer. *Unknown, c. 1895*

Opposite page: The cool drama of caves, cascades and rockpools drew many picnickers to favourite spots such as this one, possibly at Leura, NSW, where Daisy Ethel Andrews sits on other people's graffiti contemplating Nature while her husband composes the picture. *E. Garfield Andrews, c. 1910*

222

Opposite page: Pleasures are often a question of bringing together those with much in common. Here are two characters of a kind. Unfortunately, the meeting offers pleasure to only one of them. If this groper is on display advertising bait, then those live worms are worth every penny of their inflationary price: the equivalent of half a lobster.
NSWGP, 1909

Left: The cheapest way to provide public baths is to put a fence around water already there—for seawater swimming in a harbour (with sharkproof fence) or for freshwater swimming in a river. These Perth City Baths were erected in 1897 and advertised as 'fresh and salt water baths', this mystery is not explained unless in a tidal waterway that is fresh with the outgoing tide and salt with the incoming tide. Underneath, along the edge of the pool, a grille of timbers may be seen; this is a typical sharkproof fence.
Unknown, c. *1900*

Below: People are admirably resourceful when it comes to devising pleasures. Absence of water in the salt lake didn't prevent this family, plus dog, taking their nifty craft for a sail.
Hemus and Hall, c. *1895*

Right: The Theatre Royal, Sydney, burnt down in 1892. The ravages of that fire produce their own tattered ostentation. And the men stand ready on stage, almost like actors themselves, guiding our way of seeing things. The original Theatre Royal, the first permanent theatre in Australia, opened in 1833 and within very few years the *Sydney Gazette* complained that it attracted a 'half-tipsy, half-strumpet audience'. The new Theatre Royal was opened in 1875 and enjoyed a much more respectable reputation.
Unknown, 1892

Below: From very early days, theatres have offered popular and serious entertainment. Her Majesty's Theatre, Sydney. Perceiving that the audience itself is a vital part of the show, the photographer focuses his camera on them, achieving an effect in itself theatrical: the simple, flowing bands of the balconies ornamented with fantastic detail of living heads and torsos. At the front, centre, stands the conductor ready to begin the overture, also the enquiring faces of some of the orchestra peering over the edge of the stage. Possibly there is an official party in the centre box—they have such a lot of room each, the men are so formal in white ties and the ladies so resplendent.
Unknown, n.d.

Left: Janet Achurch as Nora in Henrik Ibsen's *A Doll's House*, Melbourne, 1891. A contemporary critic summed up her performance this way: 'If acting at once refined and artistic; if an impersonation powerful and vivid, and also delicate in every detail; if subtlety of insight into character, and consistency, variety, and completeness of delineation could secure the success of a piece, Miss Achurch would have carried *A Doll's House* to a triumphant issue.' But, he went on to explain, the Melbourne audience could not be expected to abandon its moral scruples for a mere theatre piece. The fact that Nora paid for her thoughtless crime with dread of exposure, driven to the verge of hysteria, did not thaw the audience's antipathy towards the character – 'Though she herself appeared to be enamoured of it, and was, therefore, inspired to almost heroic efforts to communicate her affection for it.' *Stuart and Co., 1891*

Below: Dame Nellie Melba, the great operatic soprano. Late in life she had the reputation of being arrogant and disagreeable, filled with the bitterness of success and a crochetty determination to remain known as the best. Here, the bower of leaves forms a proscenium arch, even in this homely setting, and she is exposed on the stage of real life, the mat pale and circular as a spotlight. In her prime she was matchless. George Bernard Shaw, then a music critic, wrote of her 'unspoiled, beautiful voice, and, above all, her perfect intonation'. He went on, 'You never realize how wide a gap there is between the ordinary singer who simply avoids the fault of singing obviously out of tune and the singer who sings really and truly in tune, except when Melba is singing.' *Unknown, c. 1925*

Right: The making of images always has carried with it a special quality of satisfaction. The photographer, Stephen Spurling, makes his image of the image-makers among their mysteries: the room's simple parallels and planes, the panels of ornate plasterwork samples, the statuettes, busts, and that dangling arm. *Stephen Spurling, n.d.*

Below: At the National Gallery of Victoria, students being marshalled by Greek statuary. A young Norman Lindsay is seen showing off his waistcoat. Frederick McCubbin, the master, modest and bald-headed, sits among his followers. *Unknown, c. 1900*

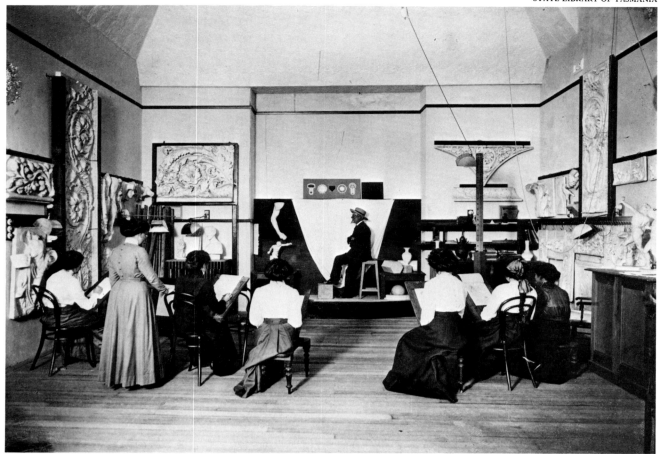

Ideas, tastes, canvases, books, instruments, all were brought as part of the European heritage. The young violinist stands by the back steps and the water tank of 'Fairseat' her family home at Bardon, Brisbane. Walter Hume, who took the photograph of his daughter Mary, was Queensland Surveyor-General. But Mary appears uncomfortable with the instrument. Taking account of her awkward posture and her weight on the wrong foot, she probably hated practising. *Walter C. Hume, 1897*

Right: Of course no other happiness is said to be like conjugal bliss. About to find out, is the latest young lady to marry into the Hopkins family, seen gathered here at their fashionable residence 'Summerhome'. The photographer has made a very heavy-handed attempt to improve his work with retouching. *Unknown,* c. *1872*

Below: Equally soon to find out—and less likely to be fooled by silly illusions—Sarah Poole marries Fred Charlewood, facing very different circumstances at the tiny goldmining and dairy-farming township of Central Tilba, NSW. And once married, married for good. Until very recent times divorce was so rare as to be scarcely feasible. The Parliament at Westminster passed its *Divorce Law* in 1857, for the first time allowing secular courts to dissolve a marriage. However, by 1870 the successful cases under this law only reached 1 in 10,000 marriages. By 1900 the number had increased to 7 in 10,000. The chances are that these particular young people stayed together, happy or not. *W. H. Corkhill,* c. *1900*

Right: For some the pursuit of happiness could hardly be said to involve much pursuing. Government House, Melbourne, recreated the easy domesticity of the English ruling class. The persons are from left to right: Haskett-Smith, Major Kerr-Pearse, Mr Bickersteth, Mrs Rupert Downes, Colonel Dangar, Lady Doris Blackwood and Miss Eva Robertson. Lady Doris obviously enjoys a relaxed attitude towards the photographer, the Hon. Victor Nelson Hood, Secretary to the Governor. The tennis refreshments stand untouched, as does the court. *V. N. Hood, 1916*

Below: Tennis, respectable at least since King Henry V's time, always offered a variety of possibilities: to sit and watch, to sit and not watch, to doze to the plokking of furred balls, to call the score and criticize fine points of play, or in extremity to play. This tennis party boasts, from left to right, Miss Reid, Miss Byron Moore, Mrs Willie Clark, Frank Clarke, Mr Crowther, Roma Clarke, Mrs Crowther, W. J. T. Clarke and V. N. H. (the Hon. Victor Nelson Hood). Taken on 27 February 1916, war or no war, life must go on, of course, and one must not allow standards to lapse. *V. N. Hood, 1916*

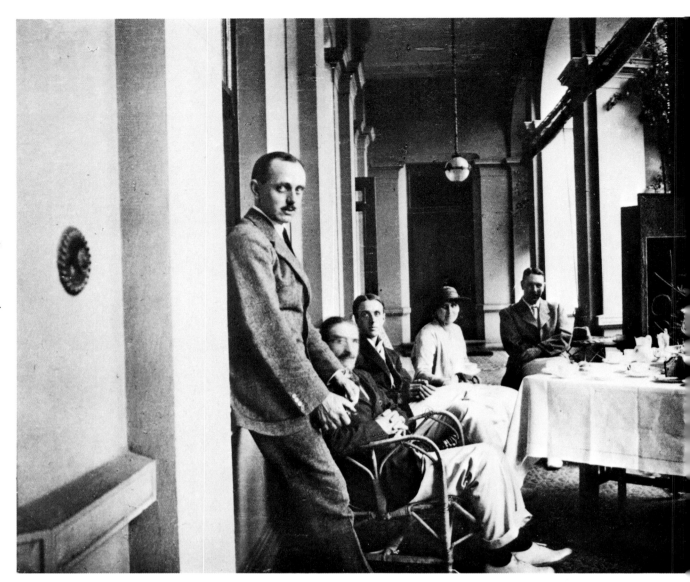

231

Below: The quality which distinguishes children's amusements from those of their elders is the wholehearted, self-denying absorption they bring to even the simplest occupation. Gordon Andrews concentrates on painting a replica of his father's T-model Ford which he made to scale from his own measurements. Retail department stores ran competitions for model making, which was very much encouraged as a hobby. In Gordon Andrews' case it had direct bearing on his subsequent career – he went on to become one of Australia's leading designers, from furniture to banknotes. One incidental detail is that as well as a thick belt, he wears Police and Firemen's braces. This recalls the traditional Australian joke that the definition of a pessimist is a man who wears both braces and a belt.
E. Garfield Andrews, c. *1925*

Right: The young Gordon Andrews in one of his homemade cars, this time powered by the somewhat volatile fuel of a younger brother, Ron. The smaller boy with his bare feet presents a picture of a typical Australian.
E. Garfield Andrews, c. *1924*

GORDON ANDREWS

Right: It is not surprising to find a keen tradition of sailing and boating races developing early; after all, the country was dependent on sailing skills for supplies and for contact with the outside world. Also the fine harbours and river estuaries offered ideal conditions, in most cases the whole year round. This tradition grew steadily. And of all classes of sailing boat, none is more spectacular than the 'eighteen footers'. Lightly constructed shells, they competed without restriction as to how much canvas they could carry or how many crew. Sydney skiffs like the *Kovik* would normally carry about 74 square metres in a race, and up to 93 with a spinnaker. To manage such a mass of sail required a crew of fifteen men, having to balance the craft by throwing their weight to windward in three rows. As designs were refined and trapezes developed, the size of the crew diminished dramatically, to the point where today's boats carry a crew of three only, all on trapezes.
Unknown, n.d.

Below: Tathra, NSW. Just over the rise is the beach and the sea. This well-known holiday resort no longer has the quiet backwater feeling the photograph shows: it is crowded with caravan parks, motels and fast-food stalls.
Max Dupain, 1950

MAX DUPAIN

Luxuries and Slums

Inevitably those first hamlets on the coast, with their barracks of soldiers and their misery of convicts, grew. And as the harbour facilities continued to be of central importance, the principal cities developed on the spot.

From being famous as the most drunken society on earth, Sydney developed to the sedate town described by Anthony Trollope in 1885: 'The first thing, then, that struck me on walking about Sydney one afternoon, looking at the place and the people, was the appalling strength of British civilization . . . The same gloomy dress, cumbrous on the women, hideous on the men . . . the same food, the same overeating, and overdrinking, and (observe how careful we are) at the same hours! . . . In Melbourne, for reasons spoken of elsewhere, this fact is not so striking. Melbourne, I have said, has something of London, Paris, New York, and of its own. The prevailing characteristic of Sydney is its Britishness. Everywhere are the thumb marks and the great toe marks of the six-fingered six-toed giant, Mr Arnold's life-long foe, the British Philistine!'

The following year F. Adams confirmed this impression. 'Melbourne has, what might be called, the *metropolitan tone*. The look on the faces of her inhabitants is the *metropolitan look*. Melbourne likes to "go ahead". . . . This I say is Melbourne—Melbourne with its fine public buildings and tendency towards banality, with its hideous houses and tendency towards anarchy. And Melbourne is, after all, the Melbournians.'

In 1883, R. E. N. Twopenny observed: 'The working class can, of course, afford to be, and are, better dressed than at home; for though clothes are in reality much dearer, they are much cheaper in proportion to wages . . . Churches abound in every Australian city, especially in Adelaide, where they are so numerous as to excite the ridicule of the less devout Victorians . . . In Australia a man feels himself an unit in the community, a somebody; in England he is one among twenty-seven millions, a nobody.' However, the obverse of this equality was a levelling of excellence. On the subject of the arts, Twopenny related an anecdote: "How on earth am I to get on in Adelaide," said a musician of considerable merit to me, "when, as you know, there is no one with whom I can provoke comparisons?" The very superiority of the man was fatal to his success.'

The charter to open the first bank in New South Wales had a tremendous impact. Commissioner Bigge in his enquiry into Governor Macquarie's administration noted: 'The evils of a paper circulation, issued upon the credit of individuals, had become the subject of universal complaint, and had defied all the measures of restraint or correction that from time to time had been applied to them.' The colony's official money was English currency. Although some order began to emerge from the chaotic financial situation, opponents of the bank possibly guessed even then that bankers would grow powerful enough to manipulate parliaments. On the other hand

Just four years after opening for business the Oriental Banking Corporation confronted Melbournians with this deadly cold neo-Classical building. Despite profitable trading in Australia, this international British bank eventually went out of business, its resources drained to meet vast losses in Ceylon and Mauritius. *Antoine Fauchery or Richard Daintree, c. 1858*

any misgivings were insignificant beside the general relief.

After the goldrushes began in the 1850s, banks sprang up all over the place, with flamboyant displays of wealth in the cities—especially Melbourne because the Victorian goldfields were the richest. The cities revelled in being clearing houses for the wealth dug out of rock, and they also welcomed their role as chief consumers and distributors of the produce of the rural districts. The greatest Australian festivals were the annual Agricultural Exhibitions. Despite the countless small shows in bush towns, the great ones were not in the country at all, they were in the State capitals. Huge buildings were put up to house these exhibitions of fruit, vegetables and machinery; and confectioners set up permanent stalls there to display sample bags of their tooth-rotting delights, a fairground jangled with entertainments day and night, capacity crowds at the great open arena watched sheep-dog trials, wood chopping, displays of horsemanship and marching bands, culminating in the Grand Parade of stud livestock by the hundred, wearing satin championship sashes, which filed into view, spelling out majestic spirals on the grass. Lasting a full week, the only rivals in richness and spectacle to these festivals were the great gatherings of the Aboriginal people.

The cities were a Mecca and drew visitors from all over the country as well as thousands of immigrants waiting to move out on to farms or diggings. In the days when travel was by ship or wagon, transit travellers could be delayed by weeks or even months. Hotels were a necessary service and each city boasted hundreds of them. As commerce expanded, office buildings and warehouses came to take over with fewer and fewer people living in the central area and commuting daily by foot or horse-drawn vehicles. Later, when electrified tramways were brought in, it was the people who'd been pushed out into the suburbs who had to pay the huge cost of installing

and running them. As for life in the outlying suburbs, the advantages were chiefly rural—even the poorest houses stood on large pieces of land and people lived a healthy, open-air existence unthinkable in European cities. The inner suburbs, crowded with modest dwellings on small allotment strips grew older, denser and dirtier, posing severe sanitation problems. By the 1860s they were already slums. Many of the residents were ex-convicts and the stigma of this was felt by the community at large.

The price of city luxuries had to be paid in the overcrowded factories and slums. In 1900 Sydney suffered an outbreak of bubonic plague and so the poor suffered doubly, because they were the ones who caught the disease. An inter-colonial plague conference was held that year, and entirely rejected the theory that bubonic plague might be carried by rat-fleas. But the Chief Medical Officer of New South Wales, Dr Ashburton Thompson, made a study of the plague in Sydney and irrefutably proved that it was spread by the fleas. This important medical knowledge has resulted in bubonic plague being brought under control throughout the world.

The problem with the health, education and cultural responsibilities of councils has been that the aldermen were most often the very businessmen whose success helped create deprived conditions for others. Over the years their wilful and systematic destruction of beautiful and historic buildings has resulted in an impoverishing of the national heritage in every capital city except Hobart.

Local councils were first set up in the 1830s using the English model where possible. The case for having them was eloquently put by the Colonial Office in Westminster in 1842.

Local Government and democracy are essentially intertwined, and it is difficult to see how the one can survive without the other . . .

The tramway became essential to the sprawl of suburban development and its advantages were immediately apparent. People could now live where they chose (provided they could afford it) and travel to work, rather than having to live near enough to walk. *Unknown, c. 1909*

States, where national democracies are not supported by the practice of local self-government, will not develop that wide and solid political capacity in their citizens which is the chief bulwark against autocracy.

Initially the councils were elected to administer markets and toll roads. This gave them a certain income, which was later increased by adding rates and penalties—they then had to take responsibility for providing roads, education, public buildings, parks, and maintaining a police force. Unfortunately this took little account of the geographic spread of many shires (which resulted in roads, for example, being immensely expensive per capita), or of genteel corruption. From the outset the right to vote was restricted to men, but by no means all men. Only land owners had the vote.

As local councils took shape, the central governments began to see they would have to take back some of the powers given them. Responsibility for many areas of administration was resumed by the State and special authorities were set up to run all ports and harbours, roads and road-making, town planning, water and electricity supplies. So at a time when city councils might have become professional bodies, paying their members as members of parliament are paid, they fell back into the hands of amateurs whose financial success in life allowed them the time to sit on committees. Brisbane, to this day, is the only Australian city that pays its Lord Mayor and aldermen a full professional salary.

Management of city affairs was at best unimaginative, at worst it accentuated the instabilities of general government policies.

Within six years of R. E. N. Twopenny's complimentary remarks about Melbourne, that city was very differently portrayed in an article on the 1890 Depression: 'Three hundred starving women, with babies in arms, paraded through the streets of Melbourne last Wednesday . . . These women then proceeded to the *Age* office and gave three groans for that capitalistic sheet . . . On Friday about 400 of the unemployed knocked on the gaol door and demanded admittance, but the governor said that was impossible unless they broke the law . . . Families are being evicted and landlords are taking the goods and chattels of the unemployed. Some go to the auction rooms and take back by force their comrades' furniture.' This report first appeared in a provincial newspaper glorying in the title The *Wagga Wagga Hummer*.

On the other hand, cities are not just buildings and regulations, they are people, and every city grew its special character. Throughout the nineteenth century each colony tended to develop self-contained industries. Everything from shoes to trams was of distinctive local design. Basic household commodities were produced in a range of choices far beyond that offered today. For example, with an ordinary item such as soap, there were not just the brands put out by transnational corporations, each with its white soaps in competition with its yellow and pink soaps, but independent products widely different in quality and price. Backyard manufacturing operations were common in the cities and even in small towns. In Port Adelaide, Anderson Mitchell & Co. advertised that they made every kind of soap, candles and drysaltery goods, such as Blue Bell Mottled Soap. It is a fair bet that this brand was unheard of in Sydney or Perth. Also they offered candles in wax, stearine, and composite.

The cities began to be plastered with advertisements, bold lettering and gaudy colours, and often enough it was hit or miss who would succeed or fail. Brooke's Monkey Brand toilet soap was a case in point. It may well have been a good soap, but its name and slogan made disastrous inroads into the sales until the company folded altogether. Professionalism in advertising is one of the marks (dubious though it may be) of the twentieth century. It is hard to imagine who could have thought up the Monkey Brand sales pitch:

We're a capital couple, the Moon and I,
I polish the Earth, he brightens the sky,
And we both declare, as half the world knows
Though a capital couple, we 'WON'T WASH CLOTHES'.

The artist puts the finishing touches to the advertisement for Monkey Brand soap. *Dora or Mabel Hookey, c. 1900*

Members of the Victorian Police Wireless Patrol guarding the public's safety. *Unknown, 1948*

Sussex Street at Grafton Wharf, Sydney. Like a Dutch Renaissance painting with its loving detail of brickwork and its celebration of contemporary life. The wharf itself runs alongside the ship that may be seen nudged in among the sheds at the right. *Charles Kerry*, c. *1900*

Left: The dome of the Garden Palace, erected to house the Sydney International Exhibition of 1879, despite a public outcry that so large a structure would obscure harbour views. The dome was over 30 metres in diameter and 27 metres from the ground floor. In the centre was an eye of stained glass 6 metres across. The framing was wood covered by corrugated galvanized iron.
Charles Bayliss, 1880

Top: The Garden Palace. After 20 April 1880 when the Exhibition closed, the building was used to house sculptures, a mining and technology museum, and certain government department records. When it burnt to the ground exactly three years after being first opened, many believed the fire had been started on purpose to destroy convict records — of which people were then ashamed, but which would now be accepted as priceless

national and personal treasures. A few years later the ground was reland-scaped and the site became part of the Botanic Gardens; the only trace of the building was the waterpipe of a fountain. *Unknown, c. 1880*

Above: As if a bomb has gone off and Jacquemart's statue is saying, 'Ssh, did I hear something?' This is all that remained of the Garden Palace after the 1882 fire. These powerful gentlemen have decked themselves out correctly. As the poet Victor Daley would have it:
  Who rules the world with iron rod?—
    The person in the Tall Silk Hat.
  He is its sordid lord and god—
    Self-centred in a Shrine of Fat.
Unknown, 1882

243

Right: Clad in corrugated iron, but nevertheless bowing to tradition with Tudor brackets over the doors and windows, this Congregational Church stood in Bourke Street, Sydney. *Unknown, 1870*

Below: In photographing these echoes of the Italian Renaissance in the Largs Pier Hotel, SA, the photographer has folded the arcaded coolness round a centre of balance. It was relatively easy in the early days to give buildings this monolithic feel while they stood uncluttered by surrounding structures. *J. Gazard, c. 1905*

Left: Sun streaming into the roofless Sydney Town Hall, not yet quite complete. Local government authorities expressed their self-esteem in the offices in which they housed themselves. However, the character of the place was modified by the environment; Sydney's public buildings, built of sandstone, have a quite distinct feel from the granite of Melbourne or the limestone of Brisbane. *A and A Photo Company,* c. *1875*

Below: City photography offered rich opportunities with the geometry of light and shadow. The columns of Parliament House, Sydney, frame samples of other city buildings: the church, the old Georgian-style terrace houses indistinguishable from those in many an English city and, at left, the new Sydney-style terrace with small shady verandahs. *NSWGP, 1871*

245

Right: In case it should be thought the foundation of Sydney University was solely in the service of reason and enlightenment, architect and stonemasons provided gargoyles to recall the dark night of gothic fears. The stone is triassic sandstone, common in the Sydney area and remarkably easy to work. *Unknown, c. 1857*

Below: The whole university building taking shape, a tribute to the enlightened citizens who argued so energetically for its establishment, but taking shape nonetheless as a nightmare of rigid echoes from Oxbridge. Designed by Edmund Blacket, the building was begun in 1854 and finished in 1860. He also designed fifty-eight churches, including St Andrew's Anglican Cathedral. His favoured style was nostalgic gothic. Blacket was self-taught as an architect so a lot of credit must go to the engineers and masons that many of his buildings are still standing. *Unknown, c. 1857*

ARCHIVE OFFICE OF NSW

Left: Stonemasons from many parts of Europe came to work in Australia. Those from Italy were especially sought after. These masons are working on the construction site of the Royal Prince Alfred Hospital, Sydney. The foundation stone, laid in 1876 bears the legend: 'Founded to commemorate the gratification of the people of New South Wales at the recovery of the Duke of Edinburgh from the wound inflicted by an assassin at Clontarf in 1868.' This was the same Prince Alfred who had shaken the hand of William Lanne, the last full-blood Tasmanian male Aborigine, at a regatta in Hobart. The hospital was completed in 1882.
Unknown, c. 1880

Below: Doubtless, cricket was inevitable in a British colony. But fielding must have been an unenviable chore in this game at Strathalbyn, SA.
S. W. Sweet, c. 1880

The unrehearsed information in a street scene is often the most fascinating part of it. The figures in this fine picture of King William Street, Adelaide, are full of interest, with their wide skirts and narrow trousers, stooping, communicating, strolling, hurrying, running to leap on a horse-drawn tram, cycling, and being tracked by a methodical dog. The slowness of the traffic is clear in the free use being made of the street by those pedestrians wandering among the vehicles.
J. Gazard, c. 1899

Right: The Exhibition Building in Melbourne, which is still standing, was opened with even more grandiloquence than the Garden Palace in Sydney. The famous poet Henry Kendall wrote an ode for the occasion:

Dressed is the beautiful City—the spires of it
Burn in the firmament stately and still
Forest has vanished—the wood, and the lyres of it,
Lutes of the seawind and harps of the hill.

As it went on, alas, the blight of official pomposity grew worse if anything. The Muse was not in the mood to be made use of:

Here, on the waters of majesty near to us,
Lingered the leaders by towers of flame:
Elders who turn from the lordly old year to us
Crowned with the lights of ineffable flame.

A more refreshing feature was this German Beer Court. *Unknown, 1888*

Below: And if the exhibition buildings connected the city with the country, so did the city markets. This interior with its beautiful gaslamps is the Victoria Markets, Sydney.
Star, n.d.

2918. GEORGE STREET.
BY MARKET ST.

KERRY PHOTO SYDNEY.

The copper domes of the Victoria Markets in George Street, Sydney. Described with enviable certainty in *Samuell's Guide to Sydney* of 1899 as 'superior to any structure in the world', the market housed fruit and vegetable stalls in the basement, various small goods shops on the ground floor, while upstairs were a lending library, concert room, banquet hall, offices and artists' studios. Vehicles could be driven in and carried up and down by a hydraulic lift. The horse-drawn omnibus in the street outside is the shuttle run from Circular Quay to Central Railway Station. The original omnibuses were licensed to carry 18 passengers for a fare of three pence a head. This form of public transport operated in the city for half a century, from 1870 till 1920. (The Queen Victoria Building has been restored to its former glory. It now houses specialty shops and cafes.) *Charles Kerry*, c. *1912*

251

At the approach to the river port of Brisbane, stands its Customs House, an impressive specimen of confusions. The ghost of Christopher Wren haunts Charles Maclay's design—built in 1888–9. But how is it to be approached? Petrie Bight curves towards it at a tangent. The apse of the building (which the vocabulary of architecture teaches us to read as the back) opens through a small door to the east. This church-like layout suggests a main entrance at the western end, but here the building abuts another. The entrance at the side between the columns, which *is* the way in, is bewilderingly inconsistent on the riverfront. From whatever viewpoint it is approached, its pompous elements appear lopsided. Follies of this kind have been tolerated gladly in that hot, friendly city. Here, a local standing beside the Victorian postbox enjoys his moment of being centre-stage. *Albert Lomer, 1889*

253

Pyrmont Bridge, Sydney. Pyrmont was named in 1806 after the German spa near Hanover for its pure and uncontaminated spring. But before long it was densely populated and became, in the words of one commentator, 'the most exclusively working-class suburb of Sydney', eventually to be dominated by the chimney stacks of the powerhouse.

This picture looks east from Pyrmont across Darling Harbour. At the far end of the bridge was the city's fruit and vegetable market. Judging by the dense traffic and the loads being carried, this photograph was probably taken on a day when the market was open.

The bridge, designed by Percy Allan, is now threatened with demolition and is no longer in use. *Charles Kerry, 1902*

K & CO.
329. PYRMONT BRIDGE

Right: The price of city luxuries is paid in the slums. This photograph of Exeter Place off Wexford Street, the Rocks, Sydney, was taken during the outbreak of bubonic plague. From the grime of their homes, the people stand back and stare through an invisible barrier of infection at the pho-tographer who is risking his privilege of safety. The first case of plague was identified on 19 January 1900. *J. Degotardi Jnr, 1900*

Below: Certain districts were held in quarantine during the plague, and a civic cleansing operation set in motion. The backyard of No. 2 Walton Place, Sydney, with its occupant and its out-door lavatory, presents a sample sanitary problem. A measure of administrative concern is that similar places are still to be seen today. *J. Degotardi Jnr, 1900*

Left: When they weren't in their backyards, the children of the poor were most often playing in the streets. A world away from the beauties of other harbourside suburbs and the expansive lawns of the prosperous, this street is as bleak and treeless as any in the midlands of England. *Unknown, 1900*

Below: The problems of the poor have not been solved by the vastly increased wealth of the nation over the past two centuries. This family faced council eviction from a Redfern slum dwelling, the property having been condemned. They were offered no alternative housing. Shortly after the picture was taken, the building was demolished to make way for a Housing Commission development of four-storeyed flats. No smooth talk can unsay what is written in the face and body of this worn-out woman, recalling lines from a Max Williams poem:

> Next day I watched an old lady
>   crying
> and demolition workers putting
>   back the sky.

There was nothing special about the date, 1949, no depression. Indeed, the boom years had begun for some. *David Moore, 1949*

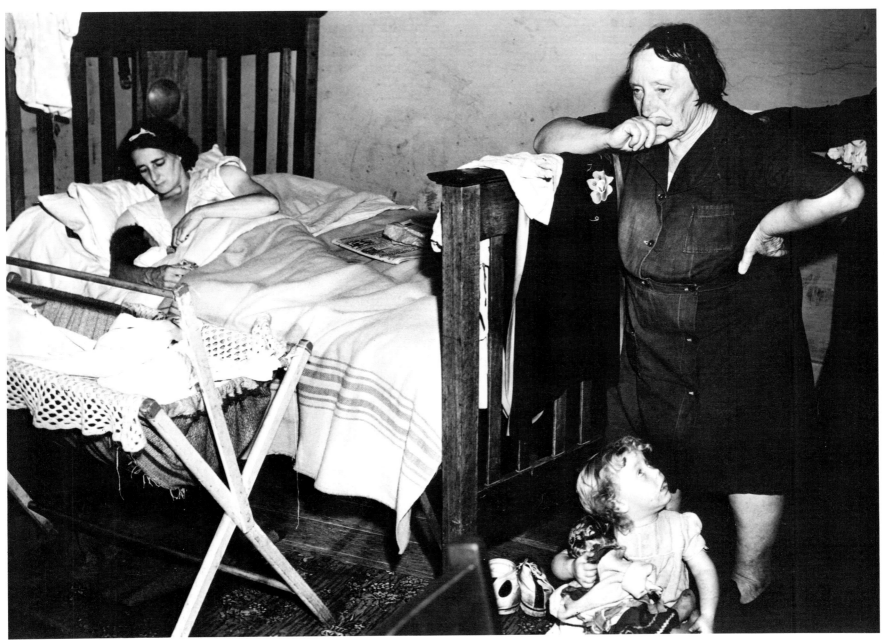

257

Right: This is the fire at Tattersall's Hotel, Kalgoorlie, on the Western Australian goldfields. On this glass plate the photograph captures a moment of drama, with the street blocked by onlookers, and that heavy rush of smoke. It's doubtful whether the photographer's rival, Roy Millar, was competing for this shot since his studio was likely to be the next casualty. *J. J. Dwyer, pre 1900*

Below: Fires in the country attract a crowd of volunteer fire-fighters. Fires in the city attract a crowd of spectators. The first professional fire services were run by insurance companies and, being commercial concerns owned by rivals, they only went out to save the property of clients. Each building insured displayed a plaque screwed to the wall identifying the insurer. In the 1850s voluntary brigades formed and sold their services racing each other to reach a fire; whoever arrived with 'first water' received the payment. It was not until 1884 that the services came under public control. *Unknown, n.d.*

Horsedrawn fire engines out on parade. This is No. 3 Fire Station, Sydney, in George Street North, at the Circular Quay end. By the time this picture was taken in 1892 steam-powered fire engines had been in use for over twenty years and although the watch-tower still remained, the telephone had taken over as the major means of alerting firemen to the location of a fire. *NSWGP, 1892*

This excavation for the underground railway at St James, Sydney, was later roofed with the lawns and trees of Hyde Park. Taken on 16 October 1922, the picture shows only one machine digging. Even at so recent a date, the rest is done by horse and manpower. This electrified line was part of a bold city transport plan which included the Sydney Harbour Bridge to provide direct rail connections between north and south Sydney. The chief engineer and author of the scheme was John Job Crew Bradfield — his name giving some indication of what his parents expected of him. The whole huge plan was put into effect between 1920 and 1932.
Unknown, 1922

16·10·22.

Right: Dr Bradfield, born at Sandgate in Queensland and trained at Sydney University, designed two alternatives for crossing the harbour, a cantilever bridge and an arch bridge. Tenders were then called and the final design was made in England by Sir Ralph Freeman for Dorman, Long & Company, who built the bridge. The supervising engineer was Lawrence Ennis. Standing dangerously near the edge of the growing structure is Sir Ralph Freeman, next to him Sir William Cullen and then Dr Bradfield, between the two bowler hats. Behind is the dogman's platform suspended from a crane—their vehicle for reaching this spectacular lookout. *Unknown, 1930*

Below: The promise of a great structure: the roadway of the incomplete bridge looms above a huge steel unit being lifted into place. This powerful, previously unpublished photograph was taken by Henri Mallard who worked for nine years to record in detail the construction of the bridge. *Henri Mallard, 1931*

Gordon Andrews, seen at an earlier age on page 232, looks to the future of the completed arch with his brother, Ken.
E. Garfield Andrews, 1930

The tone of Sydney, which has grown into the country's most exciting city, is undoubtedly set by the harbour. The solution to crossing the harbour had to be a special structure, and it was. The bridge was opened with much ceremony, with sailing and speedboat displays and aircraft flying over. One of the more modest and original contributions was the Wallaga Lake Gumleaf Band who marched to the ceremonies barefoot, playing their gumleaves and wearing only loincloths; they had travelled over 400 kilometres from their Aboriginal reserve to take part. *E. W. Searle, 1932*

Independent, More or Less

In 1899 the new Governor, Lord Beauchamp, committed an error of tact even before he landed to take up office. When his ship anchored in Sydney Harbour he responded to the welcoming party with a short, hamfisted verse of his own composition, the first line of which conceded patronisingly, 'Your birthstain have you turned to good.' Undoubtedly the convict past was regarded as a stigma—and even fifty years later wealthy families were paying to have any convict connections of their ancestors expunged from the records. This lapse of good manners on Lord Beauchamp's part helped fan the flames of nationalism.

Ever since 1788, the colony had been splitting itself amoeba-like into separate territories. At first there was New South Wales which incorporated everything known, including Van Diemen's Land. Then Tasmania was granted separate status, and so the divisions began. They continued till 1859 when Queensland was proclaimed a colony in its own right.

However, no sooner had they split than the movement to reunite them was under way. In 1842, to help provide an administrative framework, Governor George Gipps was appointed with an all-embracing title: Captain-General and Governor-in-Chief of New South Wales and Van Diemen's Land and their Dependencies. His failure was partly owing to his disastrous unpopularity. A future Premier of New South Wales, William Forster, published a satire on him within a year of his taking office. Not only did the satire make savage attacks on his administrative ability, but on his personal meanness.

> Sit down. And I hope you've taken tea—
> The hour for that meal being past with me;
> I'd offer you grog, but I sadly fear
> My cupboard is locked, and the key's not here.

The all-embracing title was withdrawn on Gipps's retirement four years later. The Victorian independence movement was particularly clamorous at this time. The following year Earl Grey (celebrated for his favourite blend of tea) proposed a national assembly for Australia, and when Victoria achieved official separation in 1849 it was within the frame of some future federal authority. But according to one member of the pastoral Manifold family, 'two well-placed men with muskets could have kept Queen Victoria out of the Western District' (of Victoria). And at an even more anarchistic level bushranger 'republics' were declared fleetingly in different parts of the country. Perhaps it could all have come to a head at Eureka Stockade when the diggers rebelled against the authorities in an armed clash, if it had been better timed and better planned.

The case for national status grew with the rapid development of a firm financial base in rural industries. As an example of economic

Artist Tom Roberts poses with his painting of the opening of the first Australian Parliament in Melbourne, 1901. The canvas was eventually completed in London in 1903. *T. Humphrey and Co.,* c. *1901*

expansion, wool production yielded £245 in 1807, £750 million a century later, and almost double this figure by 1950. Also as time went on, the artificial boundaries drawn between the colonies began to look more and more arbitrary and ridiculous. As settlement expanded and roads were put through, it was no longer a case of single isolated cities, each with a cluster of shires round it and 1000 kilometres of bush to the next nearest administrator.

The outside pressures took a fresh turning. In the 1870s German traders and plantation owners moved into New Guinea, Australia's nearest neighbouring country, and official moves were made by Berlin bankers to urge Chancellor Bismarck to annex New Guinea altogether. The Australian colonies took fright and Great Britain moved in, dividing the territory with the Germans. From 1888 to 1906 Britain and the Australian States shared joint control of Papua-New Guinea, and from 1906 control of this part of the island passed to the Commonwealth of Australia.

The issue as to whether or not to federate was put to the people in a referendum in 1898 and another in 1899, in all States except Western Australia. The results showed that the firmest support was in the most metropolitan State, Victoria, and the greatest opposition in the State with the largest proportionate rural population, Queensland. When a vote was finally taken in Western Australia on 31 July 1900 heavy support for Federation in the goldfields areas gave a 'yes' vote of 44,800 to a 'no' vote of 19,691. It wasn't long before the Western Australians decided to change their minds and voted to secede from the Commonwealth. For thirty years, Intercolonial Conferences had haggled over petty property rights and nurtured trivialities till they burgeoned into insuperable obstacles. Federation, when it finally came in 1901, was already too late and too much compromised. A disgruntled public was grateful, though, for any solution giving them some degree of national independence.

Eighty years later, the inadequacies of the Federal constitution are still being felt, the country is not yet fully independent, and a republic seems a long way off.

The moment Federation was first debated, one of the central arguments was which city should be the capital. This was solved by the decision to build a new capital on land belonging only to the new Commonwealth and not to any of the rival States. The problem then was to choose such a neutral site. In Canberra they found one and announced an international competition for a design. It was won by an American, Walter Burley Griffin. Griffin designed the city round an artifical lake, the streets and buildings in interlocking circles, the spokes of which would radiate out to all parts of the nation. Put into effect, this concept has a certain mandala quality. The city area was then lavishly planted with trees, giving it the character of the world's biggest garden and the buildings lost in greenery. As a result the city is widely spread out, vehicles of one sort or another are essential. It is a city of cars: an American dream. Interestingly enough, in 1981, the contest for a design for a new Parliament House was also won by an American firm of architects.

The role of the Governor-General underwent change following the 1927 agreement on Dominion status. Previously he had been the appointee of the Westminster Parliament and responsible to them—in fact something close to a British High Commissioner today. From 1927, the Governor-General became a strictly vice-regal representative and a separate High Commission was opened in Canberra.

Perhaps the most fundamental issue that had to be resolved when setting up a new Australian Parliament was who should be allowed to vote in the elections. The wealthy establishment insisted that voting must be the exclusive right of men with property and that they ought to have multiple votes according to the extent of their land. The radicals argued for one man one vote, for the payment of members, and votes for women—all of which were hotly opposed by the conservatives. The first fully organized and constituted Labor Party contested forty-five seats in the New South Wales election in 1891 and won thirty-six. During the next ten years, the three party system was consolidated, with two parties representing vested interests (one based on city finance and the other on landed farmers) and the Australian

The speaker of the House of Representatives, Charles 'Fighting Mac' McDonald, hammers in the second survey peg on the site of the new Federal capital. King O'Malley, who drove in the first peg, inspects the job while Lord and Lady Denman look on from a safe distance. *NSWGP, 1913*

Labor Party representing the working class and the unions.

In the first Commonwealth general election the ALP won sixteen seats in the House of Representatives and eight in the Senate—far from government, but enough to hold the balance of power. However, when it came to the great test, they were shown to have no effective policy. The Nationalist-Country Parties had presided over a disintegrating financial situation before being brought down in 1929. The Labor Party was put in power at a critical time (though without control of the Senate), but hadn't the conviction to move towards a definite socialist policy. They proved incapable of understanding the economic forces that were driving the country to ruin. Their success was a handout system of food tickets for the destitute.

From this time on, no pretence was credible: the unemployed saw this one thing clearly, that the Australian Government was in office but not in power. And that has remained the case ever since. Those with the real power are seldom known to the public and are never voted for.

In August 1930 Sir Otto Niemeyer of the Bank of England arrived from the shambles of his own country to express every confidence in Australia's resources, 'but the country would have to set its house in order, and not depend entirely on financial assistance from abroad'.

While thousands starved and tens of thousands were homeless, the newspapers comforted their middle-class readers with headlines about Dole Frauds and Military Alerts. 'It seems hardly credible,' wrote an articulate miner to the editor of The *Sydney Morning Herald*, 'that there is a body of men who though offered work refuse to accept it.' Talk of nationalizing industry was common and some people put the case for governmental controls, at least, on commerce and the marketing of primary produce. The reaction was immediate. The wheat farmers of New South Wales decisively rejected a proposal that their wheat be pooled for three years for planned disposal at home and abroad. They replied angrily that this would subject them to a yearly threat of loss of trade and they feared this was the beginning of socialization of production and distribution.

The personal tragedies were what lodged in the memories of those who suffered. And these they would never forgive. In a few cases groups of the unemployed tried collective resistance, and The *Sydney Morning Herald* reported on 21 July 1931:

HOUSE WRECKED
COMMUNIST OUTRAGE
Riotous conduct by members of a militant organization of unemployed men, who had objected to the departure of a woman and her children from a house from which they were to have been ejected for non-payment of rent, culminated today in the wrecking of the building. The demonstrators tore down a picket fence, pushed over a paling fence at the side, smashed windows, tore down doors and destroyed fittings. The wreckers dispersed before the police arrived.

Anyone who attempted to stand up for himself and protect his family was a target for further punishment and abuse.

During its first half-century, the Australian Parliament had to face three major crises spanning the years 1914–49—the First World War, the Great Depression, and the Second World War. Only one of these took place at home and the helplessness of the government in the face of economic collapse marked the end of a brief period of public faith.

The clumsiness of the Federal system became painfully obvious, with State and Commonwealth legislatures frequently in conflict and working against each other's interests. The Head of State is still the British monarch and there are still fifteen Houses of Assembly, upper and lower, round the country jealously guarding their fragments of the power left over by big business.

The spirit of the people has been tempered in these fires. At each blow it was not a beaten populace who emerged, but a tough resilient breed, committed to the loyalties of mateship about which Henry Lawson wrote so eloquently.

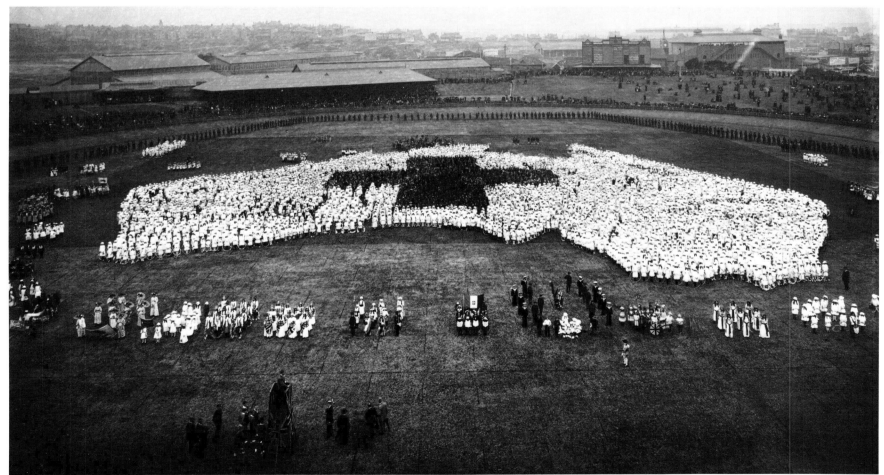

Sydney's schoolchildren show their support for the Red Cross in Sydney in 1915 whilst at Gallipoli Australian servicemen were being slaughtered in their thousands for the glory of the Empire. Either Tasmania has wandered, or it has been forgotten by the co-ordinators. *NSWGP, 1915*

269

Below left: Firing the *feu de joie* to salute the Union Jack, Motumotu. *Unknown, 1884*

Below right: And so, on 6 November 1884, the flag was hoisted at Port Moresby, destined to become the capital of New Guinea. The main building is the Rev. Lowe's house and headquarters of the London Missionary Society (the most famous of whose missionaries was Dr Livingstone in Africa). Behind it stands the schoolhouse. As usual, political annexation followed once the first religious wedge had been driven in. Commodore Erskine stands at the centre of the verandah, announcing his proclamation in a language totally meaningless to all but a handful of the inhabitants. *Unknown, 1884*

Right: One sign of the nation's self-confidence was the annexation of more territory. At 9 a.m. on 22 October 1884 Commodore James Erskine left Sydney in HMS *Nelson* with a fleet of other naval vessels. The harbour waters had to be navigated with great care as the *Nelson* was a large ship drawing an impressive 8.2 metres. They sailed north outside the Barrier Reef, in waters, as the narrative explained, 'very little frequented by ships, and on this occasion not one was sighted between Moreton Bay and New Guinea. No birds followed the ship, or were anywhere in sight, so that altogether the sea bore an aspect of great desolation.' The squadron landed at Motumotu in south-eastern New Guinea from a calm sea. This picture defines the brink of land as if this were the first landing, the expectant discovery, the blameless moments before contact. So it might have been with Captain Cook a century earlier at Botany Bay. *Unknown, 1884*

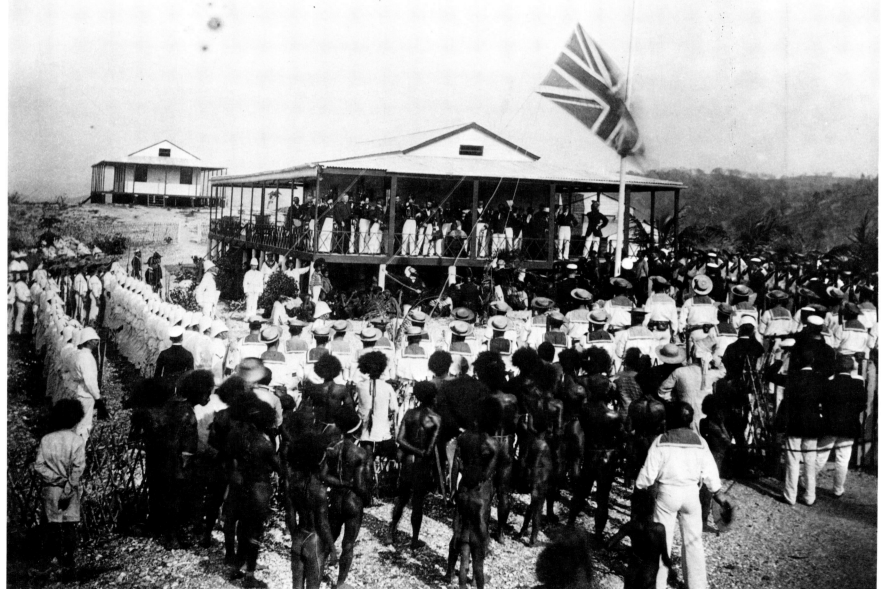

Below: John Pascoe Fawkner (1792–1869), a fiery, pugnacious man of affairs and one of the founders of Melbourne. His father was transported as a convict but allowed to bring his family (still free) with him. Granted freedom and land in Van Diemen's Land in 1806 and further land by Governor Macquarie in 1813, the Fawkners began the long, hard toil back to respectability and prosperity. The son was convicted of assisting some convicts in building an escape vessel, given 500 lashes and transported to Newcastle. He was released in 1817 and settled in Launceston where he established a radical newspaper. In 1835 he and his wife and a party of friends arrived in Port Phillip, made their way up the Yarra and decided to establish a village on the site of the present Spencer Street. He built a hotel, started another couple of newspapers, became a councillor and later a politician. A lifelong member of the Congregational Church, he was a dogged fighter for education reform, temperance, for the rights of the poor, and for separation from New South Wales. Such separatist movements, though successful, were short-lived and gave rise to many of the anomalies of Federalism in present day Australia. *Batchelder and Co.*, c. 1860

Right: As a result of much agitation and endless meetings during which the various colonies squabbled over the terms of unification, a federal system was accepted. The Duke of York and Cornwall (later King George V) was sent out from London to perform the ceremony of opening the first Australian Parliament in the Melbourne Exhibition Building, 9 May 1901. *Unknown, 1901*

272

Right: Martin Place, Sydney. A series of triumphal arches was erected at various key points, for example the German community's arch at Park and College Streets, the Commonwealth arch at Park and Elizabeth Streets, the Agricultural arch in Bridge Street, and this elaborate structure outside the Post Office in Martin Place, bearing Lord Hopetoun's name. Hopetoun didn't stay long. Appointed in 1900 at a salary of £10,000 he demanded more, was paid a further £10,000 to cover the exceptional costs of the Duke and Duchess of York and Cornwall opening parliament, but when refused an extra £16,000 a year, he resigned in 1902. His only friction with the new government was his unwillingness to sign the assent for the Alien Immigration Restriction Bill of 1901, destined to bring into effect the White Australia policy. After long deliberation he did sign. *Unknown, 1901*

Below: The pavilion built in Centennial Park, Sydney, for the swearing-in of ministers of the new nation, 1 January 1901. The ceremony was performed by Australia's first Governor-General, Lord Hopetoun, a Scotsman. *Unknown, 1901*

Sir Edward Nicholas Coventry Braddon, KCMG, Premier of Tasmania in the 1880s, brother of Miss Braddon the novelist and great-grandfather of another popular author, Russell Braddon. Like all Premiers of the period he represented moneyed interests and conducted the affairs of State rather like a business manager but with the pious demeanour of a judge. He had served his executive apprenticeship in the family's mercantile firm in India. A convinced Federalist, he was eventually elected as a Tasmanian member of the first Commonwealth Parliament, joining with the Free Trade Party in opposing Prime Minister Barton. The principal opposition in politics was between the free traders and the protectionists. One clause in the Constitution on customs revenue bears his name, the Braddon Clause.
Unknown, 1880

Left: Sir Henry Parkes, looking as much like Walt Whitman as he was able—doubtless to the chagrin of Alfred Deakin (who became Australia's second Prime Minister and had a lifetime's longing to be a poet). Parkes himself published six volumes of verse. Between 1872 and 1891 he was five times Premier of New South Wales and a passionate advocate for Federation. Perhaps his most significant legislative successes were the *Public Schools Act* of 1866, which made moves towards literacy as a right, and the *Hospitals Act* of 1866 which, among other things led to his arranging with Florence Nightingale to send trained nurses to New South Wales. Whilst in England in 1882 propounding Federalism he argued that it would benefit the Empire, 'the softer the cords, the stronger will be the union between us'. The most valued friendships he made there were with the poet Tennyson and the historian Carlyle. This picture was taken at Faulconbridge in the Blue Mountains, where he died a few years before Federation became a reality. *NSWGP, 1880*

Below: Not just a study in well-fed ambition, this is the Parkes Ministry. Though they solidly supported Federation it came too late, the peak of patriotic optimism had crumbled with the 1890's depression. *NSWGP (?), 1889*

Opposite page

Above: Citizens in each State voted on the issue of Federation. The results board outside the *West Australian* newspaper office in Perth, 31 July 1900, shows small centres sometimes returning a clear No to Federation, but the bigger towns emphatically in favour. The four divisions of Coolgardie show a 20 to 1 majority. This trend was typical throughout the nation. For some years there had been official moves to exclude Western Australia from the Federation, as a result of which there was even a petition to Queen Victoria to have the goldfields established as a separate State and part of the Australian Commonwealth. The final result was Yes: 44,800, No: 19,691. *Unknown, 1900*

Below: Though the voting on the Federation issue was accepted seriously all over Western Australia, the country people brought their own cheerful touch to recording the results, quite distinct from the sombre businesslike returns of the city. The Aborigine invited for the photograph didn't, of course, have the right to vote. There's a certain holiday atmosphere still to be found at election times in the country. *Unknown, 1900*

Left: William Morris Hughes, opening a fete in Killara, Sydney, presenting a skin of leather cured in mud. And a thick skin he undoubtedly needed. A prominent Labor supporter of Federation, he was elected to the West Sydney seat in the first Commonwealth Parliament. He became Prime Minister in 1915 and conducted this office as a Welshman, fervent in his call for conscription and total war against Germany. At the Versailles Peace Conference he clashed with President Wilson of America and sided with the French in demanding the vengeful terms against Germany that helped sow the seeds of the Second World War. He had already compromised the National Labor Party and sold out to the Opposition. *Unknown, 1934*

Below: 'A Monarch on a Monarch' reads the original caption. A karri tree cut down for the benefit of Prime Minister Billy Hughes to use as a platform for his truculence. *Claude McKinley, n.d.*

Opposite page: The provisional seat of government in 1901 was Melbourne and Melbournians were determined the permanent capital would not move to Sydney; Sydney-siders were equally definite that it wouldn't stay in Melbourne. So the senators of the nation scoured the territory between in search of a neutral site. Here they have reached Orange, NSW. *Unknown, 1902*

Left: Having had the general direction pointed out, Sir William Lyne, Minister for Home Affairs and former Premier of NSW, gets in some practice at sitting on the fence. *Unknown, 1902*

Below: King O'Malley, Minister for Home Affairs and a key figure in the establishment of Canberra as the capital, stands next to Lady Denman who is officially naming the site. Beyond her stands the Labor Prime Minister Andrew Fisher who had already made something of a reputation for enlightened developments, including a transcontinental railway and maternity allowances. On the right of the group is Lord Denman, the Governor-General. Interestingly, not one member of the official party was Australian: the Denmans were English, Fisher was a Scot and O'Malley a Canadian. Down below, the Australian troops can be glimpsed. *NSWGP, 1913*

Once the flapdoodle of officialdom had had its fun, the professionals moved in to survey the site for the national capital and begin the work of pegging straight lines. The pattern of settlement throughout the country was enormously affected by surveyors and their orderly respect for the points of the compass. This group portrait is of Mr M. Scrivener and staff. *NSWGP, 1910*

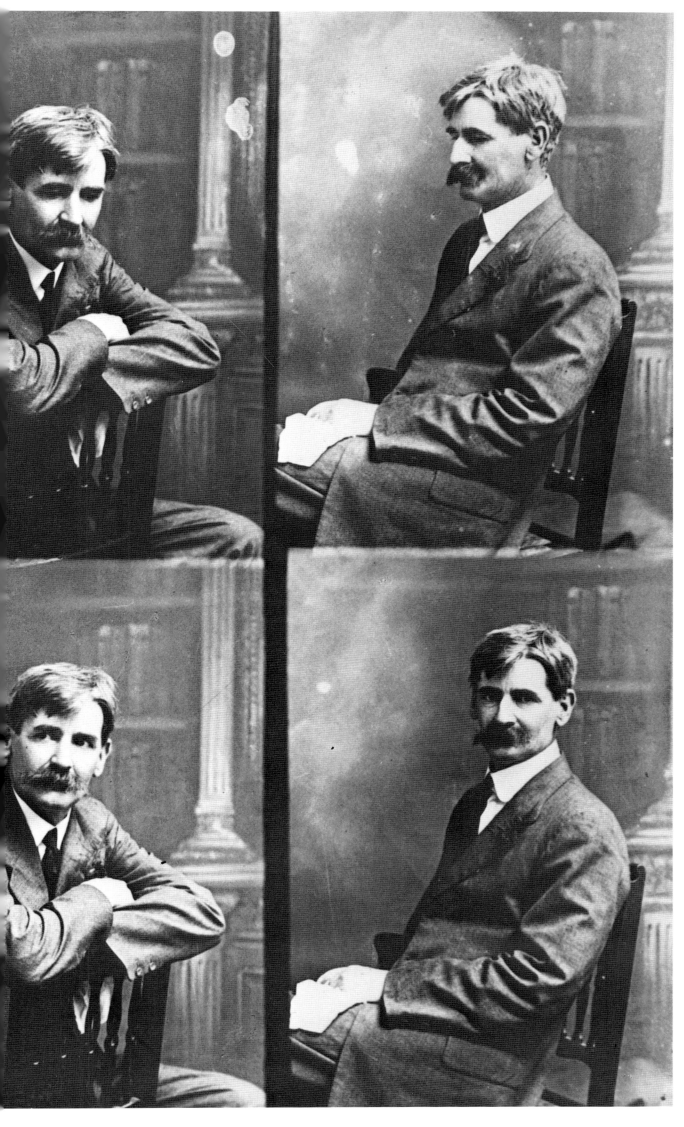

No author since the 1788 invasion has had so profound an effect on shaping our national character as Henry Lawson. Born in a tent on the goldfields at Grenfell, NSW, in 1867, his mother was a journalist and a leading feminist of the time. Lawson was a shy, modest person, afflicted by near-deafness, but he had a tremendous capacity to make friends. His poems and short stories are filled with battlers heroically or comically surviving loneliness in the backblocks or poverty in the cities. These photographic proofs of a portrait sitting capture a quality of animation—something of his mercurial mood at the height of his fame.
Unknown, c. 1910

Right: The Depression first hit Australia in the country districts. In 1929 rural industries and mining lost their markets abroad. And though the government devalued the currency by 25% to help alleviate this blow, it achieved little. So the tens of thousands of men from the cities who migrated on foot to search for work on the land found the situation there worse, if anything, than at home. At the height of the Depression, one third of the nation's workforce was unemployed, and nothing like full employment was restored until 1933. Only those workers whose produce was predominantly for consumption on the home market (such as fishermen) remained in more or less stable employment. Here are two fishermen at Bermagui, NSW.
E. Garfield Andrews, c. *1929*

Below: The Great Depression. Unemployed men on relief work arrive at a former Army training area, Blackboy Camp, WA. Five thousand of them were housed here in tents, hessian huts and makeshift shelters. What is it that makes them smile? Is it the expected response to the camera? Or is it that leap of the spirits when men are united in adversity and each journey has something of the desperate insecurity of adventure? *WAN, 1930*

Left: 1931—the unemployed stage an orderly march along Wellington Street, Perth, on their way to Parliament House and the Treasury Building. Once again, out of the desperation of their hunger and helplessness, they smile for the camera. The single figure marching beside the column calls to memory that many of these men are veterans of the Great War, just as the street sweeper who is looking on is a reminder that some people were in employment. *WAN, 1931*

Below: In all States intolerable humiliation drove the unemployed on to the streets and inevitably to clashes with the police. Here in Perth, outside the Treasury on 12 March 1930, the crowd demanded to see the Premier, Sir James Mitchell. When he declined to meet them, the ugly scenes that followed became known as 'The Treasury Riot'. *WAN, 1930*

The Grant family posing at their cottage in Lenah Valley, Tas., at the height of the Depression. *Michael Sharland, 1927*

Left: Backyard community soup kitchen, Tas. Agencies such as the Salvation Army set up these kitchens and gave out free soup in return for Government meal tickets. In Sydney, Lady Game, wife of the Governor, visited the Buckland Street Emergency Shelter for Men and saw for herself the Salvation Army's attempts to help nearly three hundred unemployed. The shelter housed the men and offered them two meals a day—'breakfast and tea'. Baths, showers and even fumigating rooms were provided, and clothing given out where needed.
The *Mercury*, c. *1930*

Below: With nothing to write on and no faith in the government to rescue the situation, this class of young men attends to the blackboard in spite of the Tasmanian winter.
Michael Sharland(?), c. *1930*

Bottom: It is possible to make the rich and the employed seem too callous. If they wouldn't part with their money, some of them parted with food. Here in Hobart, they are seen bringing succour to the less fortunate.
Michael Sharland(?), c. *1930*

MERCURY NEWSPAPER LIBRARY

Left: Western Australia had been the last State to agree to join Federation, and then the decision was far from wholehearted. Prime Minister J. A. Lyons makes an impassioned plea to a Perth audience to remain in Federation. Despite his exhortation, the West voted solidly to secede. However, their ace was trumped by Westminister, the British Parliament refusing to accept the secession—demonstrating how appropriately the platform for this political battle was decorated with the backdrop to a play. The novelist H. G. Wells visited Australia in January 1939 and referred to Adolf Hitler as 'a certifiable lunatic'. When this was reported in the press, Lyons, as Prime Minister of the nation, rebuked him. Three months later, Lyons was dead, so he didn't have the opportunity of weighing his political acumen against Wells' when the Second World War broke out in September that year.
Unknown, 1933

Below: R. G. Menzies taking a one-eyed view of the world. Having been ignominiously deposed as wartime Prime Minister in 1941, Menzies made a come-back and went on to become Australia's longest-serving Prime Minister. Historian Donald Horne wrote of him that his success lay in his being 'very slow to decide anything, monumentally suspicious, cunningly guarding his own power, his theatrical skills, and his luck in having an electoral system that in 1954 and 1961 kept him in office despite the fact that in those two elections a majority of voters wanted him to go...Menzies' great talent was that he learned how to preside over events and look as if he knew what they were all about.'
Ministry of Information, London, 1941

AUSTRALIAN WAR MEMORIAL

You Win Some,
You Win Some More

In the early days of the last century, veterans of the Duke of Wellington's campaigns against Napoleon might have met to reminisce over tankards of ale in the hotel at Windsor (NSW). Troopers from the American Civil War recognized each other in Melbourne. Survivors of the Opium War arrived from the new Hong Kong concession in 1842. Heroes of the united European defence of Turkey against Russia in the Crimea told their yarns round drovers' campfires from 1856 onwards. Always there was a war in the recent past to be remembered and another looming in the present to be fought. Throughout the period people voiced fears of a 'Yellow Peril', the vast nations of Asia to the north. These grew more alarmist with news of the horrifying T'ai-P'ing Rebellion—a modestly named war in which twenty million people were massacred (more than twice the entire toll of the First World War).

Then came Australia's earliest official war. In 1863, General Cameron led a contingent to New Zealand to fight in the Maori Wars; their most celebrated engagement was at Rangariri where 130 of the Australians were killed. By the time the war ended in 1872, 2,500 Australian volunteers had gone there to fight. Thirteen years later volunteers again enlisted and set sail in the troopships *Australasia* and *Iberia* for Suakin on the Red Sea coast for Britain's war of attrition in the Sudan. Then in 1899 it was to South Africa, again as members of the British Imperial Forces, this time to suppress the Boers. And although Federation was declared whilst this war was being conducted, no change was made to Australian involvement. This was the war where a distinctively Australian style of action was developed based on the high proportion of horses to men—16,175 men went and 16,314 horses—speed and mobility were the key, the campaigns being fought chiefly with small arms. Many veterans who survived the fighting in the Transvaal and Orange Free State eventually joined up for the Great War in 1914, mistakenly expecting the mounted infantry to be similarly effective in Turkey and France.

Where defence at home was concerned, other European powers had always been regarded as potential enemies. Ever since La Perouse sailed into Botany Bay a few days after the arrival of the First Fleet in 1788, the French, the Dutch, the Portuguese and the Germans might obviously threaten British claims in the South Pacific. However, they were familiar. They were not that limitless unknown, the hordes of Japan and China. Among the first acts of the new Commonwealth Parliament in 1901, the *Immigration Restriction Act* was designed to refuse entry to non-English speaking immigrants. At this time also, the New South Wales and Victorian governments offered contingents to serve British interests against the nationalists in the Boxer Revolution in China. Once again we went.

Astoundingly, after all the sacrifice of Australian lives in English causes round the world during the nineteenth century, after the protestations of loyalty, the ecstatic welcomes given various royal

Enjoying the euphoria of embarkation, troops of the 6th Division leave for the Middle East. *Unknown, 1940*

visitors since the first in 1867 (Queen Victoria's second son, Prince Alfred, was given a wonderful time, apart from being shot and wounded by an Irish fanatic in Sydney), the British Fleet withdrew from the Pacific under a new agreement with the Japanese. Here was the Yellow Peril in person. Newspapers were vocal in their alarm. The young nation rushed into the protective arms of the United States of America. In 1908, at the arrival of the American Navy, the Great White Fleet, the country went rapturous with relief, quite unaware that the comforting embrace immediately hardened to a ruthless grasp. The *Sydney Morning Herald* editorial of 22 August 1908 correctly predicted the military future of the Pacific: 'It is likely that the United States of America will be our first line of defence against Asia.'

Soon afterwards, The Great War offered another test of how real our independence was. Here again was a chance to formulate policies that would demonstrate a responsible self-sufficiency. Instead, Australia's politicians galloped for the precipice.

The fervour triggered by the onset of the 1914 war is hard to account for. Certainly many young people saw it as an adventure and a call to the courage. The Australian and New Zealand Army Corps—the famous ANZACS—were the only fully volunteer army to fight in the war. Their first battle casualties occurred in New Guinea when German wireless stations had to be seized.

The war imposed massive costs at home, met by heavy borrowing and new taxes. Wheat and wool were produced in record yields, but prices rose and the relative value of wages fell. By 1915 the country was rife with discontent and strikes. As an internal security measure, alien nationals were interned in camps, the largest being at Liverpool where thousands of foreign-born immigrants were shut away and denied contact with their families. They were not even allowed money that might be worth anything outside the camps, being issued with worthless discs bearing a nominal value.

Once the war was over the returned soldiers, back in this peaceful, fundamentally modest community, carried their memories of wastelands of shell-pocked mud, the senseless butchery for the sake of advancing and retreating and advancing again over the same desolate strip of France, of soldiers freezing to the ground in their sleep. They had fought the first modern mechanized war on horseback; they had served in tanks that chewed up roads and crushed all signs of civilization in their path; they had fought man-to-man duels in the air; and their howitzers had blasted the dead horizon. They had been

NSW GOVERNMENT PRINTING OFFICE

A visiting Japanese admiral photographed at Government House, Sydney, June 1916. Given Australia's fear of the 'yellow peril' it is little wonder this visit was not reported in the popular press. *NSWGP, 1916*

urged to go by romanticized visions of heroism, by hysterical advertising campaigns. There had been flags, crowds, bands and bonfires and 420,000 enlisted out of a total population of four million. Of those who signed up 330,000 were sent overseas on active service, two-thirds of them became battle casualties, 4,000 were taken prisoners of war and 60,000 were killed in action: one in five who went.

Among other things, the Great War provided a peerless training-ground for rhetoric. Before it was even over, apologists trumpeted that this was the coming-of-age of the nation. In fact it was the most desolating proof that the apron strings had not been cut. The shame of the country, the massacre of those sixty thousand young men and women was paraded as a mark of glory. The course was set for at least the next sixty years, and the ship of state put on automatic pilot.

Till this time and in all these conflicts, God, for some reason, had always been on our side, according to the propaganda. The 1914 war had been a murderous stalemate between empires in rivalry for the same expansionist spoils. But in 1936 with the Spanish Civil War, the Australians who went found themselves in a rehearsal for a confrontation with fascism on a terrifying scale, an ideological system deeply repellent to most people. When another World War started in 1939, this time the community knew it was, to an important degree, a war of political ideologies. This set it apart from all previous wars Australians had been involved in: the war against the Aborigines had been a largely civilian campaign of occupation, and even the Sudan campaign had been not so much political as religious, suppressing the rise of insurgents whose Arab nationalism was only the label we gave their Islamic fervour.

Another extraordinary aspect of the Second World War was that it was brought right here. Between February 1942 and November 1943 Australia's most northerly city, Darwin, was bombed 59 times. In all, 238 people were killed and much of the town lay in ruins. And in Darwin Harbour the Japanese sank five of our merchant ships as well as three warships, and damaged thirteen other vessels. Tiny as these losses were in terms of the suffering in the rest of the world, they frightened the public at home into a clearer understanding of what war was about than had ever been achieved in the First World War. Bombing attacks were also made on Broome, Port Hedland, Derby and Wyndham. Industry, commerce and the labour market were regulated, prices and rents were fixed, and food, petrol and clothing rationed. A massive effort was concentrated on strategic work, factories, road building and airfields. And a Civil Construction Corps was formed for armed services building programmes at home. These men were drawn from two groups: those between 45 and 60, too old to be conscripted for active service, and interned aliens.

Many of the jobs previously thought exclusively men's work were taken over by women. The Land Army did rural labouring and female workers in munitions and shipbuilding coped magnificently with things they were supposed not to be able to do. By the end of the war nearly three-quarters of a million women were employed in industry.

The United States confirmed her role as Australia's saviour in May 1942 when the Japanese Navy was defeated at the Battle of the Coral Sea, and General Douglas MacArthur arrived as Commander of the Allied Forces in the South-West Pacific to set up his headquarters in Brisbane.

George Johnston, a war correspondent, reported the New Guinea campaign: this was a vital war for Australia, to keep the Japanese invasion at bay. 'It would never have done to admit the truth of things,' he wrote in his private diary. 'New Guinea was the only bastion against invasion, and so one painted a picture in vivid colours and larger than life of this little tropical fortress of heroes.' On 3 October 1942 he reported: 'MacArthur up on the [Kokoda] track today—only as far as the road went through!' And on 16 October: 'Everyone is incensed with the new censorship bans, including MacArthur's personal censorship of stories of his visit here which have

been slashed to ribbons to convey the impression (a) that he went right up to the front line (which he certainly did NOT) and (b) that this was NOT his first visit to NG. Censorship is not just plain Gestapo stuff!'

MacArthur's publicity releases suggested that the Japanese had been pushed back across the Owen Stanley Ranges by his Americans, but Johnston records on 12 November: 'The fact remains that no American ground soldier has fired a shot in this campaign so far,' and praises the extraordinary fortitude and courage of the Australian troops slogging through the jungle and fighting in 'the worst battlefield in the world'.

Long after the war finished in 1945, the scars remained, but the mood of the country seemed practical and hopeful. And there was a determination that this time the period of rehabilitation would not be followed by a depression as happened previously. However, politicians were already busy with the so-called 'Cold War', and the wars of interference in Malaya, Korea and Vietnam were to be the direct outcome, maintaining our remarkable record of aggression without provocation. The real coming-of-age of the nation is more likely to be achieved by sparing our force of arms for a cause that is our own.

JOHN FAIRFAX AND SONS LTD

Men of the Civil Construction Corps on the job during the war. *Unknown, 1942*

NSW GOVERNMENT PRINTING OFFICE

Right: Middle Head Battery, Sydney. North Head and South Head, where other gun emplacements were mounted, can also be seen in the background. In the 1790s a French invasion was expected. A hundred years later, and after many awaited invasions had failed to happen, the Germans moved into the northern part of New Guinea. The belief that it was only a matter of time before they moved south to take over Queensland and New South Wales, helped push the States into a federation. *NSWGP, 1871*

Below: In the 1860s the Chinese were rumoured to be the real threat. Twenty years later it was the Russians. On that occasion, at colossal expense, the coastline was equipped with gun emplacements which were never used. This one is at Warrnambool, some 225 kilometres west of Melbourne. *Unknown, c. 1880*

MITCHELL LIBRARY

Volunteers' encampment, Centennial Park, Sydney. There's something of the character of a picnic about this scene. However, the recruit in the background might well have espionage in mind while he appears to be listening at a field lavatory. *Unknown, 1888*

Buttoned up against the heat a
detachment of New South Wales
Artillery volunteers parade under the
British flag at Victoria Barracks,
Sydney. The barracks were designed by
George Barney, the architect responsible
for the horse-shoe shaped quay at the
south end of Sydney Cove, known since
as Circular Quay. He was also
responsible for fortifying the tiny
Pinchgut Island in Sydney Harbour as
Fort Denison. *NSWGP, 1887*

SOUTH AUSTRALIAN ARCHIVES

Right: South Australian volunteer forces—infantry and artillery—in a showy confusion of uniforms and doubtless rival commands. The unmilitary way some are lounging about gives the impression that vanity is the prime motive of certain serving officers. These peacocks belonged to a society convinced that native peoples throughout the empire gave proof of their barbarity by making war in feathers and paint. *Unknown,* c. *1865*

Below: Departure of the Sudan Contingent, Sydney, on 3 March 1885. Marching to the tune 'The Girl I Left Behind Me', 734 men went with 200 horses. They saw scarcely any action: six of them died – from fever. They returned three months later. The exuberance of the crowd is tremendous, balancing on spars, clambering over unfinished warehouses (tiles stacked on the roof), and that one figure marvellously at the top of a light pole looking straight down on the river of white helmets. *Thomas H. Boyd Studio, 1885*

MITCHELL LIBRARY

Left: A couple of willing, if slightly rumpled, buglers of the South African War contingent. The slouch hat was to become the most famous item of Australian army uniform.
Unknown, c. 1900

Below: Scottsdale Railway Station, Tasmania—local lads leaving for the South African War, to fight for the Crown against the Boers, people in a situation far closer to their own than the English. The small group lines up for a public accolade. That earlier enemy, the forest, stands mutely in tatters as a background to the neat, unimaginative building.
T. R. G. Williams (?) c. 1900

Left: Before embarkation for active service, men of the South African Contingent attend a luncheon in their honour at the Exhibition Building, Adelaide. Right under Queen Victoria's nose, the band takes a break. It is essential to the conduct of war that the soldier fighting it has no idea what it is all about, unless it is a religious war or a defence of the homeland, otherwise he might doubt the rightness of what he does and even come to question his orders. It is hard to imagine that the conversation at this luncheon had anything to do with the Boer farmers as thinking people. *J. Gazard*, c. *1900*

Below: Resplendent in his ceremonial uniform, complete with feathered helmet and medal, an officer of the South Australian Artillery.
Unknown, 1901

Opposite page: Girls with American and Australian flags stage a display at the Sydney Cricket Ground for welcoming the Great White Fleet in August 1908. The band of dark figures encloses them like an inexplicable shadow. The scoreboard shows a blank, except for the word 'CANADA' upside down. The arrival of the United States Navy was greeted with immense relief and rejoicing as this Navy was to be Australia's protection and first line of defence. *NSWGP, 1908*

Left: American sailors on shore leave having commandeered a car, just as their colleagues commandeered girls during the Second World War. They were a novelty then and were made unreservedly welcome. *NSWGP, 1908*

Below: Crowds taking the Watson's Bay tram to the mouth of Sydney Harbour to watch the American Fleet sail in. Whatever protest the tramways official at left is making, his chances of having any effect seem minimal. The photograph was taken at King's Cross, an area famous for unruly behaviour. *James Stening, 1908*

307

Above: 1914: a recruitment march through New South Wales, led by a single drummer. Marches like this gathered volunteers as they went. Sometimes the distance covered from their hometown to the State capital was hundreds of kilometres, and at every township they were feted. This picture shows the 'Kangaroos' at Wallendbeen. The *Sydney Mail*, c. *1914*

Opposite page: Reinforcements leaving Sydney for France, and facing the prospect with different feelings to judge from their expressions. Considering that they were going in defence of British capital, it is curious that they should call themselves 'diggers', a popular name for prospectors on their goldfields which came to enjoy Republican overtones during the diggers' rebellion at the Eureka Stockade in 1854. *Unknown*, c. *1915*

Rear-Admiral Sir William Rooke Creswell, credited with being the founder of the Australian Navy. After an undistinguished career in and out of the British Navy he retired and went to South Australia in 1885 to begin another naval career. For the next twenty years he agitated for a navy to be established. In 1904 he was appointed director of the Commonwealth Naval Board. He died in 1933. *Unknown, n.d.*

Opposite page
Above: During the First World War internment camps for alien nationals were set up in all States. These German prisoners, held on Torrens Island, used the time in the cultivation of their bodies. *Dubotzky*, c. *1916*

Below: 19 July 1919. Peace celebrations, Macquarie Street, Sydney—the Navy marches past. This sort of theatre-piece earned tumultuous applause, but what happened to the participants when the curtain went down? The adjustment to being forgotten every day except Anzac Day became a lifelong injury to many returned servicemen. *Unknown, 1919*

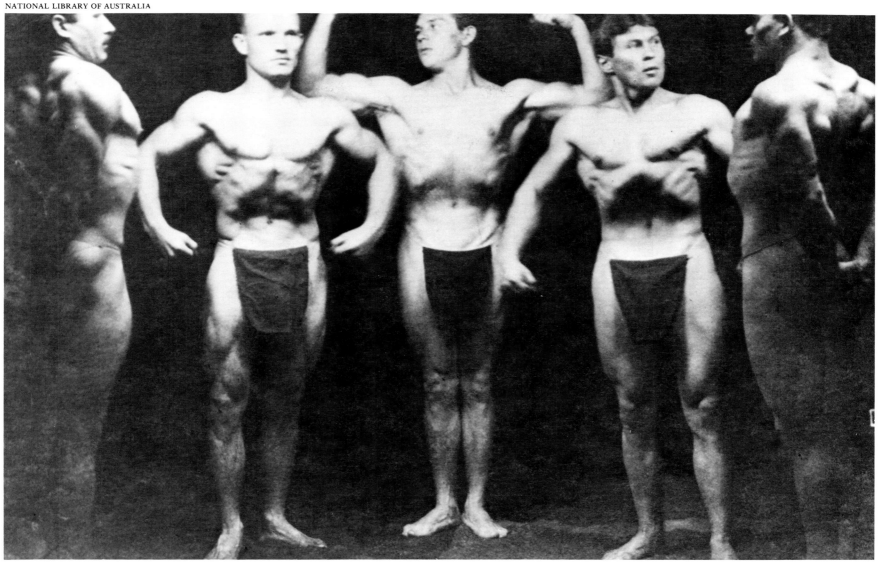

Top: Dubious though their motives had been in urging young men to fight, the genuine relief of the crowds when it was ended was unmistakable. Here the public in Martin Place, Sydney, receives news of the Armistice. Those who did not come back numbered 59,258. For what had they died? Not a single military threat was made against Australian territory in the course of the war. The *Sydney Mail, 1918*

Above: Millinery class for soldiers' widows. The market for frivolities already guessed at, the furious onset of flapperdom and the twenties, these sober women equip themselves with the skill to support and rear their children ready for the next World War. *Unknown, c. 1919*

In ancient Egypt when the Upper and Lower Kingdoms ceased warring some peacable task had to be found to occupy two demobilized armies. They were used as a labour force to build the pyramids. Our own version of the pyramids was every bit as inscrutable and frustrating to those involved. Vocational training was offered as rehabilitation after the Great War. Here an applicant is being interviewed. The beautiful particularity of light catches his ex-serviceman's badge.
Unknown, c. 1919

Opposite page
Above: Recreation at an Air Force Base during the Second World War. The lighter side of 'one in, all in'.
Unknown, c. 1941

Below: A good deal of the training programme was enjoyable to men who already had a taste for outdoor life and sports. This exercise with inflatables on the Yarra River is not as far as it may seem from the balance of life and death at the front line. And Australian training programmes for this war did prove remarkably effective.
E. Cranstone, c. 1940

Left: Department of Air, Directorate of Public Relations, No. 2 Mobile Entertainment Unit, drew large crowds at every performance in the north-west of Western Australia. A member of the unit, Leading Aircraftman Jack Glenn, with his bass, epitomizes the incongruities of war. *Dept of Air, 1945*

Below: Recruiting drives for the 1939–45 war were conducted on very different lines from the white feather campaigns of the previous World War. Here, 'Superman' switches uniform to do his bit for recruitment in Queensland. The *Courier Mail*, c. 1940

Opposite page: Australian Imperial Force [*sic*] recruits are inspected by Lieutenant-General Sir Thomas Blamey, December 1939. A resourceful and gallant officer, Blamey's great achievement was to stop the Japanese land thrust across New Guinea. When he arrived there in 1942 they were still advancing south. He turned them back from the Kokoda Trail and, by the end of the campaign, Buna had been recaptured and the invading forces repulsed. The picture was taken by Damien Parer. An official photographer with the AIF, he accompanied the first contingent to the Middle East. Then in 1942 he joined the troops fighting against the Japanese in New Guinea. Not only did he take superb action pictures, he was also a great movie cameraman. His name became a byword among the profession for boundless courage and dedication. He lived and moved, unarmed, where the risk was greatest among the front-line troops recording life and death. In this way he was killed at the Peleliu landing on 20 September 1944. *Damien Parer, 1939*

Above: The original caption read, 'Nice work: — Instructors are pleased when pupils can hold an accurate formation such as this "echelon right". There is more to it than merely looking pretty in a parade ground way, accurate flying is the foundation from which tactical manoeuvres are developed.' The aircraft are Australian-made Wirraways. In fact only one Wirraway destroyed an enemy aircraft: on 26 December 1942 over Papua a Japanese Zero was shot down by one of these wood and fabric planes. Built by the Commonwealth Aircraft Corporation, based on a couple of American models, its maximum speed was 350 km/hour. Pilots were assured that the Japanese had such narrow eyes they would not be able to see properly to fight. *Unknown, c. 1940*

Left: Not giant lipsticks. These munitions workers are inspecting anti-aircraft shells prior to the charge being fitted. *Douglas Darien-Smith, 1942*

Below: AIF (Australian Imperial Force). Individuality is often sacrificed for a war effort. So these three lads let their hair be used, just for a lark. Deeper meanings are also suggested in their temporarily mutilated appearance: baldness, a renunciation; the cutting off of hair, an ancient symbol. There's more to this than a cheery carelessness with self. Through the joke and the tribute something threatening is suggested as well. The troops are embarking for Malaya, September 1941. *Unknown, 1941*

Bottom: Troops ready to be transferred on board ship arriving in Sydney by a train bearing messages. *Unknown, 1941*

Right: Relatives and friends make a last lingering farewell to the *Strathallan* with their loved ones aboard, as she sails down Port Phillip Bay, Melbourne, suggesting the remoteness of wars and the agony of separation. *Unknown, c. 1939*

AUSTRALIAN WAR MEMORIAL

Right: The bombing of Darwin, 1942. This was the first time since 1788 that the country had faced foreign invaders. The picture shows the frailty and ineffectuality of firefighters behind their asbestos shield hoping to make headway against the inferno of bombed fuel storage tanks. *Unknown, 1942*

Opposite page: US General Douglas MacArthur arrives in Canberra on 17 March 1942 to be met by Prime Minister John Curtin. They are followed by several of the war cabinet and, seen between them, Sir Frederick Shedden, Secretary of the Defence Department. MacArthur, pampered and fashionable, awaits the higher call to lead his own country. Seen as a white knight coming to the aid of a vulnerable virgin land, he immediately set his propaganda machine into operation and conducted the war as a public relations campaign for himself. He was rumoured to have decided on a 'Brisbane Line' allowing everything north of Brisbane to be temporarily surrendered to the Japanese if they invaded successfully. He was much hated for this, especially in Queensland, but no documentary evidence of such a policy has been produced. *Unknown, 1942*

AUSTRALIAN WAR MEMORIAL

320

Right: One of three Japanese two-man miniature submarines which attempted a raid on shipping in Sydney Harbour, 31 May 1942. This daring intrusion struck even more alarm in the community than the Darwin bombings—Darwin, after all, being as far from Sydney as Cairo is from London. Each submarine was some 30 metres long, powered by batteries and manned by a crew of two. They had been developed from a British design during the First World War. This submarine was sunk by depth charges and ramming. One Japanese torpedo, aimed at the US cruiser *Chicago*, sank the requisitioned ferry *Kuttabul*. Of the naval ratings asleep aboard HMAS *Kuttabul*, 19 were killed and 10 injured. Here the wreck of the submarine is being raised from the Harbour floor the following day. *Unknown, 1942*

Below: Air-raid exercise for Adelaide school children, anti-blast training. Unlike previous wars, this one was being waged in the Pacific also, and the possibility of invasion was always there. A portrait of helplessness; children with dummies, identification tags and Red Cross bags. *Krischock, 1942*

Left: The mysteriously inappropriate signs are not the most remarkable oddity of this Western Australian choir singing in 1945. Their thanksgiving was for VE Day (Victory in Europe). The war in the Pacific still raged. It was nearly four months after the defeat of Germany before Japan surrendered on 2 September. *Unknown, 1945*

Below: Field Marshal Montgomery, Chief of the Imperial General Staff, waving to crowds on Hay Street, Perth, July 1947. He was on his way to a reception. Already on the platform and waiting to greet him was Stephen Bevan who, thirty-three years earlier had been a stretcher-bearer in the First World War rescuing a critically injured officer, who turned out to be Montgomery. The war was still a theatre of character performances. *Unknown, 1947*

JOHN FAIRFAX AND SONS LTD

MAX DUPAIN

Left: The 7th Division, AIF, marching in Martin Place, Sydney, 19 April 1944. The roadway, speckled with leaves or petals, has become an ambiguous surface, more like water catching the early morning sun than asphalt. The cenotaph, with rain stains dribbling down the dry stone, could be a floating barge. This was the first time the 7th Division had marched through the city since their return from service in the Middle East and New Guinea. They were led by Brigadier K. W. Eather. On this very day, other Australian troops still at the front were closing in on Bogadjim—northern coast of New Guinea—meeting signs that the Japanese invaders were planning a withdrawal to the west. The other main war item in the papers was news that the large icebergs mysteriously appearing in the North Sea between England and Holland were a new Nazi weapon—the Germans themselves claimed to have developed a chemical to kill everything within a 500-metre radius by instant freezing. Throughout the war there was a recurring image that mere men (such as these) were up against a super-science machine.
The *Argus*, 1944

Top: Victory over Japan, 'VJ Day', Sydney, 15 August 1945. Part of the power of this photograph is that the woman dancing with the American sailor looks so very nearly Japanese.
Unknown, 1945

Above: Meat queue, 1946. Women at the butcher's shop queue for rationed meat, parading their dour wartime clothes, showing in their faces what it is to bear the responsibility of bringing up healthy children on rations. The shock waves of the war continued to be felt for some years after it was over.
Max Dupain, 1946

Cadet midshipmen in training for the Australian Navy, 4 February 1950. They look to the future, their caps making plain they bear an awesome responsibility they can't possibly understand. There is something touchingly quixotic about them, as there was about the men who went off to fight the First World War on horseback. In the British tradition the Navy is still regarded as the senior service yet, apart from its submarines, it faces obsolescence in warfare. In one important respect the armed forces have a history which recalls the early explorers who sailed from Europe to meet a challenge on the wrong side of the world. Nearly every arena where Australians served has been in the northern hemisphere; the country's youth travelling huge distances to strange and remote places to do battle for the interests and ideals of Britain and, later, America. However, one day, cadets like these will find they are the country's first line of defence and the responsibility for planning and helping keep the future secure will be theirs.
The *Argus, 1950*

Archive Credits

The following individuals and organizations provided photographs and gave their permission for their reproduction in this book:

Front cover: John Oxley Library, Brisbane, 22133;
Front endpaper: Kodak (Australasia) Pty Ltd;
Page 1: La Trobe Collection, State Library of Victoria, Blackburn Papers, manuscript collection;
Page 2: Mitchell Library, MIN 205;
Pages 8–9: Kodak (Australasia) Pty Ltd;
Page 10: Mitchell Library, ONCY 25, Box 55 (iii);
Page 11: Library Board of Western Australia, Battye Library Pictorial Collection, 392OB/96:
Pages 12–13: Mitchell Library, small picture file;
Page 14: National Library of Australia, Rex Nan Kivell Collection, NK 2039;
Page 15: Tasmanian Museum and Art Gallery, HCC No. 1840 16 Q 6185;
Page 16: Mitchell Library, small picture file;
Page 17: La Trobe Collection, State Library of Victoria, H 34899;
Pages 18–19: National Library of Australia, Album 116 NL 10383;
Page 20: Mitchell Library, Neg. 18443, Box 5;
Page 21: Mitchell Library, small picture file;
Page 22: South Australian Archives, B12210;
Page 23: Archives Office of Tasmania, NS 80/12;
Pages 24–5: Mitchell Library, small picture file;
Page 26: Mitchell Library/Macarthur Stanham, Macarthur Album 4358-1;
Page 27: *al* Mitchell Library/Macarthur Stanham, PXA 4358-1; *ar* National Library of Australia, Album 131; *b* National Library of Australia, Album 116;
Page 28: La Trobe Collection, State Library of Victoria, Fauchery/Daintree Album, p. 1;
Pages 28–9: National Library of Australia, Album 219;
Page 30: Library Board of Western Australia, Battye Library Pictorial Collection, 884 B;
Page 31: *a* Library Board of Western Australia, Battye Library Pictorial Collection, 6923B/91; *b* West Australian Newspapers Ltd, Hist. 811;
Page 32: South Australian Archives, B17890;
Page 33: *a* South Australian Archives, B1512; *b* Mitchell Library, small picture file;
Page 34: Mitchell Library, MIN 50;
Page 35: *a* Mitchell Library, ML P1/B Dixson Library ZDL PXX 3; *b* La Trobe Collection, State Library of Victoria, H872 MC 5/3/2;
Page 36: Mitchell Library/Macarthur Stanham, PXA 4358-1;
Page 37: *a* South Australian Archives, B12; *b* NSW Government Printing Office *1101;
Pages 38–9: NSW Government Printing Office, *1098;
Page 40: *a* Mitchell Library, small picture file; *b* National Library of Australia, Album 120;
Page 41: Mitchell Library, small picture file;
Pages 42–3: Mitchell Library, small picture file/Taree Photographics;
Page 44: Herbert Chargois;
Page 45: National Library of Australia, Album 283;
Page 46: Mitchell Library/Macarthur Stanham, PXA 4358-1;
Page 47: Dame Mary Durack Miller, 1903–9;
Page 48: Mitchell Library, small picture file;
Page 49: *a* Archives Office of Tasmania, St David's Cathedral Album NS 407/54; *b* Reproduced from a copy held by the Australian Institute of Aboriginal Studies, Canberra/Australian Consolidated Press, AIAS No. 75–458, King No. 1313;
Page 50: *a* Paul Popper Ltd, London, 40955/15; *b* South Australian Archives, B470;
Page 51: *a* National Library of Australia, Album 426; *b* Mitchell Library, small picture file;
Page 52: National Library of Australia, Album 229;
Page 53: National Library of Australia, Album 229;
Page 54: *al* Archives Office of Tasmania, 30/4595; *ar* Queen Victoria Museum and Art Gallery, Melbourne, 1958-78-16 QVM File 441; *bl* National Library of Australia, Album 226;

Page 55: *1* Mitchell Library, small picture file; *b* Archives Office of Tasmania, 30/4112;

Pages 56-7: Archive Office of NSW, 729;

Page 57: National Library of Australia, Album 229;

Page 58: *r* La Trobe Collection, State Library of Victoria, Copyright Collection, envelope 5, No. 43; *bl* La Trobe Collection, State Library of Victoria, Copyright Collection, envelope 5, No. 5; *br* La Trobe Collection, State Library of Victoria, Copyright Collection, envelope 5, No. 22;

Page 59: Both photographs La Trobe Collection, State Library of Victoria, *a* Copyright Collection, envelope 5, No. 28, *b* H13586;

Pages 60-1: Foreign and Commonwealth Office, London, Vol. 15;

Page 62: Reproduced from a copy held by the Australian Institute of Aboriginal Studies, Canberra/National Trust, Alice Springs, N 1778-27a;

Page 63: Mitchell Library, small picture file;

Pages 64-5: Mitchell Library, small picture file;

Page 66: All photographs reproduced from copies held by the Australian Institute of Aboriginal Studies, Canberra/Australian Consolidated Press, *ar* AIAS 1733-35, Kerry No. 1400; *bl* AIAS No. 1995-20, Kerry No. 611; *br* AIAS No. 75-48, Kerry No. 1364;

Page 67: *a* Australian Museum, Neg. No. 7810; *b* Mitchell Library, small picture file;

Page 68: *a* South Australian Archives, B1672; *b* La Trobe Collection, State Library of Victoria, Copyright Collection, envelope 22, No. 51;

Page 69: National Library of Australia, Album 262;

Page 70: Kodak (Australasia) Pty Ltd;

Page 71: Australian Consolidated Press, Kerry No. 2503;

Page 72: *a* La Trobe Collection, State Library of Victoria, H27251, Bay 2, Rose Postcard Collection; *b* Australian Consolidated Press, Kerry No. 3227;

Page 73: *a* NSW Government Printing Office, *3653; *b* Royal Geographical Society, London (Maproom);

Page 74: *a* National Library of Australia, Album 232; *b* National Library of Australia, Album 212;

Page 75: Mitchell Library, small picture file;

Page 76: State Library of Tasmania, CG65;

Page 77: *a* South Australian Archives, B24184; *b* Archive Office of NSW, 1071;

Page 78: *a* Mitchell Library, small picture file; *b* NSW Government Printing Office, S.H.408;

Page 79: Mitchell Library, small picture file;

Pages 80-1: Mansall Collection Ltd, London, 2418;

Pages 82-3: John Oxley Library, Brisbane, 22133;

Page 84: Mansall Collection Ltd, London, 2424;

Page 85: Mitchell Library, small picture file;

Pages 86-7: South Australian Archives, B417;

Page 88: *a* John Oxley Library, Brisbane, 13127; *b* La Trobe Collection, State Library of Victoria, H 15058;

Page 89: Both photographs National Library of Australia, *a* Album 420; *b* Album 219;

Page 90: *a* National Library of Australia, NL 23247; *b* Mitchell Library, Holtermann 12 × 10 series;

Page 91: Mitchell Library, small picture file;

Page 92: *a* La Trobe Collection, State Library of Victoria, H 29955, Bay 5/19/11, envelope 3; *b* Library Board of Western Australia, Battye Library Pictorial Collection 5323B/1069;

Page 93: *a* Kodak (Australasia) Pty Ltd; *b* NSW Government Printing Office, *1136;

Page 94: *a* South Australian Archives, B22742; *b* La Trobe Collection, State Library of Victoria H27471 MC 4/10 in Illustrations of Victorian History Vol. 20, No. 1, LTA 194 f.2;

Page 95: Mitchell Library, small picture file;

Page 96: Library Board of Western Australia, Battye Library Pictorial Collection, 72B/126;

Page 97: *a* National Library of Australia, Album 280B; *b* Library Board of Western Australia, Battye Library Pictorial Collection, 5323B/1815;

Page 98: *a* John Cato Collection; *b* Archives Office of Tasmania 33/14;

Page 99: Kodak (Australasia) Pty Ltd;

Pages 100-1: Australian Consolidated Press, Kerry No. 930;

Page 102: *a* National Library of Australia, William Henry Corkhill Tilba Tilba Collection; *b* NSW Government Printing Office, *1122;

Page 103: National Library of Australia, William Henry Corkhill Tilba Tilba Collection;

Page 104: *a* South Australian Archives, B7794/17; *b* John Oxley Library, Brisbane, 23249;

Page 105: *a* Herald and Weekly Times Ltd, Bushfires, Victoria envelope; *b* Mitchell Library, small picture file;

Pages 106-7: John Oxley Library, Brisbane, 22173;

Pages 108-9: *a* Mitchell Library, small picture file; *b* Foreign and Commonwealth Office, London, Vol. 18/B2;

Page 110: Both photographs South Australian Archives, *a* B27196; *b* B7639;

Page 111: *a* National Library of Australia, Album 219; *b* Mitchell Library, small picture file;

Pages 112-13: Department of Mapping and Surveying, Brisbane, PR/044558. Photograph supplied by the Surveyor-General, Queensland, and reproduced by arrangement with the Queensland Government. Crown copyright reserved.

Page 114: Dame Mary Durack Miller;

Page 115: The Mercury Newspaper Library, 994.6, Sharland, Box 16;

Page 116: *a* Archives Office of Tasmania, 30/4449; *b* La Trobe Collection, State Library of Victoria, Copyright Collection, envelope 28, No. 51;

Page 117: *a* South Australian Archives, B6282; *b* South Australian Archives, B11187;

Page 118: Both photographs La Trobe Collection, State Library of Victoria, *r* Copyright Collection, envelope 23, No. 52; *b* H29545;

Page 119: *a* John Oxley Library, Brisbane, 20215; *b* Queen Victoria Museum and Art Gallery, Melbourne;

Page 120: South Australian Archives, B25174;

Page 121: *a* Archive Office of NSW, 753; *b* South Australian Archives, B7608;

Pages 122-3: Both photographs La Trobe Collection, State Library of Victoria, *b* Copyright Collection, envelope 7 in Illustrations of Victorian History; *r* LTA 144 H 35678, Album p. 24;

Page 124: *a* National Library of Australia; *b* Northern Regional Library, State Library of Tasmania, Historical Society Room (Chinese);

Page 125: La Trobe Collection, State Library of Victoria, H32730;

Pages 126-7: Royal Geographical Society, London, G/013502;

Page 128: John Oxley Library, Brisbane, 20265;

Page 129: Both photographs Archives Office of Tasmania, *a* 30/5154; *b* 30/5155;

Page 130: *a* West Australian Newspapers Ltd, Hist. 1496; *b* NSW Government Printing Office, *3485;

Page 131: *a* National Library of Australia; *b* Cyril Hume Collection;

Page 132: Archives Office of Tasmania, NS 786/102;

Page 133: NSW Government Printing Office, *5270;

Page 134: *a* Mrs Gordon Pullar; *b* Tasmanian Museum and Art Gallery, C301 Smith;

Page 135: South Australian Archives/J. T. Cowin, B6799;

Page 136: Mitchell Library, small picture file (portraits);

Page 137: *a* John Oxley Library, Brisbane, 6641; *b* Library Board of Western Australia, Battye Library Pictorial Collection, 25166 P;

Page 138: Mitchell Library, small picture file;

Page 139: Australian Archives CRS A3560, Item 631;

Pages 140-1: Australian Consolidated Press;

Page 142: Archives Office of Tasmania, 30/4615;

Page 143: *a* Mrs Gordon Pullar; *b* South Australian Archives, B8168;

Page 144: La Trobe Collection, State Library of Victoria, Copyright Collection, envelope 28, No. 5;

Page 145: South Australian Archives, B1032A;

Pages 146-7: The Mitchell Library, small picture file;

Page 148: *l* NSW Government Printing Office, S.H. 1346; *r* James Flood Charity Trust, 4514Q;

Page 149: Post and Telecom Museum, 776-F;

Pages 150-1: Mitchell Library, small picture file;

Page 152: John Cato Collection;

Page 153: NSW Government Printing Office, S.H. 400;

Page 154: *a* Archive Office of NSW, 1194; *b* Mitchell Library, small picture file;

Page 155: South Australian Archives, B7964;

Page 156: *a* Western Morning News Ltd, Plymouth, 244/A; *b* Cyril Hume Collection;

Page 157: Cyril Hume Collection;

Page 158: *a* Mitchell Library, small picture file; *b* La Trobe Collection, State Library of Victoria, LTA ef 17f8;

Page 159: *a* NSW Government Printing Office, *1165; *b* South Australian Archives, B16681:16;
Page 160: *a* National Library of Australia, 27479; *b* South Australian Archives, B7055;
Page 161: *a* South Australian Archives, B26156; *b* Dr Peter J. Phillips, 17;
Page 162: State Rail Authority of NSW, 93/2;
Page 163: *a* State Library of Tasmania, CG470/1877; *b* La Trobe Collection, State Library of Victoria, H 1077 Madden Album, Vol. 1, p. 228;
Page 164: *a* Library Board of Western Australia, Battye Library Pictorial Collection, 24711P; *b* Archives Office of Tasmania, NS 786/113;
Page 165: *a* South Australian Archives, B22763; *b* John Oxley Library, Brisbane, 23197;
Page 166: *a* NSW Government Printing Office, 3953; *b* John Oxley Library, Brisbane, 23195;
Page 167: *a* Stuart Gore, 7; *b* West Australian Newspapers Ltd, Hist, 2000;
Pages 168–9: John Oxley Library, Brisbane, 2680;
Page 170: Both photographs National Library of Australia;
Page 171: *a* Cazneaux family/National Gallery of Australia; *b* West Australian Newspapers Ltd, Hist. 6343;
Page 172: *a* Qantas Airways Ltd; *b* National Library of Australia;
Page 173: Herald and Weekly Times, Herald 'personal';
Page 174: David Moore Collection, X 18–35;
Page 175: David Moore Collection, X 14–1;
Pages 176–7: Archives Office of Tasmania, 30/4442;
Page 178: South Australian Archives, B26038;
Page 179: The Mercury Newspaper Library, 994.6;
Pages 180–1: Archives Office of Tasmania, NS 241/21;
Page 182: NSW Government Printing Office, *482;
Page 183: *a* La Trobe Collection, State Library of Victoria, Copyright Collection, envelope 25, No. 22; *b* Archives Office of Tasmania 30/744;
Page 184: Both photographs State Rail Authority of NSW, *a* 669/2; *b* 549/20;
Page 185: Australian Consolidated Press, Kerry No. 330;
Pages 186–7: All photographs South Australian Archives, *a* B23893; *b* B19609; *r* B12590;
Page 188: Library Board of Western Australia, Battye Library Pictorial Collection, 2240B/51;
Page 189: *a* Library Board of Western Australia, Battye Library Pictorial Collection, 2240B/54; *b* NSW Government Printing Office, *462;
Page 190: Both photographs NSW Government Printing Office, *a* 665; *b* 664;
Page 191: Tasmanian Museum and Art Gallery, C300 Hob-Legrands;
Page 192: Mansall Collection Ltd, London, 2512;
Page 193: *a* Library Board of Western Australia, Battye Library Pictorial Collection, 816B/1527A, Series A; *b* NSW Government Printing Office, *2354;
Page 194: Australian Consolidated Press, Kerry No. 2027;
Pages 194–5: NSW Government Printing Office, *1323;
Pages 196–7: Australian Consolidated Press, Kerry No. 226;
Page 198: *a* Mansall Collection Ltd, London, 2513; *b* Foreign and Commonwealth Office, London, 74;
Page 199: *a* Royal Commonwealth Society, London, Y 3086/M; *b* Mansall Collection Ltd, London, 2520;
Pages 200–1: Mitchell Library, small picture file;
Page 202: *a* John Oxley Library, Brisbane, 22153; *b* Mitchell Library, small picture file;
Page 203: *a* Dame Mary Durack Miller; *b* Mitchell Library, small picture file;
Page 204: *a* Queen Victoria Museum and Art Gallery, Melbourne, S 208; *b* National Library of Australia, Album 570;
Page 205: National Library of Australia, Album 564;
Page 206: *a* South Australian Archives, B12316; *b* NSW Government Printer, 8096;
Page 207: National Library of Australia, Cazneaux Drawers;
Pages 208–9: National Library of Australia, Film Archive No. 2;
Page 209: National Library of Australia, Film Archive No. 3;
Pages 210–11: National Library of Australia, Film Archive No. 6;
Page 212: National Library of Australia, Album 288;
Page 213: South Australian Archives, B9850;
Page 214: *a* W.L. Crowther Library/State Library of Tasmania, Abbot Album 158; *b* Mitchell Library;

Page 215: *a* South Australian Archives, B7437; *b* Archives Office of Tasmania, 30/2078;
Pages 216–17: NSW Government Printer, *1657;
Page 218: Both photographs Queen Victoria Museum and Art Gallery, Melbourne, *a* S 361; *b* QVM AS S 362;
Page 219: Both photographs Mitchell Library, small picture file;
Page 220: *a* National Library of Australia, Album 224; *b* Mitchell Library, small picture file;
Page 221: Gordon Andrews Collection;
Page 222: NSW Government Printing Office, *4487;
Page 223: *a* West Australian Newspapers Ltd, Hist. 4819; *b* Library Board of Western Australia, Battye Library Pictorial Collection, 4393P;
Page 224: Both photographs Mitchell Library, small picture file;
Page 225: Both photographs Mitchell Library, small picture file (portraits);
Page 226: *a* Northern Regional Library, State Library of Tasmania; *b* La Trobe Collection, State Library of Victoria, LTA 144 'Lorne Album', p. 54;
Page 227: Fryer Library, University of Queensland, J.O.L. Neg. No. 22146;
Page 228: National Library of Australia, William Henry Corkhill Tilba Tilba Collection;
Pages 228–9: Archives Office of Tasmania, NS 655/3;
Pages 230–1: Both photographs La Trobe Collection, State Library of Victoria, *a* LTA f 5, p. 85c; *b* LTA f 5, p. 88c;
Page 232: Gordon Andrews Collection;
Pages 232–3: Gordon Andrews Collection;
Page 234: Max Dupain Collection;
Pages 234–5: National Library of Australia, Album 106;
Pages 236–7: La Trobe Collection, State Library of Victoria, Fauchery/Daintree Album, p. 14;
Page 238: South Australian Archives, B4398;
Page 239: *a* Tasmanian Museum and Art Gallery, Q2954; *b* Herald and Weekly Times Ltd, Herald: Police, Vic., historical.
Pages 240–1: Australian Consolidated Press, Kerry No. 3210;
Page 242: Foreign and Commonwealth Office, London;
Page 243: Both photographs Mitchell Library, small picture file;
Page 244: *a* Foreign and Commonwealth Office, London, Vol. 12, No. 142; *b* South Australian Archives, B8807;
Page 245: *a* Mitchell Library, small picture file; *b* NSW Government Printing Office, S.H. 550;
Page 246: Both photographs Archive Office of NSW *a* 1564; *b* 422;
Page 247: *a* Archive Office of NSW, 1525; *b* South Australian Archives, B3093;
Pages 248–9: South Australian Archives, B16681:16;
Page 250: *a* La Trobe Collection, State Library of Victoria, LTA 144 'Lorne Album', p. 52 or p. 53; *b* Mitchell Library, small picture file;
Page 251: Australian Consolidated Press, Kerry No. 2918;
Pages 252–3: John Oxley Library, Brisbane, 22188;
Pages 254–5: Australian Consolidated Press, Kerry No. 329;
Page 256: Both photographs Archive Office of NSW *a* 1664, *b* 3259;
Page 257: *a* Archive Office of NSW; *b* David Moore Collection, X27–4;
Page 258: *a* Library Board of Western Australia, Battye Library Pictorial Collection, S816B/104; *b* Mitchell Library, small picture file;
Page 259: NSW Government Printing Office, *349;
Pages 260–1: State Rail Authority of NSW, 817/17;
Page 262: *a* Mitchell Library, small picture file; *b* Australian Centre for Photography;
Page 263: Gordon Andrews Collection;
Pages 264–5: National Library of Australia, Album 125;
Pages 266–7: Mitchell Library, Tom Roberts Papers;
Page 268: NSW Government Printing Office, *4999;
Page 269: NSW Government Printing Office, *5705;
Page 270: *b* National Library of Australia, Album 440A;
Pages 270–1: *a* National Library of Australia, Album 440A;
Page 271: *b* National Library of Australia, Album 439;
Page 272: La Trobe Collection, State Library of Victoria, H 4305;
Pages 272–3: National Library of Australia, Album 324;
Page 274: *a* National Library of Australia, Album 322, *b* Foreign and Commonwealth Office, London, Vol. 42, Pt.2;
Page 275: Mary Andrews Collection;
Pages 276–7: NSW Government Printing Office, S.H. 1365;

Bibliography

Page 277: Archive Office of NSW, 998;

Page 278: *a* West Australian Newspapers Ltd, Hist. 1220; Library Board of Western Australia, Battye Library Pictorial Collection, 3881B/184;

Page 279: *a* Mitchell Library, small picture file (portraits); *b* Jean McKinley Collection;

Page 280: National Library of Australia, Album 301;

Page 281: *a* National Library of Australia, Album 301; *b* NSW Government Printing Office, *5029;

Pages 282–3: NSW Government Printing Office, *1122;

Pages 284–5: Mitchell Library, small picture file (portraits);

Page 286: *a* Gordon Andrews Collection; *b* West Australian Newspapers Ltd, Hist. 5870;

Page 287: Both photographs West Australian Newspapers Ltd, *a* Hist 5867; *b* Hist. 5866;

Pages 288–9: The Mercury Newspaper Library, 994.6, Sharland, Box 16;

Page 290: The Mercury Newspaper Library, 994.6, Hobart Hist;

Page 291: Both photographs the Mercury Newspaper Library, *a* 994.6, Sharland, Box 16; *b* 994.6, Hobart Hist;

Pages 292–3: West Australian Newspapers Ltd, Hist. 5753;

Page 293: Australian War Memorial, Neg. No. 7036, by permission of the Trustees of the Imperial War Museum;

Pages 294–5: Australian War Memorial, Neg. No. 44609/ John Fairfax and Sons Ltd;

Page 296: NSW Government Printing Office, 5878;

Page 297: Argus Collection, State Library of Victoria, Box 17B, envelope 23,/ John Fairfax and Sons Ltd;

Page 298: *a* NSW Government Printing Office, S.H.1; *b* Mitchell Library, small picture file;

Page 299: Mitchell Library, small picture file;

Pages 300–1: NSW Government Printing Office, S.H. 496;

Page 302: *a* South Australian Archives, B5592; *b* Mitchell Library, small picture file;

Page 303: *a* South Australian Archives, B26151; *b* Archives Office of Tasmania, NS 786/40;

Pages 304–5: South Australian Archives, B8828;

Page 305: Australian War Memorial, Neg. No. A3852;

Page 306: NSW Government Printing Office, AM 27;

Page 307: *a* NSW Government Printing Office, AM 221; *b* State Rail Authority of NSW, 1053/5;

Page 308: Australian War Memorial, Neg. No. H11586;

Page 309: Mitchell Library, small picture file;

Page 310: South Australian Archives, B11220;

Page 311: *a* National Library of Australia, Album 648, No. 13; *b* Mitchell Library, small picture file;

Page 312: *a* Australian War Memorial, Neg. No. H11563; *b* National Library of Australia, Album 602;

Page 313: National Library of Australia, Album 602;

Page 314: *a* National Library of Australia, Album 613; *b* Australian War Memorial, D.O.I. Neg. No. 10255;

Page 315: *a* Argus Collection, State Library of Victoria, Box 17H, envelope 6; *b* Australian War Memorial Neg. No. 180541/the *Courier Mail*;

Page 316: Australian War Memorial, D.O.I. Neg. No. 332;

Page 317: *a* Australian War Memorial, D.O.I. Neg. No. 14344; *b* South Australian Archives, B7798;

Page 318: Both photographs Australian War Memorial, *a* D.O.I. Neg. No. 9809; *b* D.O.I. Neg. No. 9649;

Pages 318–19: Australian War Memorial, Neg. No. 30411;

Page 320: Australian War Memorial, Neg. No. 157291;

Page 321: Australian War Memorial, D.O.I. Neg. No. 72967;

Page 322: *a* Australian War Memorial, Neg. No. 60696; *b* South Australian Archives, B21652;

Page 323: Both photographs West Australian Newspapers Ltd, *a* W 2462; *b* Hist. 5757;

Pages 324–5: Argus Collection, State Library of Victoria, Box 7c;

Page 325: *a* John Fairfax and Sons Ltd; *b* Max Dupain Collection;

Page 327: Argus Collection, State Library of Victoria, Box 39;

Back endpaper: NSW Government Printing Office, *3340;

Back cover: National Library of Australia, William Henry Corkhill Tilba Tilba Collection.

BURKE, KEAST, *Gold and Silver*, Heinemann, Melbourne, 1973.

CLARK, C. M. H., *A History of Australia*, Vol. 1, Vol. 2., Melbourne University Press, Melbourne, 1962.

_____ *Select Documents in Australian History*, Angus & Robertson, Sydney, 1969.

_____ *Sources of Australian History*, Oxford University Press, London, 1957.

DALLAS, K. M., *Trading Posts or Penal Colonies*, Fullers Bookshop, Hobart, 1969.

ELLIS, VIVIENNE RAE, *Tracanini, Queen or Traitor?* O. B. M. Publishing Co., Hobart, 1976.

GILCHRIST, J. T. and MURRAY, W. J., *Eye-witness; selected documents from Australia's past*, Rigby, Adelaide, 1968.

GORDON, HARRY, *An Eyewitness History of Australia*, Rigby, Adelaide, 1976.

GRZIMEK, BERNHARD, translated by J. Maxwell Brownjohn, *Four-legged Australians*, Hill & Wang, New York, 1967.

JOHNSTON, GEORGE, private war diary, National Library of Australia, to be published by William Collins, 1984.

MACARTHUR-ONSLOW, SIBELLA, *Some Early Records of the Macarthurs of Camden*, Angus & Robertson, Sydney, 1914.

MANIFOLD, J.S., *Who Wrote the Ballards?*, The Australasian Book Society, Sydney, 1964.

MULVANEY, D. J., *Cricket Walkabout*, Melbourne University Press, Melbourne, 1967.

REYNOLDS, HENRY, *The Other Side of the Frontier*, James Cook University, Townsville, 1981.

WRIGHT, JUDITH, *The Cry for the Dead*, Oxford University Press, Melbourne, 1982.

Many other periodicals and unpublished sources were consulted in the National Library of Australia, including the Gazetteers of the separate colonies, also the files of newspapers, particularly the *Argus* (Melbourne) and the *Atlas* (Sydney). I must thank the staff of the National Library for their helpfulness over a period of several years, especially Catherine Santamaria.

A further unpublished source was a lecture given at the Humanities Research Centre of the Australian National University on 6 May 1981 by Dr Helen Watts, Map Librarian of the British Library.

Index

Aborigines 214
  Barron River 66
  children 49, 51
  Clermont district, Qld 134
  conflict with 43-59
  Daisy Bates 135
  disease 44
  first contact 13-16
  in chains 47
  Lake Tyers Reserve 152-3
  Myall Creek massacre 44
  names 63
  Prince of Wales Island 67
  reserves 44
  Tasmanian 16, 44, 49, 134
  three generations 64-5
  woman of the Workia tribe 66
Achurch, Janet 213, 225
Adelaide
  air-raid exercise for school children
    322
  King William Street 248
Adelaide Advertiser 117
Advertising 178, 239
  biscuits 179
Aircraft 170-3
  Second World War 317
Airlines, QANTAS 172
Air races 149
Alice Springs 22
Alpha Cottage 31
Alps 72-3
Ambulance, horse-drawn 154
America, relations with 296
American fleet 307
Andrews, Daisy Ethel 221
Andrews, Gordon 232-4, 263
Andrews, Ken 232-3, 263
Animals 62, 95
Antarctica 213
ANZACS 296
Armistice 312
Arts 226-7
Ashton, Julian 59
Australian Imperial Force 316, 318

Bagot, Captain Charles Harvey 32
Bairnsdale, Vic., kiln for drying hops 92
Ballarat 19
Banks 21, 85, 90, 238
  Oriental Banking Corporation 236-7
Banks, Joseph 15, 16
Baobab tree 69
Barambah Aboriginal Settlement,
  Murgon, Qld 50
Barkly, Sir Henry 28
Barnet, William 120
Barney, George 300-1
Barron River 66
Barry, Sir Redmond 17
Basalt 62
Bass Strait 177
Bates, Constable 178
Bates, Daisy 135
Bathurst 148
Bayliss, Charles 10
Beauchamp, Lord 267
Beer 20

Belltrees Station, Scone, NSW 197
Bendigo 19
Bermagui, NSW 102
Bethesda Mission Station 51
Bevan, Stephen 323
Beyers, Louis 90
Black Boy Camp, WA 286
Blackett, Edmund 246
Blackheath 78
Blacksmiths 177
Blamey, Sir Thomas 316
Blaxland, Gregory 20
Blue Mountains 60-1, 78
  crossing 62
  road over 153
Boer War 295, 303-4
Bonython, Sir John Langdon 117
Bookbinding 190
Books 190-1, 213
Botany Bay 150
Boxer Revolution, China 295
Boyd, James 54
Boyd Town 114
Braddon, Sir Edward Nicholas Coventry
  275
Bradfield, John Job Crew 260-1, 262
Brassey, Lord 126
Bridges 16, 110, 160
  Hawkesbury River Bridge 184
  Mitcham 147
  Pyrmont Bridge 254-5
  Sydney Harbour Bridge 262-5
British Imperial Forces 295
Broken Hill Proprietory Limited 189
  blast furnace 207
Broken Hill silver mine 179
Broome, WA 178, 203
  Eastern Extension Cable Company
    137
Budgerigars 61
Buffalo Gorge, Vic. 76
Buffalo Ranges, Vic. 76
Buildings 16
  Congregational Church, Bourke
    Street, Sydney 244
  Customs House, Brisbane 252-3
  Exhibition Building, Adelaide 304-5
  Exhibition Building, Melbourne 250
  Government House, Brisbane 113
  Largs Pier Hotel, SA 244
  No. 3 Fire Station, Sydney 259
  Oriental Banking Corporation 236-7
  Parliament House, Sydney 245
  Queen's Hall, State Library of
    Victoria 17
  Royal Prince Alfred Hospital,
    Sydney 247
  Sydney Town Hall 245
  Sydney University 246
  Victoria Barracks, Sydney 300
  Victoria Markets, Sydney 250-1
Bullock teams 148, 193, 197
Bundaberg, Qld 202
Bunyip aristocracy 113
Burke, Robert O'Hara 36
Burke and Wills expedition 16, 21,
  34-5, 35
Burrawong, NSW, shearing shed 194

Burrinjuck Dam 204-5
Bush 61
Bushfires 84
    Crafers, SA 104
    Gippsland 105
Bushrangers 21, 45, 58-9, 83
    republics 267
Business 21
Byrne, Joe 59

Cadet midshipmen 326-7
Camden Park 20, 27
Camels 45, 80, 84, 88, 89
Campaspe River 147
Campbell's warehouse 27
Canberra 268, 281
    site for 282-3
Cars 148, 166-9, 232-4
    car rallies 149
    Ipswich, Qld 169
    reliability trial 148
Cash, Martin 51
Catholic Archbishop of Hobart 119
Cattle 136, 147
Cazneaux, Harold 11, 207
Centennial Park, Sydney 274
    volunteers' encampment 298
Central Tilba, NSW 103
Charleville, Qld 137
Charlewood, Fred 228
Child labour 187
Chillagoe, Qld 88
Chinese 115
    funeral at Cooktown, Qld 126
    Royal visits 124-7
Churches 114
Circular Quay 40-1
Cities, growth of 237-65
Clark, Bessy 48
Climate 16
Coaches 85, 148, 152-3
Coal 62
Coal Mine Bend 162
Coalminers 93, 182
Cobb & Co. 148
    first mail motor car 167
Cobham near Gilderoy, Vic. 99
Colebrook, Tas., harvest time 198
Condon, WA 97
Congregational Church, Bourke Street,
    Sydney 244
Conscription 279
Constitution 20
Convicts 17, 21, 45
    convict labour 43
    end of transportation 20, 27
    Port Arthur 54-5
Cook, Captain James 14-15
Cooma bus 166
Cooper's Creek 16
    memorial 35
Coral Sea, Battle of the 297
Crafers, SA 104
Cremorne Point, NSW 182
Creswell, Sir William Rooke 310
Cricket 213, 214-5, 247
Crowther, Dr W.L. 16
Cullen, Sir William 262

Cumjam 44
Curtin, John 321
Customs House, Brisbane 252-3
Cycles 154, 155, 218

Dams 204
    Burrinjuck Dam 204-5
Darmody, Miss Bridget 88
Darvall, Sir John 21, 40
Darwin 297
    bombing of 318-9
Dawe's Point 27
Defence 21
Defries, Colin 149
Denman, Lord and Lady 268, 281
Depression 269, 286-91
Deserts 61
Dinosaur, relics of 68
Dr Barnardo's Homes 131
Donahue, Bold Jack 83
Donaldson, S.A. 20
Donaldson, Stuart 40
Dorrigo, NSW, sawmill 193
Drovers 137, 147
Duck Reach power station 204
Duigan, J.R. 170
Duke and Duchess of York and
    Cornwall 124
Durack family 114
Dust storm 111
Dutch explorers 14

Eather, Brigadier K.W. 325
Ebenezer Coal Mine 178
Ebor Falls, New England Tableland 70
Echuca, NSW 147, 160, 161
Education, free 114
Edward, Prince 122
Elections 268-9
Electricity 149
Entertainment 178 see also Arts; Films;
    Music; Social life
    films 209
    Second World War 315
    Snow White and the Seven Dwarfs
    115
Erskine, Commodore 270-1, 271
Eureka Stockade 267 242-3
Exhibition Building, Adelaide 304-5
Exhibition Building, Melbourne 250
Exhibitions
    agricultural 238
    International 242-3
Explorers 16, 21, 61

Farming 14
    experimental 177
Faulconbridge, Blue Mountains 277
Fawkner, John Pascoe 272
Federation 268, 272-5, 293
    search for a federal capital 280
    voting results, WA 278
Ferguson, Charles 102
Films 178, 208-9
    Painted Daughters 210-11
Fire engines, horse-drawn 259
Fires 258-9
Fisher, Andrew 281

Fishing 222
Flinders Island 44
Flogging 45
Floods 84, 105, 219
    Queensland, 1893 104
Football 215
Forests 62, 177
    clearing 98-100
    karri 193
    timber cutting 192
Forster, William 267
Foxes 215
Fox hunting 215
Freeman, Sir Ralph 262
Funerals 126-7

Gaols 21, 50-1
    Port Arthur 55
    Success 52-3
Garden Palace, Sydney 242-3
Gardens 109
George, Prince (George V) 122, 272
Gilbert, John 21
Gipps, Governor George 267
Gippsland, Vic., Croajingolong district
    94
Gippsland bushfires 105
Glassford, George 55
Glenelg train in King William Street,
    Adelaide 159
Glenn, Jack 315
Glenrowan 45, 58
Gold 17, 62, 85, 90, 115, 188-9
    prospecting 8-9, 188
Goldfields 20, 21, 124, 178
    disembarking at Port Melbourne
    28-9
    Hill End, NSW 33, 90
    Mt Ragged rush 96
    New England 185
    Victorian 238
    Western Australia 92
Goldfields Express, Kalgoorlie, WA 11
Goldstein, Miss Vida 1
Government 267-93
    first Australian Parliament 266-7,
    272
    local 238-9
    representative 17, 20
    self 20
Government House, Brisbane 113
Government House, Melbourne 230
Govett's Creek 60-1
Granite 62
Graves, John Woodcock 17, 49
Great Barrier Reef 62
Great Britain 214
Great War 295, 308-13
Griffin, Walter Burley 268
Grose River, NSW 60-1
Guillaux, Maurice 171
Gulf Country 44
Gulgong, NSW 20

Hackney tram, Adelaide, SA 165
Hall, Ben 45, 84
Hall, Edward Smith 44

Hall, Ken G. 208
Harbours 16
Hargrave, Lawrence 149, 170
Harpur, Charles 63
Hart, Steve 59
Hart, W.E. 149
Hawkesbury River, NSW 147, 216-17
Hawkesbury River Bridge 184
Hayes, Sir Henry Browne 20
Henning, Rachel 20
Herald 36
Hereward 157
Her Majesty's Theatre, Sydney 224
Hidges, Florence 105
Higgins, Arthur 209
Hill End, NSW 178
    Clark Street 33
    Holtermann's claim 90
    Star of Hope gold mine 90
Himalaya 174-5
Hinkler, Bert 149
Hobart
    court buildings 15
    gaol 15
    Murray Street 15, 17
    Queen's Park 22-3
Holman, W.A. 172
Holtermann, Bernard Otto 10, 90
Hopetoun, Lord 274
Hopkins family 228
Hopwood, Henry 147, 160
Horses 84, 148, 177, 215, 248, 254-5,
    259, 295
    harvesting wheat 201
    hauling wheat 199
    horse-drawn omnibus 251
    horse-drawn trams 238
    horse racing 218
Hotels 40
    six o'clock closing 144-5
Howie, David 54
Howitt, A.W. 16
Hughes, William Morris 279
Hume, Mary 227
Hume, Walter 227
Humour 17, 84
Hunter River, NSW 147
Hydroelectricity 204-5

Immigrants 21, 114, 130-1, 238
    interned 296, 311
    White Australia Policy 295
Ipswich, Qld 169
Irish 17
Irrigation 202, 205

Japanese 296
    miniature submarines 322
Japanese Admiral 296
Jennings, Mr T.D. 211, 212
Jerilderie Plains, Vic. 159
Johnson, Amy 173
Johnston, George 297
Johnstone, Barnett 17

Kalgoorlie, WA 11, 45, 189
Kanakas 202
Kangaroos 61

Kapunda copper mine 178
Kapunda Football Club 215
Katherine Telegraph Station, NT 77
Kelly, Dan 59
Kelly, Ned 45, 58
Kelly Gang 84
Kendall, Henry 250
Kidman, Sir Sidney 136
Killalpaninna, SA 51
King, Governor 20
King, Henry 49
King, John 16, 35
King, Philip Gidley 20
King George Sound, WA 46
King's Cross, Sydney 307
Kingsford-Smith, Charles 149
Kokoda Trail 297, 316
Koroonda, SA 178
Kovik 234-5

Labor Party 268
Lake Poppii, a bush hut 94
Lambing Flat Riot 115
Lane, William 131
Lanne, William 16-17, 48
La Perouse, Jean 150
Largs Pier Hotel, SA 244
Lavender Bay, Sydney 10
Law 21
Lawson, Henry 284-5
Legrand, Mr 191
Leura, NSW 221
Lindsay, Norman 226
Lithgow Valley, NSW, coalminer's
    house 93
Lithgow Zigzag railway 162
Lizard's Head, Chillagoe, Qld 75
Loch, Sir Henry 116
London Missionary Society 271
Lorne, Vic, Erskine House group 122-3
Lowe, Rev. 271
Lyne, Sir William 281
Lyons, J.A. 293

Macarthur, Captain John 20
Macarthur, Elizabeth 20, 36
Macarthur, James 27
Macarthur family 20, 27
MacArthur, General Douglas 297, 321
McCubbin, Frederick 226
McDonald, Charles 'Fighting Mac' 268
Mackie, Reverend George 118
Maclay, Charles 253
Macquarie, Governor 20
Macquarie Harbour 45
Mail services 85
    by air 171
    letter carriers 148
Manning, Judge 21
Mantuna 44
Maori Wars 295
Maroubra Beach, Sydney 157
Matilda 110
Mawson, Douglas 213
Mead, William 102
Meadowbank Engineering Co. 206
Melba, Dame Nellie 213, 225
Melbourne, Swanston Street 124

Menzies, R.G. 293
Middle Harbour, Sydney 21
Millinery class 312
Miners 186, 187
Mining 178
Missionaries 44
Missions 50
Montgomery, Field Marshal 323
Moonta copper mine, SA 186
Motumotu, New Guinea 270-1
Mount Feathertop, Vic. 73
Mount Kosciusko, NSW 63, 73
Mount Lyell smelters, Queenstown,
    Tas. 180-1
Mount Ragged 96
Mount Templeton, SA, harvesting
    wheat 201
Mowbray Racecourse Company 218
Mueller, Baron von 177
Munitions workers 317
Murphy, Daniel 119
Murray cod 222
Murray River 160, 222
Murray-Darling River 147
Murrumbidgee Irrigation Area 139, 205
Murrumbidgee River 147
Music 211

Namoi 216-17
Narrandera, NSW 111
National Gallery of Victoria 226
Nationalism 267
Navy, Australian 326-7
Nellie 160
New Australia Movement 131
New Guinea 268, 325
    annexed 270-1
    Second World War 296
New Norfolk Hotel, Tas. 215
New South Wales
    Executive Council 40
    self government 20
New South Wales Corps 20
Newcastle Iron and Steel Works 207
North Sydney 10
Northern Territory
    Katherine Telegraph Station 77
    Overland Telegraph, 24-5

O'Malley, 'King' 268, 281
Onslow, Arthur 36
Onslow, G.I. 26
Oriental Banking Corporation 236-7
Outback 19
    transport 149
Overland Telegraph Line 24-5, 77,
    86-7, 149

Paddle steamers 147, 160-1
    Namoi 216-17
    Nellie 160
Papua New Guinea 268
Parachilna, SA 88
Parer, Damien 316
Parkes, Sir Henry 277
Parkes Ministry 277
Parliament 266-7
Parliament House, Sydney 245

Parramatta 19
    first brewery 20
Parrots 61
Pattly 48
Pearce family 288-9
Pearl divers 178, 203
Perth 30
    City Baths 223
    Hay Street 323
    unemployed march along
        Wellington Street 287
Picnics 213, 220
Pittsworth, Qld, Yandilla Street 106
Plague 238, 256
Plants, introduced 62
Polding, Archbishop 118
Police Wireless Patrol 239
Politicians 267-93
Poole, Sarah 228
Port Adelaide 37
Port Arthur 54-5, 74
    chapel of the Model Prison 55
Port Macquarie 66
Port Melbourne 28-9
Port Moresby 271
Ports 19
    Adelaide 37
    Darwin docks 203
    Sydney 40
Portuguese explorers 13
Pottinger, Sir Frederick 84
Presbyterian Church 119
Pyrmont Bridge, Sydney 254-5

QANTAS 149, 172
Queen's Hall, State Library of Victoria
    17
Queensland native cedar 62
Queenstown, Tas., Mount Lyell
    smelters 180-1

Rabbits, exported to England 202
Racing 218-19
Radio 149
Railways 19, 147, 148, 158-9, 260-1
    construction gang, central Qld 82-3
    derailments 162-3
    Flinders Street to Hobson's Bay Pier
        28-9
    linking small settlements 97
    Lithgow Zigzag 162
    signalman 206
    Transcontinental Railway 89
    viaducts 158
Red Bluff 12
Red Cross 269
Referendum on Federation 278
Remarkable Cave, Tas. 76
Reserves, Aboriginal 50
Ridley, John 201
Rivers 147
Roads 16, 84, 85, 147, 148, 153
    city street 257
    North-West Highway 167
Roberts, Tom 178, 266-7
Rocks, the 20, 40
    backyard of No. 2 Walton Place 256
    Exeter Place off Wexford Street 256

Rodney 156
Roe, J. Septimus 30
Roman Catholic Bishop's Palace 31
Roper River, NT 86-7
Rowing 213, 219
Royal College of Surgeons, The 16
Royal Prince Alfred Hospital, Sydney
    247
Royal Society, The 16
Royal Tar 131
Royal visits
    Duke and Duchess of York and
        Cornwall 124
    Princes Edward and George 122
Rugby 213
Rum, trade 20

Sacred nugget 189
Sailing 213, 234-5
    in a salt lake 223
Sailing ships *see* Ships
St George, Qld 90
St James Station, Sydney, underground
    railway 260-1
School of the Air 114
Schools 114, 132, 291
    Montessori 133
Scottsdale Railway Station, Tas. 303
Scrivener, Mr. M. 282-3
Sealing 16, 177
Second World War 297, 314-325
    embarking for the Middle East 294-5
Sentimental Bloke, The 209
Settlement 21
Shearers 147, 194-5
Shedden, Sir Frederick 321
Sheep 137, 147
    merino 20, 177
Shingle splitters 21
Ships 19, 44, 156, 174-5
    Great Britain 214
    Herald 36
    Hereward 157
    Himalaya 174-5
    Rodney 156
    Royal Tar 131
    Sobraon 21, 37, 38-9
    Strathallan 318-9
    Success 52-3
    Thermopylae 156
    Vernon 18-19, 39
Shops 20
    Brisbane, Qld 128
    Hill End, NSW 33
    Launceston, Tas. 129
Smallpox 44
Smith, Fanny Cochrane 134
Smith, Keith 172
Smith, Ross 172
Snow 72-3
Sobraon 21, 38-9
Soccer 215
Social life 142-3, 211-35, 220, 230-3
    marriages 228-9
    the poor 257
    see also Entertainment
Soldiers 294-327
    Imperial army officers 121

officer, South Australian Artillery 305
recruiting drives 308, 315
rehabilitation 313
reinforcements leaving for France 309
salute the Union Jack, Motumotu 270
Seventh Division 325
South Australian volunteer forces 302
Sudan contingent 121, 302
see also Wars
Soup kitchen 290-1
Spanish Civil War 297
Sport 213-35
Squatters 43
Stanthorpe, Qld 119
Stanwell Park, NSW 170
Star of Hope gold mine 90
Steel 189, 207
Steele, Sergeant 45, 58
Stephen, Miss Elanor Elizabeth 2
Stokell, Dr 17
Stone family 31
Stonemasons 247
Strathalbyn, SA 247
Strathallan 318-9
Streeton, Arthur 178
Strikes 186
Strzelecki, P.E. 63, 73
Stuart-Whyte, F. 210-11
Sturt, Charles 16
Success 52-3
Sudan 295
Sugar 202
Surfing 141
Swagman 110, 147
Swan River Colony, St George's Terrace, WA 31
Swimming 223, 314
Sydney 40
 Macquarie Street 311
 Martin Place 274, 312, 325
 Middle Head Battery 298
 Park Street 41
 Pitt Street 41
 Sussex Street at Grafton Wharf 240-1
Sydney Cove 27
Sydney Cricket Ground, welcome to American fleet 306
Sydney Harbour 10, 21
 raid on shipping 322
Sydney Harbour Bridge 262-5
Sydney Town Hall 245
Sydney University, gargoyles 246

Tamworth, NSW, ploughing with a traction engine 199
Taradale Viaduct near Castlemaine, Vic. 158
Tasmanian Aborigines, see Aborigines
Tasman's Arch, Eagle Hawk Neck, Tas. 74
Tathra, NSW 234
Tattersall's Hotel, Kalgoorlie, WA 258
Tench, Captain Watkin 43
Tennis 230-3
Theatre 224-5
Theatre Royal, Sydney 224
Thermopylae 156
Thompson, Dr Ashburton 238
Three Sisters, Blue Mountains 78
Thunderbolt 63
Timber 16
Timber cutting 177, 192-3
Timore Caves, NSW 63
Todd, Alice 22
Todd, Sir Charles 22, 24-5, 86-7, 149
Tower Hill 68
Trade unions 179
Trams
 crowds taking the Watson's Bay tram 307
 Hackney tram, Adelaide, SA 165
 horse-drawn 238, 248
Transcontinental Railway 89, 281
Transport see Bullock teams; Camels; Cars; Coaches; Cycles; Horses; Paddlesteamers; Railways; Roads; Ships; Trams
Trees
 Big Ben, Great Dividing Range 74
 karri 279
 tree-stump house 93
Truganini 48
Twofold Bay, NSW 83, 114, 183

Unemployment 269, 286-7
 the Treasury Riot 287

Vaucluse House 20, 26
Vernon 18-19, 38-9
Viaduct over Stonequarry Creek, Picton, NSW 158
Victoria Barracks, Sydney 300
Victoria Bridge, Laura, SA 110
Victoria Markets, Sydney 250-1
Voting 268

Wallace, George 208
Wallaroo Mine, SA 186
Wallendbeen recruitment march 308
Wallerawang, NSW 108
Walls of Jerusalem, Lincoln County 66
Warburton, Vic. 8-9
Ward, Frederick 63
Warrnambool, Vic. 68
 gun emplacement 298
Wars 294-327
 Boer War 295, 303-4
 Boxer Revolution, China 295
 First World War 311
 Great War 295, 308-13
 Maori Wars 295
 peace celebration 311
 Second World War 297, 314-325
 Spanish Civil War 297
 see also Soldiers
Water 61-81, 205
 artesian 102
Waterfall Gully 68
Waterfalls
 Blackheath, NSW 79
 Ebor Falls, New England Tableland 70
 Leura, NSW 221
 Waterfall Gully, SA 68
Weldborough, Tas. 124
Wentworth, W.C. 20, 26, 62
Wentworth Falls, Blue Mountains, NSW 78
West Maitland, NSW 105
Western Australia tries to secede 292-3
Westralia Hotel, Kalgoorlie, WA 84
Whaling 16, 183
 Twofold Bay, NSW 114
Wharf labourers 203
Wheat 198-201
Wheat Belt 201
White Australia Policy 274, 295
Wildflowers 220
Williamson, J.C. 213
Williamstown Volunteer Rifle Company, SA 33
Wills, William John 36 see also Burke & Wills expedition
Wilson's Promontory 62
Wine industry 20, 177
Women
 equal educational opportunities 21
 in the workforce 178
 meat queue 325
 recreation during the Second World War 314
Wool 16, 20, 161, 177, 194-7, 268
Woolabrah bore, Moree District, NSW 102
Wright, Judith 43
Wyndham Gaol, WA 47
Wynstay, south Gippsland, Vic., tree-stump house 93

Yarra River, soldiers training 314
Yenda, NSW. 139